Learning to Listen, Ready to Talk

Harry:

With appreciation for your commitment to promoting Christian scholarship, and for your faithful service to Christian higher education.

Best wishes,

Harold

$10.00
03/23

Learning to Listen, Ready to Talk

◆

A Pilgrimage Toward Peacemaking

Harold Heie

iUniverse, Inc.
New York Lincoln Shanghai

Learning to Listen, Ready to Talk
A Pilgrimage Toward Peacemaking

iUniverse books may be ordered through booksellers or by contacting:

iUniverse
2021 Pine Lake Road, Suite 100
Lincoln, NE 68512
www.iuniverse.com
1-800-Authors (1-800-288-4677)

ISBN: 978-0-595-45546-1 (pbk)

ISBN: 978-0-595-89855-8 (ebk)

Printed in the United States of America

Dedicated to
David L. Wolfe
Mentor and Friend

We should listen with the ears of God that we may speak the Word of God.

—Dietrich Bonhoeffer
Life Together

Talking with one another is loving one another.

—Kenyan proverb

The greatest single antidote to violence is conversation.

—Jonathan Sacks
The Dignity of Difference

But speaking the truth in love, we must grow up in every way into him who is the head, into Christ.

—Ephesians 4:15

Do not repay evil for evil or abuse for abuse.... Always be ready to make your defense to anyone who demands from you an accounting for the hope that is in you; yet do it with gentleness and reverence.

—I Peter 3:9, 15

Let everyone be quick to listen, slow to speak, slow to anger.

—James 1:19

And what does the Lord require of you but to do justice, and to love kindness, and to walk humbly with your God?

—Micah 6:8

Contents

Thanks

I have stood on the shoulders of giants. Arthur Holmes and Nick Wolterstorff have over many years made the most profound contributions to my understanding of the nature of Christian higher education. George Marsden has made the greatest contribution to my understanding of the nature of Christian scholarship and the proper role of Christian scholars in the larger academy. I have no illusions that I can improve on what the three of you have said in your many fine publications. It is my modest hope that I have been able to tease out some of the concrete implications of your insightful thinking. I extend to you my thanks. You have inspired me and countless others to devote our lives to the causes you have championed.

Thanks to a number of Christian leaders under whom I have worked at Christian colleges: Sam Barkat, Friedhelm Radandt, Jim Bultman, Stan Gaede, Mark Sargent, Dick Gross, and Jud Carlberg. In your varied ways, you provided me with welcoming spaces to work creatively under your direction, helping me to understand better the ways in which I could create welcoming spaces for others.

Thanks to my fellow mentors at many faculty development workshops sponsored by the Council for Christian Colleges & Universities: Arthur Holmes, Susan Gallagher, and Stan Gaede. I learned much from each of you during these workshops about the nature of Christian higher education. And thanks for our many informal times together as friends, consuming many scoops of ice cream with workshop participants.

Thanks to past and present staff members at the Center For Christian Studies at Gordon College: Debbie Chrysafides, Amy Kvistad, Debbie Drost, Toby Hanchett, Jeremy Martin, and the new CCS Director, Dan Russ. Your encouragement and support of my work at the CCS has been and continues to be exemplary. Thank you for the countless, unheralded, behind-the-scenes tasks you have carried out with distinction for my various CCS projects.

Thanks to all my friends mentioned by name in my narrative. Each of you has made an important contribution to my own learning and growing.

Thanks to Christina Wassell, who made a marvelous contribution to the shaping of this book. In addition to your typing a number of the earlier drafts of this manuscript and providing splendid editorial assistance, the greatest help you provided was your uncanny ability to ask many probing questions about the content of the manuscript, questions that caused me to rethink and revise what I had said in earlier drafts. Thank you also for helping me to see more clearly that my journey can best be characterized as "A Pilgrimage Toward Peacemaking."

Thanks to Kim Van Es, a faculty member in the English Department at Northwestern College (IA), for your splendid copy editing of the penultimate draft of this book, and your meticulous proofreading of the final draft. And thanks to Beth De Leeuw for your excellent help in formatting the final draft for publication.

Thanks to many friends who read a second draft of the manuscript and offered generous advice for refining the narrative: Marsha Borgman, Paul Borgman, Kevin Filocamo, John Heie, Bruce Herman, Doug Jacobsen, Rhonda Hustedt Jacobsen, Dan Johnson, Tim Johnson, Jonathan Lauer, Ron Mahurin, Tim Sherratt, Jim Skillen, John Skillen, and Dick Stout. Your comments and suggestions were very helpful. It is my hope that most of you will notice the results of your good ideas in this published draft, even if I didn't have sense enough to follow all your suggestions.

Thanks to Michael King, the head of Cascadia Publishing House. In his commitment to fostering "loving dialogue" about the thorny issue of homosexuality within the Mennonite Christian community, I found a true kindred spirit. Michael helped me to understand better the challenges of trying to create a seamless blend between memoir and intellectual treatise. He provided sage advice on how I could try to meet that challenge. I have tried my best to create a blend between genres that most would consider to be mutually exclusive.

Thanks again to Stan Gaede, a trusted colleague and friend over many years, for writing a generous *Foreword* to this book. Your excellent modeling of being a very effective teacher, a productive scholar, and a wise administrator continues to inspire me. We have learned much from each other.

I cannot find words to adequately express my thanks to my wife Pat and our three children, Jonathan, Janice, and Jeffrey. I have learned much from each of you, and you have been a constant source of love and support throughout our years together. Special thanks to Pat, for your patience during the many hours I have spent at my desk writing and rewriting this manuscript.

Finally, thanks to David Wolfe, to whom I have dedicated this book. Your inspiration and example was the catalyst that launched me on a lifelong pilgrimage of learning after I was finished with school. For that excellent mentoring I am most grateful. I value your friendship more than words can say. Thank you for reading multiple drafts of this manuscript and for your helpful suggestions for refinement. And thanks for the many lively, enjoyable, and respectful conversations we have had over the years, some sitting by a roaring fireplace in your renovated Vermont farmhouse, drinking much good strong coffee and eating not a few Dunkin Donuts. Life doesn't get much better than that.

It is fitting that when I wrote the first draft of this section of my manuscript, it was the morning of Thanksgiving Day.

Foreword

This is an important book—not only because of what the author says, but also because of who he is, and the times in which we live.

The reality is, Harold Heie is a great friend. That fact has not required us to be in agreement at all times, however. Indeed, before consenting to write the *Foreword* for this book, Harold encouraged me to pay particular attention to one chapter. "You may not like it, Stan," he said. "You might even want to reconsider your offer to write the *Foreword*." I smiled but kept at the task—without blinking, I might add. Why? Because our friendship is not based on agreement, for one thing. But even when I don't see eye-to-eye with Harold, I always learn something.

And it is precisely for that reason that this book warrants our attention: Harold Heie practices what he preaches, even in moments when it's not easy (such as the times in which we live). The fact is, we argue more poorly today than at any moment in my lifetime. The "we" includes all of us in the culture, by the way. Christians and non-Christians alike. In the academy. In the church. At the courthouse. Under the Capitol dome. The location appears not to make much difference. We don't seem to know what to do with our enemies.

Interestingly enough, Jesus is rather clear on that score. We are to love them. And if he is our model, that love does not mean agreeing with them. Jesus was fairly direct in his approach to his opposition, pointing out their flaws as well as their need. But he did know how to listen, and he was ready to talk. Why? He was a teacher, for one thing, who wanted very much to communicate. And that requires both understanding and undertaking. But he was also the Son of God. The Truth. Our Savior and Redeemer. His teaching, therefore, was born of the same love that took him to the cross. By comparison, listening well is a rather small price to pay.

Why is it that we have such trouble engaging in conversation with our challengers … or even our adversaries? We say it is because of our commitment to the truth. But the Truth tells us another story. He says walk the second mile. Share your cloak. Even turn the other cheek. We don't listen because we love too little and we talk too much. Truth be told, the Truth is not in us. But it has found a good home in its servant, Harold Heie. Those of us who have known him can testify to that fact. This is a man who has embodied his own teaching. He has listened, when the listening was painful. He has shared, even at his own expense. He has given his life to the cause that has birthed this book.

Learning to Listen, Ready to Talk: A Pilgrimage Toward Peacemaking is Harold's cross and his glory. And we, his companions, get to bear witness. Thanks be to God.

Stan Gaede, Scholar-in-Residence
Gordon College

President, 2001–2006
Westmont College

Preface

"Harold, what makes you think anyone wants to read about your life?" That question ruined my day, since I didn't have a good answer for my sister-in-law. Now, about three years and many drafts later, I have a response.

It isn't that I think the story of my life will dazzle you. But, I want to make a point: *learning and living are of one piece*—an intertwining that defies *telling about* in a few words, but which can, hopefully, be *shown* in the story of one life. What I have learned about some important issues cannot be understood adequately or evaluated fully outside the context of my life story. And, I dare to claim that the same is true for you. This conviction emerged after all of my formal schooling, during which I had viewed learning as primarily for the purpose of preparing for a career, a series of jobs. I had created a destructive bifurcation between learning and everyday life. I now reject that bifurcation. As you will soon see, the most important things I have learned, my *lived beliefs,* have emerged from my daily attempts to live well.

As a result of my conviction that there is an inextricable linkage between how I am living and what I am learning, my narrative in this volume attempts to create a seamless blend between "memoir" (my story) and what one reader of an earlier draft called "intellectual treatise" (my present beliefs about some important contemporary issues). I am attempting to create a synergy between the personal and the scholarly. It is important for me to attempt to create this synergy because that goal reflects how I have come to understand myself, and I want this book to be true to who I have become, whether or not that fits the expectations of others. A good friend in the academy, who knows me well, said the following upon reading a first draft: "It's you, Harold." That made my day.

To give you fair warning, I have been advised by many people, including a few publishers, that the synergy I am attempting to create will be difficult, if not impossible, to attain. Nevertheless, I persist in not heeding such advice (possibly just being stubborn). You will have to judge whether I have been able to create the coherence between living and learning to which I aspire.

In addition to my experience of an indissoluble connection between living and learning, there is another reason for my trying to create a blend in this volume between memoir and intellectual treatise that goes deep down to my primary purpose in writing: to extend an invitation to "respectful conversation." The punch line for this volume is that to most effectively engage another person who disagrees with you about any important issue, you should first develop a personal relationship of mutual trust, and such mutual trust has the best chance of emerging when you take the time to get to know one another. So, as quaint, hopelessly naive, and even corny as it may sound to the modern ear, I am hoping that by your reading my story, you will get to know me well enough to trust me in certain ways. You will see that I, like you, do not have all the answers to life's riddles. I am a finite, fallible human being trying to live well in light of my present understanding, without trying to browbeat you into believing as I do. I hope you will see that whereas I am committed to beliefs that reflect my Christian faith, I am open to the possibility of being wrong about any number of things, and I am open to refining my beliefs in light of what I can learn from those who disagree with me. I hope you find my narrative to be totally honest and transparent. Finally, I hope that in your getting to know me in this way, you will conclude that what I have to say about some important contemporary issues are ideas about which we should be able to talk respectfully, even if you believe that many of my beliefs are all wrong. If in the personal dimension of my narrative I tell you more things about me than you could possibly want to know, I hope you can find it within yourself to bear it and grin a few times.

In light of my daunting intention to create a seamless blend between memoir and intellectual treatise, it may be helpful for me to provide a road map though this volume.

Part I is the story of my pilgrimage. My story will reveal that at various points in my life certain "seeds" were sown, rudimentary ideas that were not yet well thought out, ideas that I would struggle with and elaborate on later in my pilgrimage. These seeds, identified at the end of the chapters in Part I, include the importance of creating welcoming spaces for respectful conversation; the importance of establishing personal relationships of mutual trust with those with whom you disagree if you want to have fruitful conversations about your differences; the status of claims to knowledge, and consideration of how to adjudicate competing claims; the meanings of justice and peace, and how to be an agent for the fostering of these values; and the meanings of the elusive phrases "the integration of faith, learning, and living" and "holistic education" that are so prominent in the rhetoric of institutions of Christian higher education.

The chapter in Part I toward which all the previous chapters converge is chapter 16 ("Respectful Conversations"), in which I extend to all readers an invitation to create forums for respectful conversation in their various spheres of influence, including politics, public policy practice, religious communities, and especially the academy.

Parts II-IV presents progress reports on my more nuanced understandings of the "seeds" that I introduced in Part I. In light of my overarching purpose of extending an invitation to respectful conversation, Part III ("Can We Talk about Justice and Peace?") is presented in the unusual form of simulated conversations about justice and peace.

With this road map as a guide, it is my hope that you will come to see a compelling synergy between memoir and intellectual treatise (between the personal and the scholarly) that reflects this pilgrim's experience of living and learning as being of one piece.

Introduction: An Invitation to Respectful Conversation

It will eventually become apparent that, starting with a small seed that was sown around the dining-room table in my boyhood home in Brooklyn, my life has converged on a passion for fostering respectful conversation among those who disagree with one another.

The respectful conversation I envision is in stark contrast to the usual format of a TV talk-show where two pundits present diametrically opposed positions on a hot issue of the day. They typically argue from "fixed positions." Battle lines are drawn. The pundits' goals can be expressed in metaphors of war. They hope to *win* the argument, to *attack* the opponent, to *demolish* his point of view (see Lakoff & Johnson 1980, p. 4). Neither pundit is open to really listening or learning from the other. The only purpose of talking, beyond entertaining the TV audience, is to convert others to one's unyielding position.

My vision rejects the fixed positions model for public discourse in favor of a learning model. I envision numerous public conversations in which persons having strong disagreements sit around the same table, saying words like the following:

> I now understand your position and why you hold it. In fact, in light of what I have heard you say, I think you could actually strengthen your argument by.... What do you see as the strengths and weaknesses of my point of view? Our differences are significant, but we seem to agree on the following.... What have we learned from each other?

How unrealistic is that? In this model, those in conversation aren't required to give up their positions. But, at the end of the conversation "they would know something they didn't know at the beginning ... either about themselves and why they believe what they believe, or about their opponents, or about what's possible" (Rodin & Steinberg 2003, p. 86). One possible sign of the "success" of such a conversation may be that "the speakers say things they never said before and think things they never thought before" (84). One speaker may even "burst out with something like 'Oh, now I understand your position,' or at least 'Oh, *now* I can see that we can get somewhere as we talk together'" (Booth 2005, p. 9).

The fixed positions model is not limited to TV talk shows or other forms of journalism. It is pervasive in the political realm, the community of scholars comprising the academy, and certain religious groups. The result is public discourse that is increasingly shrill, confrontational, and, at times, very nasty. In response to this ubiquity of verbal confrontation, this book is an invitation to respectful conversation that will open up the possibility of us learning from those with whom we disagree. While others have written more eloquently about the philosophical and theological bases for the call to respectful conversation, my invitation will consider the nuts and bolts of "how to do it," and will articulate some prior conditions for making such conversation fruitful in politics and public policy practice, in religious communities, and especially in the academy.

The intended audience for my invitation to respectful conversation can be envisioned in terms of concentric circles, starting with Christians and then extending out to all other human beings—those committed to other religious traditions and those who consider themselves to be secularists. First, a word to Christian readers.

I am a Christian. As my story will soon reveal, my own commitment to fostering respectful conversations was gradually forged during a lifetime of learning about the implications of my faith commitment. We Christians do not have a stellar record of knowing how to talk with each other respectfully and charitably about our disagreements. For example, current debates within and across Christian denominations regarding homosexuality threaten to tear the Christian church apart. I hope that the reading of this book will help Christians to navigate such troubled waters.

I do want to go beyond Christians talking only to one another. I want to challenge Christian readers to initiate respectful conversations within the larger human community. My call to Christians for respectful conversation is not just a potential means toward a worthy end. It is a worthy end in itself. Jesus Christ calls all Christians to love others. I firmly believe that a deep expression of loving another person is to listen to her and give her a voice, to provide her with a welcoming space to express her point of view (however contrary that may be to my own Christian beliefs), and to treat her with kindness and respect in the process of talking about our agreements and disagreements.

The primary subcategory of Christians to which I extend my invitation to respectful conversation consists of administrators, faculty, and students involved in Christian higher education. The phrase "integration of faith, learning, and living" is prominent at Christian colleges and universities. What is the meaning of this slogan? In serving for over forty years at four Christian colleges, I have been exposed to much "telling" about its meaning. I intend for my narrative to go beyond "telling" to "showing."

Some Christian readers may wonder where I am coming from theologically. It will soon become apparent from my story that I have learned about what it may mean to live well as a Christian from multiple Christian traditions: the pietist Lutheran, evangelical, Reformed, and Anabaptist traditions. But the most prominent influences in my life have come from the Reformed and Anabaptist traditions. In oversimplified terms, on which my narrative will elaborate, I am Reformed in my deep commitment to a broad view of God's redemptive purposes and my belief that I am called to be an agent for God's purposes in all areas of life, including the political. I am Anabaptist in my deep conviction that the means I choose for such agency should be those of a peacemaker, which includes, but is not limited to, orchestrating respectful conversations.

To embrace aspects of both the Reformed and Anabaptist traditions is to live with considerable tension. For many who adhere to the tenets of either tradition, my attempt to synthesize what I understand to be the best insights of each tradition may be seen as corrupting both traditions (witness my eventual claim that I aspire to be a peacemaker, but whether I am a pacifist is debatable). However, I encourage the Christian reader in each tradition to be open to the possibility that my attempt at synthesis has the potential to enrich both traditions.

Hopefully, this word to Christian readers will encourage them to read on. But my dreams for this book are more grandiose than that. I believe that my story and invitation have the potential to be relevant to all human beings. Allow me a word of explanation to those readers who do not share my commitment to the Christian faith.

First, I believe that to be able to talk together in a welcoming space for respectful conversation is important for all human beings. This need reflects our common humanity. In a world where those who disagree strongly about issues are more likely to violate each other than to talk, we all need to learn how to talk respectfully about our differences. Therefore, it is my fondest hope that not only will Christians invite you to their table, but you will also invite Christians to your table. Although our differing stories may have led us to embrace different value commitments and other beliefs about the world and our place in it, these sets are probably not mutually exclusive. Whether we sit together at my table or yours, it is my hope that through respectful conversations we may find some common ground about how to live well as human beings, both within and across our respective traditions.

Another aspect of our common humanity is that learning and living are inseparable. In my own pilgrimage, I have learned that living is a dynamic process. It is in the very process of my seeking to live faithful to my Christian commitment that I gain greater insight into how to continue living faithfully. My discovery that living is a dynamic process is not idiosyncratic to me or other Christians. Every human being has a worldview, a set of beliefs about the world and the place of humans in the world, however implicit or unarticulated that worldview may be. The nature of living for all of us, whatever our worldview, is that our beliefs cannot be separated from our lives and social locations, and it is in the very process of living faithful to our present understanding that we can learn to continue living in faithfulness. It is my hope that the contours of this dynamic process of living that emerge from my own Christian story will be helpful to those readers whose stories are embedded in non-Christian traditions who aspire to live faithful to their own traditions.

Another grandiose dream I have is that by reading my story, those who do not share my Christian faith will learn to be suspicious of some of the caricatures of Christians that are so prevalent in our popular culture. One such caricature is that Christians are arrogant, close-minded know-it-alls who want to impose their views on others. There are enough Christians like that for us to expect that caricature. But that doesn't describe me. I hope that non-Christian readers of this book will see that there are Christians who embrace being human beings, with all the limitations, ambiguity, and uncertainty that are integral to the human condition. There are actually Christians who do not claim to know it all, because no human being knows it all. There are Christians who believe that a deep response to the call of Jesus Christ to love others is to provide a welcoming space for others to express their beliefs.

Although the narrative in this book converges on a methodology for respectful conversation (that emphasizes the need to first develop personal relationships of mutual trust with those with whom we disagree), embedded in its pages are many beliefs that I hold relative to substantive issues regarding the nature of faiths (Christian or secular), the nature of higher education (particularly faith-based education), political involvement, the nature of inquiry (particularly scholarly inquiry in the academy), the meanings of justice and peace, the nature of leadership, and strategies for the Christian church to facilitate conversations about the contentious issue of homosexuality. There is something in these pages for everyone to disagree with. But laying bare disagreements serves well my purpose in writing, provided my narrative has prepared you to listen well and to be ready to talk respectfully.

For those readers who accept my invitation to respectful conversation and wish to orchestrate conversations about the major themes that will emerge in this book, I include two bibliographies. The first is an annotated bibliography of works cited in this manuscript. The second is a bibliography of recommended readings that are relevant to nine themes that emerge from my story, including those issues dealt with in Parts II-IV. It is my hope that future conversations regarding these themes will reject both dogmatism and relativism, and will exemplify the "dialogic pluralism" that I (and others) have proposed, in which all perspectives on a given issue, religious or secular, will be listened to and will be talked about respectfully on the basis of publicly accessible standards for evaluating competing claims.

By now, readers who hold to their beliefs with deep conviction may be alarmed. Am I suggesting that you park your deeply held beliefs at the door when you enter the room for conversation with those who disagree with you? Not at all. But, I do suggest that preconditions for the possibility of respectful conversation will include healthy doses of charity, humility, and patience. I also call for that relatively rare combination of deep commitment to one's own beliefs *and* openness to the possibility of refining those beliefs by learning from others. I will remind those who share my faith that these preconditions reflect Christian virtues. It is my hope that the same preconditions will be embraced by those committed to other religious or secular worldviews who wish to engage in respectful conversation.

I can imagine moans of incredulity toward my hope for many more respectful conversations in public discourse. "Get real, Harold." "You surely are living in La-La Land." Despite this skepticism, or because of it, I extend this invitation to you.

PART I

Faithful Learning

Every once in a while, you hear someone say, "If only I knew then what I know now." Such wishful thinking fails to grasp the dynamic nature of living well. Our knowledge as finite, fallible human beings will always be partial. You cannot wait to live until you understand all of life. The secret to living well is to be faithful to your present understanding, while always seeking to improve that understanding. That attempt is *faithful learning*.

1

Mom, Pop, and the Girls

o o o o o o o o o o o o o o o o o o o o o o o o o o o o o o

When Mom's views, possibly on the pot roast, were the subject of criticism, Mom smiled, listened patiently, and gave a gentle response.

Our home in Brooklyn was a welcoming space for the "girls." That is what Mom called her unmarried female friends, who, like mom, had emigrated from Norway in the 1920s and taken positions as maids and cooks in fine homes in New York City and Long Island.

Aagot, Elisabeth, Sophie, Johanna, and others flocked to our home on weekends for good food and good conversation, staples in the lives of Norwegians in Brooklyn. They were a lively group, some having strong opinions on most everything, including whether the pot roast was done well enough. I sensed that they didn't have much opportunity to give voice to their points of view during the working week, possibly due to their perceived subordinate stations in life or their struggles with the English language. Mom's facility with English had come a long way since her first job as a maid shortly after arriving in the states. One day when the lady of the house fell down on a flight of stairs, Mom blurted out one of the few English phrases she had learned, "Good for you!" For emphasis, Mom said it a second time.

In our home, these women were given the space to say whatever was on their minds, sometimes half in Norwegian and half in English. Even at those times when Mom's views, possibly on the pot roast, were the subject of criticism, Mom smiled, listened patiently, and gave a gentle response. Pop mostly listened, as did my twin brother John and I.

Mom, Pop, and these lively guests are no longer with us. In ways I have only come to realize fully recently, those good experiences of a welcoming space for all of us around the table had a profound formative influence on me. I never thought much about that gracious hospitality at the time because it was just the way things were in our home, like the air we breathed.

However, there was also a painful underside to my experiences at home, especially during my teenage years, when for no obvious reason, visits from the girls became less frequent. While Mom created a welcoming space for the girls, she didn't always create such space for Pop. Part of the reason may be that while Mom loved to talk, Pop was the quietest person I have ever known. In later years, when John and I were out of the house, we used to compare notes on our telephone conversations with Pop. His typical response to our comments was "yup." Sometimes we had a 5-yup conversation. When Pop was particularly effusive, the yups would go into double digits.

Besides personality differences, a deeper reason for Mom's lack of openness to Pop's points of view had to do with their differences about religion. In Norway, Mom had made a strong commitment to the Christian faith under the influence of the pietist Lutheran Free Church. Pop was raised in the State Lutheran Church in Norway but made no personal commitment to the Christian faith. I can't remember Mom and Pop ever talking, in the presence of their two boys, about their views on the Christian faith. Although Pop was very quiet, I think that he would have been willing to talk with Mom about their religious differences if he had sensed that Mom would provide a welcoming space for him to express his point of view. Mom's views were set in cement. She didn't provide Pop with space to disagree. At the time, I wasn't mature enough to help Mom provide such space.

There were times when I wished Mom would stay home from church to be with Pop, to just listen and talk. I sensed that Pop thought there was significant contradiction between Mom's profession of Christian faith and her lack of openness to his point of view. Pop did eventually make his own commitment to the Christian faith, in his 70s, after Mom had passed away. I believe that Pop experienced the freedom and empowerment to make that choice only after Mom was gone.

Both the joyful results of there being a welcoming space for the girls in our home and the painful results of there not always being a welcoming space for Pop were the earliest seeds for a deep conviction that has matured since my boyhood days: *In my engagement with another person, I should first be a good listener, creating a welcoming space for that person to have a voice*. She needs hospitable room to express her point of view, even if I disagree. It is only within such a welcoming place that there is any hope for respectful conversation about our differences that will enable us to learn from one another.

When in later years I was shaping a practical Christian theology I could live by, it became apparent to me that my boyhood experiences with Mom, Pop, and the "girls" had a significant influence on my emerging beliefs. I have come to believe that a person's biography will have a major influence on the contours of his view of the world and his place in it.

Seeds: I learned at home that it was important to listen well. I was a better listener than talker. Eventually I would need to learn how to talk with those who disagree vehemently with me in ways that would respect them and their points of view.

2

Jesus and Me

o o o o o o o o o o o o o o o o o o o o o o o o o o o o o o o o o o o

I recall being overwhelmed with a sense that God loved me as I was, not as I hoped to be. I made a commitment to be a follower of Jesus, understanding little of the lifelong implications of that decision.

Our neighborhood in the Bay Ridge section of Brooklyn was jokingly called the third largest city in Norway, after Oslo and Bergen, because of the huge population of Norwegian immigrants and their families. It was there that Mom sent John and me off to the Sunday School program at the Norwegian Evangelical Lutheran Free Church ("59th Street Church" to us kids). Our church was one congregation of the Church of the Lutheran Brethren, a denomination whose founders in the United States traced their roots to the Hauge Revival movement in Norway in the nineteenth century. This movement was the Norwegian stream of a pietist expression of Christianity that focused on the need for a heartfelt conversion to the Christian faith (being "born again") and the corresponding call for Christians to evangelize the unconverted. Haugein principles also included a "low-church orientation" (a view that "worship is simple and informal, in contrast to ritualism and formalism") and an emphasis on active laity, with "the practice of Christian testimony in public as well as in private … to be encouraged" (Levang 1980, pp. 2–3).

At age 13, John and I and about sixty others in 59th Street Church were confirmed, having committed to memory Luther's Small Catechism (or at least having hoodwinked our pastor into thinking we had done so). But the words I memorized had no life. I could say them aloud, but I had not personally appropriated them.

This charade all changed one night in my 14th year when a traveling evangelist named Knut Heggestad spoke at our church. I don't recall his words. I do recall being overwhelmed with a sense that God loved me as I was, not as I hoped to be, and that the person and work of Jesus Christ were sufficient to enable me to enter into a personal, loving relationship with God. I didn't raise my hand in an altar call. But in the quietness of my own heart, I made a commitment to be a follower of Jesus Christ, understanding little of the implications of that decision.

I was nurtured in my home church through my undergraduate years in college primarily under the tutelage of a godly and dynamic senior pastor, Omar Gjerness, and a series of marvelous role models who served as Sunday School teachers and youth ministers. I especially remember one Sunday School teacher, Harold Tonnesen, who inspired me to immerse myself in the reading of the Bible. With the help of these mentors, I learned to cherish a number of the pietist emphases in my home church. Some of these emphases I still embrace with enthusiasm. Some others I now view as too one-sided or incomplete, needing to be supplemented.

In my pietist upbringing, great emphasis was placed on deeply felt religious experience. I embrace that emphasis. I am not a disembodied intellect (what Harvard minister Peter Gomes is reported to have called "a brain on a stick"). I feel deeply about many things, including a deeply felt sense of the presence of God in my life. My home church helped me to feel that way, for which I am grateful.

Closely related to this focus on deeply felt religious experience was an emphasis on a personal relationship with God. We talked a lot about such a relationship, although it was seldom clear to me what it meant. At times it seemed to be referring to "Jesus and me," as captured by the words of the old hymn "In the Garden" that I used to sing in the shower, far from any listening ears (which you would understand if you ever heard me sing).

> I come to the garden alone, while the dew is still on the roses ... And he [Jesus] walks with me and he talks with me, and he tells me I am his own. And the joy we share as we tarry there, none other has ever known.

I still embrace the centrality of a personal relationship with God for my Christian commitment, but the meaning I now ascribe to that relationship includes and also goes far beyond the Jesus and me motif suggested in this hymn.

Part of the Jesus and me motif evident in my church upbringing reflected a bifurcation between what we called the "Kingdom of God" (that realm where God intended to reign) and the world in which we live our daily lives. This dualism may have reflected the Lutheran tendency toward "two-kingdom" theology. Whether intended or not, drawing this firm distinction too easily led to the currently prevalent popular view that religion is a "private" matter that should not impinge on public life. I now reject that bifurcation (as will become apparent when I elaborate later on how I wish to expand on the Jesus and me motif).

An underside of the emphasis on deeply felt religious experience in my Norwegian pietist nurturing was a relative lack of emphasis on the life of the mind. My church was not overtly hostile to intellectual expressions of the Christian faith, but such expressions were not highly valued in comparison to the importance of religious experience. I now refuse to pick and choose, seeking to wed feeling deeply with thinking deeply.

What eventually proved to be my greatest difficulty with my Norwegian pietist upbringing was related to the volitional aspect of being human: dealing with practical ethical issues about how I should live my daily life. There was a healthy emphasis on "holy living." However, holiness seemed to be defined primarily in terms of what we were exhorted not to do. As the old saw goes, I didn't smoke or chew, or go out with girls who do. Neither did I drink, play cards, dance, or go to the movies. I don't think I was permanently scarred by living under these latter prohibitions. But I later regretted my inability to dance when I saw the beautiful movements of my own children dancing. The problem was that this proscriptive focus presented an extremely narrow view of what it means to live well as a Christian. What was missing was a focus on what I should do, rather than just what I should not do, with one exception.

Since evangelism was highly valued, we were strongly exhorted to witness to others about the saving grace of Jesus Christ. That encouragement was well and good. But the means provided for such witnessing were wooden and coercive. As president of our church's youth group, I was expected to set a positive example. So at times I handed out Christian tracts on the corner of 8th Avenue and 59th Street, although I disliked every minute of it. I also remember our trips to a few institutions for the mentally ill on Long Island to witness to the patients. It was difficult, at best, to talk about God to some people who already thought they were God. Getting back in the car to drive home brought a feeling of relief that bordered on ecstasy.

I am certainly open to the possibility that God could use these halting efforts of mine for redemptive purposes. But the problem, from my end, was that my witnessing did not flow out of love for those I talked at, not with. I too easily viewed those I witnessed to as possible "trophies," potential notches in my evangelism belt. It was all so impersonal. Why should those who listened to me place any trust in what I had to say? The good pietist emphasis on "personal relationships" focused primarily on my "vertical" relationship with God. Not enough emphasis was placed on the need to develop loving "horizontal" personal relationships with those to whom I witnessed. I still believe strongly in the importance of bearing witness to the grace of Jesus Christ. But the means I now choose are radically different from those of my teenage years.

Outside of the exhortation to bear personal witness to others of the saving grace of Jesus Christ, there was little positive exhortation on how to live well as a Christian. Particularly, there was little concern expressed for addressing the social ills of society. Although Hans Nielsen Hauge, the founder of the pietist Lutheran tradition in which I was nurtured, is reported to have embraced a robust social ethic, that emphasis was not passed down to my generation. I now believe that the relative silence of my church about social issues reflected too narrow a view of God's redemptive purposes for creation. I eventually came to embrace a more expansive view.

In later years, I came to realize that the Norwegian Pietism in which I was raised was not the only expression of Christian Pietism. In fact, when I eventually became a member of the Evangelical Covenant Church, I discovered a Swedish stream of Pietism that was more congruent with the beliefs that slowly emerged during my pilgrimage. In particular, this Swedish Pietism had more of an emphasis on a Christian's freedom in Christ, a concept that eventually became dear to me, as well as more of an emphasis on addressing social ills.

Despite the shortcomings, I cannot find adequate words to express my deep appreciation for the many positive lessons about the Christian life that I learned during my Norwegian pietist upbringing. It was within that community that I came to a personal decision to become a follower of Jesus Christ. I also learned the importance of a deeply felt experience of the presence of God in my life. I learned that a "loving relationship" is a major descriptor for my relationship with God. There is a profound truth to the idea of "Jesus and me," as long as my Christian faith does not end with that idea.

In brief, most of the emphases in my church were good. They were just truncated. They didn't capture the whole story of what it means to be a follower of Jesus.

Seeds: I learned that it is important for me to share my Christian faith with those who are not Christians. But I had much to learn about how to do that in a meaningful way (by developing relationships that foster mutual trust). My early Christian faith was primarily a private matter. I still had much to learn about a possible public dimension.

3

Finding Something You Love To Do

o o o o o o o o o o o o o o o o o o o o o o o o o o o o o o o

Both mentors gave me the opportunity to teach some "problem sessions" for their students. I didn't like it. I loved it.

Mom and Pop had minimal formal education. Mom completed grade school in Norway. Pop went to school evenings in Brooklyn to earn his high school equivalency degree after working long days in a factory that was initially located under an on-ramp to the Brooklyn Bridge. Pop loved to read—anything he could get his hands on.

Although we never lacked for food and the basic necessities of life, Mom and Pop did struggle to make ends meet on the one salary of a factory worker. Since a good education was seen as the road to a more comfortable life, schooling was highly valued in our home, although never in a nagging, coercive way. In general, lack of coercion was a welcome feature in our home. This openness did not mean that permissiveness reigned. There were expectations for behavior, like showing respect and concern for the "girls" and other visitors to our home. But these expectations were expressed more by example than exhortation. We were given freedom to make choices, within boundaries. This boyhood experience of a welcoming space to make decisions was a seed that blossomed over the years.

I took to schooling like the proverbial duck takes to water. I performed well in school, not because of any native brilliance, but because I loved learning and disciplined myself to work hard at learning. It wasn't that I had a voracious appetite for additional learning. I learned well what was expected of me by my teachers, no more and no less. Outside of my assigned reading for school, newspapers, and articles about Stan "the Man" Musial (the St. Louis Cardinals baseball star who was my boyhood hero), I was not an avid reader. In my spare time, I would rather play stick ball on the streets of Brooklyn than read a new, unassigned book. That tendency changed only after all my formal schooling was completed.

Since I was particularly good in matters quantitative, like arithmetic and algebra, the possibility of a career in engineering gradually emerged. On my second try, I was accepted into one of the competitive New York City schools, Brooklyn Technical High School. I was a good high school student, not excellent. After high school graduation I worked for six months as a junior draftsman for an engineering firm in Manhattan, the M.W. Kellogg Company. In the fall of 1953, I enrolled for undergraduate studies at the Polytechnic Institute of Brooklyn (now Polytechnic University) to study engineering. Originally, I indicated an interest in civil engineering but switched to mechanical engineering at the end of my sophomore year, primarily because I didn't want to go away to the summer surveying camp required of civil engineering majors between the sophomore and junior years (How is that for a profound reason for a change in major?).

My undergraduate studies went very well, and I enjoyed them. I was active with the InterVarsity Christian Fellowship on campus, serving as chapter president my senior year. I also squeezed out the time to play four years of varsity basketball, as well as playing basketball in two church leagues. I recall one stretch of time in my sophomore year when I played ten basketball games in eleven nights. I loved playing basketball, having learned it in the school yard of P.S. 105, my old grade school, sometimes after my church friends and I shoveled off the snow to play on wintry Saturday mornings. I was a decent player by smalltime college standards. But Brooklyn Poly was hardly a basketball powerhouse. I believe we won a total of less than a dozen games in my last three years. I did once score over 30 points in a game against Quinnipiac College (CT), but the person I took a turn guarding scored over 60 points. A defensive star I was not. Coach Meinhold called me "Whitey" from day one. I would now settle for hair of any color. I eventually graduated with some peers who didn't know my first name. My love for playing basketball continued through college intramural venues until about age 40.

In my senior year at Brooklyn Poly, I received a Master of Science Fellowship from Hughes Aircraft Company in Culver City, California. Having never before been west of eastern Pennsylvania, I headed for the west coast in the summer of 1957. Under the terms of the fellowship, I worked 26 hours per week at a variety of Hughes Aircraft sites, while pursuing a Masters in Mechanical Engineering degree at the University of Southern California.

I enjoyed my work as an engineer, specializing in heat transfer and fluid dynamics. This was at the very infancy of the space exploration program, and we did a bit of proposal work on the design of heat shields for space vehicles reentering the earth's atmosphere.

Besides enjoying my engineering work, I was also reasonably good at it, with one notable exception. I was, and remain, totally inept at working with my hands. Mom could never figure out why I, a mechanical engineer, couldn't fix a washing machine or anything else. "It's all in my head, Mom," I used to say. One day at the Hughes Aircraft LAX site, I was asked to stand on top of an army truck retrofitted for radar surveillance to "close up" an air conditioning unit. I didn't have a clue how to do that. It was all a tangle of wires. So, I just stuffed the wires back into the unit and screwed the lid on tight. The next day I overheard other engineers talking about the AC unit that had short circuited and burned out. I didn't say a word. And I have never confessed until this very moment.

What went on inside my head was, however, good enough for me to be awarded a Hughes Staff Doctoral Fellowship that would pay for me to pursue a doctorate full-time at any university in the country to which I could be accepted. I applied to and was accepted at Princeton University, where I began doctoral studies in the fall of 1959.

To say that my studies at Princeton were challenging is a gross understatement. I have never studied with a cohort of such bright students. Through sheer persistence and doggedness, I passed my written and oral general examinations, on the second try, and launched into my dissertation research during the 1961–62 academic year, writing on the topic "Stability of the Numerical Solution of Hyperbolic Partial Differential Equations in Three Independent Variables Using the Method of Characteristics" (I am not given to short titles). Late in 1960, I met Pat, my wife to be, who also is an identical twin, and we were married in the summer of 1962. Pat had a profound influence on my beliefs about how to live well as a Christian, in ways about which you will eventually read. By the summer of 1963 I had written a first draft of my dissertation, and it was time to look for a job. The surprising vocational direction I took was precipitated by a disappointing turn of events.

When I went to Princeton for my doctoral studies, my intent was that when I had my doctorate I would return to the aerospace industry doing work that I enjoyed and was good at. But, one day in the spring of 1961, I was called into the department head's office for some bad news, or so I thought at the time. Since my Hughes Fellowship was for two years, I had been promised a research assistantship, which at Princeton meant you were paid to do your dissertation research. The bad news was that all the research assistantships for 1961–1962 had been allocated, and I would have to settle for a teaching assistantship, which usually meant grading homework or papers for an undergraduate course. Uff da! (a Norwegian expression of disgust). This unexpected and unwelcome turn of events proved to be one of the best things that ever happened to me. I worked under two professors for the next two years. Yes, I did grade some homework (which never proved to be my favorite thing to do—I eventually claimed that I taught for nothing; colleges paid me to grade homework, exams, and papers). But both mentors gave me the opportunity to teach some "problem sessions" for their students. I didn't like it. I loved it. And from some informal student comments, I sensed that I was really good at making complex matters understandable. For the first time in my life it occurred to me that I could devote myself to teaching. This new idea was further reinforced by the marvelous modeling of excellence in teaching by one of these mentors, Dr. Forman Acton, professor of electrical engineering. Dr. Acton's lectures were exquisitely crafted and presented with infectious enthusiasm. And he cared deeply for his students. He obviously loved what he was doing and was excellent at doing it. The thought occurred to me that I would like to teach like him.

At roughly the same time that I was ruminating about this new vocational idea, I started reflecting seriously, for the first time (believe it or not) about the basis for my original decision to become an engineer, and how that decision was or was not related to my Christian faith commitment. In brief, I became an engineer because it suited my giftedness, I enjoyed the kind of work engineers do (provided I could keep my hands in my pockets), and engineering was a prestigious and well-paying profession. During my single days as a young engineer in California, I was making more money than I knew what to do with—to the point of sometimes stuffing a paycheck into the top drawer of a dresser because I didn't need it—until the Hughes accounting department called me, wondering why they were not receiving my canceled checks.

When I decided to become an engineer, I never once asked myself the following questions: Is the work that engineers do important? Are the products and services provided by engineers important, especially in light of my understanding of what the Christian faith considers to be important? To get even more specific and meddlesome: Is space exploration important? Should I work for a company that designed guidance systems for ballistics missiles?

I am not suggesting that there are easy answers to these questions. My point here is my alarm that I had never asked these questions. I now believe that the reason I hadn't asked them was that they were irrelevant to my narrow pietist view of God's redemptive purposes. After all, if God intends only to redeem individual persons, then the product or services provided by the company I work for are essentially beside the point. According to this view, my only calling as a Christian was to witness to the saving grace of Jesus to my fellow employees, accompanied by my prayer that God will redeem them, and to contribute from my substantial salary to help support other evangelistic efforts. As I suggested earlier, I do believe evangelism is one aspect of my calling, but I now believe my calling is far more expansive in light of a broader view of God's redemptive purposes, a view for which questions about the products and services of the company I work for must be addressed.

That full-orbed understanding would only emerge later in my Christian pilgrimage. In the spring of 1963, when I was looking for work, I knew that I had discovered something I loved to do even more than engineering, and that was teaching. And I also had an intuitive sense, not well thought out yet, that what teachers do, helping students to learn and grow, was important in a Christian scheme of things. So, I decided to explore teaching opportunities.

As I explored possibilities, I did receive an unsolicited overture or two from major universities to teach engineering. I think they routinely wrote form letters to graduates of our engineering program. Teaching engineering would seem to best combine my preparation and interests. But something else was stewing in my mind that took me in a radically different direction.

As I was bringing closure to my graduate study, I was developing an intuitive sense that I was an entrenched intellectual dualist. I embraced two spheres of knowledge that seemed to never intersect. As a young Christian, I had immersed myself in the Bible and eventually in an informal study of theology that exposed me to various interpretations of the Bible (the idea that there were multiple interpretations of the Bible was not prominent in my upbringing). I call the resulting sphere of knowledge my biblical and theological understanding (hereafter referred to more simply as my biblical insights). Simultaneously, I was gaining understanding through the subjects I studied in my formal schooling, which were initially limited to the natural sciences, such as physics, mathematics, and various engineering subjects. I call this sphere of knowledge my academic disciplinary understanding (hereafter referred to more simply as my academic insights). Unfortunately, I was never encouraged to explore the possible relationships between these two spheres of understanding. The secular universities at which I studied seemed to care little about my biblical insights. And my home church seemed to care little about my academic insights, possibly considering them irrelevant to Christian living or possibly even fearful that they might contaminate my biblical insights.

I didn't know much about the Christian liberal arts college scene then, but I had heard that such colleges were committed, at least on the first few pages of their catalogs, to the "integration of faith and learning" (which included the attempt to uncover relationships between my two compartmentalized spheres of understanding). I didn't have a clue about how one embarks on this quest. But I had an intuitive sense that this search for coherence of understanding was important enough for me to devote myself to it.

Pat's twin sister, Carol, had attended The King's College, a Christian liberal arts college in Briarcliff Manor, New York, just north of Brooklyn, where Mom and Pop still lived, and not far from Denville, New Jersey, where Pat's parents lived. Since being close to family was important to us, I wrote a letter to their president, Dr. Robert Cook, asking whether they needed someone to teach mathematics. They welcomed my inquiry.

Seeds: I sensed a strong need to figure out how to get beyond the intellectual dualism that compartmentalized my biblical insights and my academic insights. But, how could I begin that daunting task?

4

Learning After Schooling

o o o o o o o o o o o o o o o o o o o o o o o o o o o o o o o o o o

I used to tell friends that I wish I had a dollar for everything I learned the night before I taught it, and they thought I was kidding.

My interview for a mathematics teaching position at The King's College included time with Dwight Ryther, their beloved registrar, a crusty former military man on the outside and a teddy bear on the inside. The college was housed on a stately former resort not far from the Hudson River. Dwight took me out on the porch and said, "Harold, if you're looking for a good job at a well established Christian college, you should explore a school like Wheaton College in Illinois, but if you're looking for a challenge, you should come to King's." Those were magic words. I love a challenge.

When I met with President Cook at the end of the interview, he quoted a salary that was nothing to write home about. I said nothing, since salary was not uppermost in my mind. I gather that he interpreted my silence as dismay, since the formal salary offer I received was a bit higher. I accepted. This was my first application of some advice that the eminent golfer Jack Nicklaus is reported to have given regarding vocational choice (I hope Nicklaus actually said this, since I have been quoting him for years): "Find something you love to do so much that you would do it for nothing; then find someone who will pay you to do it." (I will suggest later that Nicklaus' advice, as good as it is, is incomplete).

In early September of 1963, Pat and I moved into a King's faculty apartment in Ossining, New York. Pat was about to give birth to our first child. Since her doctor practiced at St. Claire's Hospital in Denville, Pat moved in temporarily with her parents. At 5:00 a.m. on Friday September 13, another new faculty member, David Wolfe, knocked on my apartment door. He had just received a phone call from Mom Aldridge (we had no telephone yet), reporting that Pat had just gone into labor and suggesting that it would be timely for Harold to come quickly to the hospital. Our oldest son, Jonathan, was born on the first day of what would prove to be a forty-year career in Christian liberal arts education, and I missed the fall faculty workshop (I have met a number of faculty since then who longed for an equally compelling excuse).

Dwight Ryther's words were understated. The college was unaccredited and understaffed. The normal teaching load was four courses a semester. In my first few years of teaching my four math courses, I was asked whether I would be willing to add a physics lab course each semester. Apparently I had studied more physics in college than any other faculty member. Eager to please and excited by the challenge of this new teaching venture, I agreed. In later years when I served as Chief Academic Officer at two other Christian colleges, I worked hard to protect faculty like me against themselves. Pat and I recall that for many years, I would be up until 1 or 2 a.m. each Monday, Wednesday, and Friday morning, finishing my preparation for lectures later in the day. It wasn't just the sheer magnitude of my teaching load that was a challenge. It was also the subject matter of some of the courses I was asked to teach as half of a two-person department. For example, my significant training in applied mathematics provided no preparation for teaching abstract algebra. I used to tell friends that I wish I had a dollar for everything I learned the night before I taught it, and they thought I was kidding.

Aside from a demanding teaching load at King's, there was an enormous institutional service challenge: working toward college accreditation. Most of the senior faculty didn't relish the challenge. But I was part of a cohort of new young faculty who shared dreams of excellence, and we were willing to roll up our sleeves and work tirelessly for accreditation by The Middle States Association, a goal achieved in 1967, on a second try. We had leadership positions on major committees that we had no business serving on because we expressed a willingness to do the work and shared a vision for what the college could become.

Needless to say, during these first two years of my teaching career I was not able to concentrate on writing a final draft of my dissertation. Thanks to the efforts of my dissertation advisor, Donald Leigh, who served as a consultant at the General Electric Space Technology Center in King of Prussia, Pennsylvania, I was invited to work at that General Electric site in the summers of 1964 and 1965. During that first summer I completed my dissertation. I defended my dissertation in the spring of 1965 and received my Ph.D. in Mechanical and Aerospace Engineering from Princeton in May of 1965. I probably could have continued working for General Electric in subsequent summers, which would have been great for our pocketbook. But Pat and I decided that it was more important for me to pursue my dream for excellence in Christian liberal arts education through various summer institutional service tasks at King's. These tasks included writing two institutional self-study reports toward accreditation.

The challenges during these first few years of teaching were exhilarating and rewarding, although at times exhausting. Despite the onerous work load, we faculty took the time to be with one another. I remember with fondness my weekly informal conversations with Carl Gustafson as we drank coffee from beakers in his chemistry lab. One of our best fringe benefits as King's professors was a free lunch every school day, during which we experienced a welcoming space in the cafeteria to listen and talk about issues that crossed the rigid disciplinary boundaries typically erected in the broader academy. We didn't have the time for such marvelous conversations; we made the time.

You will recall that my primary motivation for committing myself to Christian liberal arts education was to address my intellectual dualism—to seek to develop a coherent body of knowledge that would include relationships between my biblical and academic insights. In the midst of my heavy teaching and institutional service challenges, I made slow but reasonable progress toward this goal, largely under the tutelage of David Wolfe, the young faculty member in philosophy who announced to me Jonathan's imminent birth. I will attempt to summarize the highlights of this gradual progression.

The academic disciplines I never studied in my formal undergraduate and graduate education are legion, including philosophy, history, and all the social sciences. Although my completed formal schooling in my specialization was second to none in quality, I was about as illiberally educated as one could be. This deficit never seemed problematic during my brief engineering career and my graduate studies. In brief, I was a "practitioner." I did engineering and applied mathematics. And I could do it reasonably well without reflecting much, if at all, about the significance of what I was doing or about any unexamined underlying assumptions that might have informed my doing. And in my teaching discipline of mathematics, there appeared to be little potential for drawing out relationships between my academic insights and my biblical insights. After all, 2+3=5 for everyone—Christian, Jew, Muslim, agnostic, atheist.

David Wolfe, by his words and example, teased me into reflecting on some foundational questions to which I had never given a moment's thought. For example, Is mathematical knowledge created or discovered? Initially, I thought this was the dumbest question I had ever heard. When it comes to numbers, I add them and subtract them. In moments of boldness, I even multiply and divide them. And it all works out. Who could possibly care whether knowledge about numbers is created or discovered? I eventually learned that this was a special case of a question that can be asked about any academic discipline: Are knowledge claims in any particular discipline created or discovered? To follow-up, if scholars in a given discipline make different knowledge claims, how does one evaluate the relative adequacy of these competing claims? Is any one claim to knowledge as good as any other? Or are there standards on the basis of which scholars working in the discipline can reach agreement that one particular claim to knowledge is superior to all competing claims? If so, what is the nature of such standards? Are they standards that exist external to the community of scholars working in the academic discipline? Or are they standards that the community of such scholars has simply agreed upon as the "rules of the game" for their scholarly work? (This series of difficult questions about the nature of knowledge are what philosophers refer to as epistemological questions).

But the questions were just beginning. There were also questions about the nature of the entities within various disciplines: numbers in mathematics, persons in psychology, written texts in literature, electrons in physics, groups of people in sociology (referred to by philosophers as ontological questions).

If those matters weren't complicated enough, there were also questions about the value assumptions that underlie the activities of practitioners in the various academic disciplines. Are there certain deep-rooted goals, often unarticulated and unexamined, that reflect value commitments—judgments as to what practitioners within the discipline consider to be important? I would eventually devote considerable energy to examining such axiological questions, as philosophers call them.

So many questions, so few answers (Uff da!). Mom had a saying in Norwegian about tackling such difficult questions: "Det går over min forstand, og langt inn i prestens" (It goes beyond my understanding and a long way into the preacher's). My formal schooling did not prepare me to deal with these questions. Yet, they emerged as important for me because such deep philosophical questions could be asked about both my disciplinary knowledge and my biblical and theological claims to knowledge. The two questions that would eventually occupy me most concerned the nature of claims to knowledge in the Bible and the uncovering of value assumptions (about what God considers to be important) that are explicitly or implicitly taught in the Bible. It appeared to me that there was considerable potential, at this deep level of questioning, for drawing out relationships between my biblical and academic insights.

I was a babe in the woods relative to exploring such questions. I needed much help. And David Wolfe provided that help. He pointed me to places to start reading, sometimes informally, but also through my auditing a number of philosophy courses that he taught (almost equivalent to auditing a philosophy major). A very important change took place in my life in the process. For the first time, I now read voraciously (every spare minute I could find in a hectic life) because I wanted to, not because I had to. I developed an overwhelming "need to know," not to satisfy the formal expectations of a teacher in a credit-bearing class, but because I needed to formulate my own answers to difficult questions.

While beginning to address these questions about possible connections between my biblical and academic insights, especially relative to my teaching discipline of mathematics, I was also addressing a more comprehensive question that lingered from my pietist upbringing. You will recall that holiness in my pietist tradition was defined largely in terms of proscriptions, a list of things Christians shouldn't do. This proscriptive ethical emphasis continued at the King's College. All of us, faculty and students, signed an annual pledge that we wouldn't participate in certain activities, like drinking alcohol and going to movies. In my early years at King's this pledge didn't bother me much. After all, it was consistent with my Norwegian pietist upbringing. But I increasingly came to see the negative consequences of this ethical emphasis on a set of proscriptive rules. I still remember well the question posed by one of our students when she appeared before a student discipline committee because of a minor infraction of our rules: "When are you going to let us decide some things for ourselves, so we can grow up?" Increasingly, I came to the firm conviction that such a proscriptive legalistic approach to holiness had to go. But what should I put in its place?

An inviting alternative seemed to lie in the version of "situation ethics" being proposed by Joseph Fletcher and others in the 60s. Just love! Just do what you judge to be the loving thing in the given situation. But as I read further about communities that claimed to live by this solitary maxim, I discovered that some very destructive behaviors were being perpetuated in the name of love. Some men considered women to be objects of sexual satisfaction because of a warped understanding of the meaning of love. In my mind, this apparently open-ended approach to ethics also had to go. I needed to formulate a more nuanced position between unacceptable extremes, which soon became the pattern in my intellectual pilgrimage. In summary, I started struggling with another huge question during my years at King's: What is a proper relationship between law and liberty in a Christian ethic? The pages that follow will point to the contours of the responses that slowly emerged.

Seeds: I came to realize that an approach to Christian ethics that deals primarily with proscriptions (what I shouldn't do) was inadequate. But what could I put in its place? I also realized that I had given little thought to the underlying assumptions in my academic discipline, especially assumptions about the status of knowledge claims. In particular, I had much to learn about how to sort through competing claims to knowledge.

5

Needing To Know

o o o o o o o o o o o o o o o o o o o o o o o o o o o o o o

The difference between you and me, Dr. Heie, is that you have a "need to know," and I don't.

The most important lesson I ever learned about teaching, I learned from a student. I was sitting in my office in Harmony Hall at The King's College one morning, reading *Introduction to Psychology* by Atkinson & Atkinson. A student who would flunk out of college in about six weeks, despite being very bright, walked by my door and noticed what I was reading. He came into my office, dumbfounded. For I was reading the assigned text for his Psych 101 course, the cover of which he had not yet opened. He asked me why I was reading this elementary book (after all, I had a B.M.E., M.S.M.E., M.A., and Ph.D.), and I told him: "It appears to me that the insights of psychologists will be valuable as I struggle with my 'law and liberty' question. And, since I had never studied psychology, I need to start from scratch." He then said something that revolutionized my view of teaching and learning: "The difference between you and me, Dr. Heie, is that you have a 'need to know', and I don't." His perception, unfortunately, was that the content of this book had nothing to do with his life. My contrary deep conviction was that the content of this book had a great deal to do with my life as I sought to develop an ethic that I could live by as a Christian.

This fleeting experience created a fixed point in my beliefs about how to be a good teacher. I needed to overcome the insidious bifurcation that many students, not to mention faculty, have created between learning and living, by creating within them a need to know.

In my years of teaching mathematics, my attempts to foster a need to know in my students evolved from providing external motivations to helping students become highly motivated to learn from within themselves. Providing external motivation was simple. My students needed to know how to do a lot of mathematics just to pass my courses, for I had high expectations for student performance. As laudatory student and faculty peer course evaluations revealed, I was good at helping students master the techniques for doing mathematics and helping students understand the theoretical bases underlying these techniques. I was not particularly good at helping students to be "creative mathematicians" who could build on existing knowledge and techniques in new ways, possibly reflecting the fact that I never considered myself to be an extremely creative mathematician. As a result, for those students whose mastery of existing mathematical knowledge and techniques motivated them internally to do more creative mathematics, I could not provide a lot of further help, other than pointing them to some strong graduate programs.

But my desire to create an internal need to know within my math students, and then to help them address that need, gradually took a surprisingly different direction: helping students to address some of the foundational questions about mathematics with which I was also struggling. What is the nature of mathematical knowledge—is it discovered, created, or what? Why should I do mathematics—does the doing of mathematics foster certain values that I am committed to? As I have elaborated elsewhere (Heie 2002), I gradually incorporated such questions into a variety of math courses that I taught, ranging from a freshman course on *The Nature of Mathematics* for non-math majors, some of whom had trouble adding fractions, to a senior seminar on *Philosophy of Mathematics* for math majors, dealing with such questions at levels appropriate to the intellectual maturity of the students in my classes.

But the monumental challenge was to inspire, tease, and cajole students into thinking that such questions were of any importance whatsoever. Only if students judge such questions to be important for them will they be internally motivated to pursue them. After much trial and error, I hit on two teaching strategies to help students move toward such internal motivation.

My first strategy was to start with questions about which students had a felt need to know. I then helped them to see that to deal adequately with their own questions, there was much they also needed to know about other areas of knowledge that didn't interest them initially. For example, many students in *The Nature of Mathematics* course came from evangelical Christian backgrounds and thus had a keenly felt need to know how one can present a credible witness to others about the Christian faith. Sub-questions immediately surfaced. Is the deductive nature of the mathematician useful for doing such "Christian apologetics"? If not, how do natural scientists and social scientists go about defending their knowledge claims? Should the Christian apologist reject these various approaches to gaining knowledge? Or are there ways in which the Christian apologist can learn from or adapt these means for gaining knowledge? Difficult questions, to be sure. I tried to show students that they must address such questions if they want to adequately pursue their question about "witnessing." Hopefully, this strategy inspired a few of my math students over the years to develop an internally motivated need to know that transcended particular course requirements.

My second, and most powerful, strategy for helping students to develop their own internal need to know was for me to model my own need to know. I made it clear to my students that most of the questions I was encouraging them to address were thorny questions with which I was also struggling. At the end of each offering of *The Nature of Mathematics*, I would give a progress report on the present status of my struggle with the questions they were dealing with. The last time that I taught a course dealing with *Philosophy of Mathematics* (after I became an academic administrator), I wrote a paper for my students on the same questions about which they were writing papers. On the day toward the end of the semester when they handed in their papers, I handed them my paper. We then spent a few class sessions discussing similarities and differences in our responses to these questions. A professor does indeed profess, but not prematurely. He must not subvert the need for students to formulate their own responses to important questions.

This second strategy smashed to smithereens (as we used to say as kids growing up in Brooklyn) the common destructive myth that the teacher "has arrived." He has all the answers, which he simply disseminates to his students. Nonsense! Good teachers are also on a pilgrimage. When students see this pilgrimage modeled, they are liberated to seriously pursue their own pilgrimages of learning.

A friend who read an earlier draft of this manuscript made a comment that helped me to see strategies for creating in students a need to know in a new light. Such strategies were another exemplification of my passion for creating welcoming spaces—not just welcoming spaces that will enable people to give voice to their beliefs, which will be pivotal to my eventual invitation to respectful conversation, but also *welcoming spaces for people to creatively pursue questions that are important to them.* My role is to serve primarily as a guide, assisting them in their pilgrimages in light of what I am learning in my pilgrimage.

In my twelfth and last year teaching math at King's, I taught a course that pushed this teaching methodology for creating a "need to know" to its logical extreme. The Academic Dean at King's, my good friend Sam Barkat, asked if I would teach an upper-level seminar elective course titled *Integration of Faith and*

Learning. Since I had been on my own quest for such integration for the past eleven years, I gladly agreed. I was able to shape this course in unusual ways.

First, since I was then in a Rogerian state of mind, having just read Carl Roger's book *Freedom to Learn* (Rogers 1969), I decided that students would assign their own grades at the end of the course, using criteria that they developed and I reviewed. They were good to themselves, which was a bit hard for me to swallow because I had developed a reputation for being a tough grader (where "C" really did mean "average"). But I could live with some grade inflation, because I wanted to create a learning environment that minimized the perceived importance of competing for grades, where the focus was on learning because the subject matter was important. That strategy seemed to work in this course, mostly because of a second unusual feature.

I decided that each of the fourteen students who elected this course would study a topic that was existentially important in their lives at the time, a topic about which they had a strongly felt need to know. So, on the first day of class, my homework assignment was for each of my students to write one question that they would like to address that semester, leading to a final paper that was the only formal course requirement. When I received the set of questions at the next meeting, I told the class we would meet next in two weeks, since I had much homework to do. During that time, I conferred with many of my faculty colleagues who had much more expertise than I did relative to the substance of the various questions, asking them to help me develop an individualized program of study for each student around his or her particular question. At our next meeting I handed out an individualized syllabus to each student and turned them loose. We did meet weekly thereafter, however, to discuss general matters related to the possible meaning of the integration of faith and learning, and to give the illusion of some modicum of normality to the course.

The questions posed by students were not about intellectual abstractions, nor did they fit well into any one academic discipline defined by the academy. They were concrete questions about life and how to live well, questions that transcended neat academic boundaries. The range included questions like: What is an adequate definition of love? How much can we know of the Truth? What is the Christian's role in a secular world? Is pacifism a viable position for a Christian to take? What is meant by the phrase "the will of God"? What are the roles of feeling and reason in discerning the will of God? What is Christian maturity? What is the role of prayer if God is sovereign? In an ironic twist, I would eventually struggle, in-depth, with various forms of many of these questions, suggesting that good students can also help a teacher to identify and struggle with some good questions.

My impression is that this was the best course I ever taught. A year later, when I returned to King's to speak at an Honors Convocation, one of my students from the class told me that it was the best course she ever took, since for the first time she studied something because she wanted to, not because she had to. This comment pleased me but also saddened me because this pivotal experience came so late in her formal schooling. The course was not successful for all the students. One, the son of a college trustee, was struggling with the question: How should a Christian view the present drug culture in light of his responsibility to care for his body? He stopped coming to class about halfway through the semester. When I inquired about him, I was told he had been arrested for dealing drugs.

Of course, this good experiment on my part can be carried to counterproductive extremes where students study only what they think they need to know, without due attention to what the faculty believe they need to know. Education at its best should blend what students think they need to know with what faculty think they need to know. A good teacher will learn to tease students into exploring a considerable body of knowledge starting with the questions that are currently pressing in their lives.

Once, after this extremely positive teaching and learning experience, I half-jokingly made the following proposal to an academic administrator: "Assuming that the student/faculty ratio at our college is 15:1, give me my fifteen freshmen for four years and (using the pedagogical approach sketched above) I assure you that they will graduate liberally educated." Some might argue that such graduates would be unemployable. I respectfully disagree. Of course, our typical collegiate educational structures allow no room for a large-scale application of this unusual teaching approach. But surely this pedagogy could be used more, even within existing structures. The enduring contribution of my teaching this seminar elective course to my thinking about Christian higher education was my discovery that the existential questions that my students posed about their lives were invariably what I later came to call "integrative questions." These are questions that cannot be dealt with adequately without drawing deeply from both biblical and academic insights. This was the seed of a strategy that I would emphasize later in my career for helping faculty to do "Christian scholarship."

Seeds: I came to the realization that learning is most meaningful when it can be connected to living, since this connection creates a strong need to know. I also came to see the usefulness of helping others to ask, and answer, integrative questions, as a strategy for helping them to uncover integral connections between their biblical insights and their academic insights.

6

Seeds for My Emerging Christian Ethic

o o o o o o o o o o o o o o o o o o o o o o o o o o o o o o o

Although my sabbatical studies took place in the basement of a Norwegian pietist church, the results of this study called into question the truncated view that was the focus of my pietist upbringing—that what is almost exclusively important is the salvation of individual persons.

As I struggled with my own existential question as to the relationship between law and liberty in a Christian ethic, an ethical framework for my decision-making gradually emerged. The broad contours of this framework were informed by two experiences I had while teaching at The King's College: one took place over the course of a semester, and one happened in a moment.

My extended experience revolved around my being granted a one-semester sabbatical leave at King's during the spring semester of my ninth year of teaching. At that point in my early studies in philosophy, what attracted me most were questions related to "value" (axiology), or in my own words, the primary question "What is important?" This attraction probably reflected my unease with never having asked that question in my earlier decision to become an engineer. I decided to focus on that question during my sabbatical, reading books referenced in my earlier reading and some further suggestions from David Wolfe. I also thought it would be profitable for me to read the Bible again from cover to cover, looking for hints, explicit and implicit, for what God considers to be important.

So each weekday morning during that semester, with lunch bag in hand, I walked the mile or two to my church in Briarcliff Manor, New York. Like the church I had grown up in, Faith Lutheran Church was another congregation of the Church of the Lutheran Brethren, and they had allowed me to set up a temporary study in one of the Sunday School rooms in the basement. These were full days of reading and note-taking, with much good strong coffee (the way Norwegian Americans like it, except in the Midwest). I thought I had died and gone to Heaven.

Although my sabbatical studies took place in the basement of a Norwegian pietist church, the results of this study called into question the truncated view that was the focus of my pietist upbringing—that what is almost exclusively important is the salvation of individual persons. What emerged from my study was a more expansive view of what God considers important. I concluded that all of God's creation has suffered brokenness and needs healing—what Christians call redemption (Roman 8:19–22). The comprehensive message of God's saving grace is that through the person and work of Jesus Christ, God intends to redeem all of creation (Colossians 1:15–20; see also Acts 3:20–26, Ephesians 2:13–14, II Corinthians 5:18–20). What emerged from my study was a set of beliefs that comprise at least a partial list of my understanding of what God considers to be important, expressed in terms of God's will for the collective body of those who profess commitment to the Christian faith.

- God wills that Christians be *agents for reconciliation between persons and God*, sharing the good news that people can be redeemed from the tyranny of selfish will and be restored to a proper relationship to God through Jesus Christ.
- God wills that Christians love others, with love finding expression in at least three ways:
    1. God wills that Christians be *agents of peace and reconciliation between persons and groups in conflict,* from the farthest ends of the world to our places of employment, our communities, our churches, our homes.
    2. God wills that Christians be *agents for justice*, which includes working tirelessly for fair distribution of goods and rights, especially on behalf of the poor, the marginalized, and the oppressed of the world.
    3. God wills that Christians be *agents of compassion* for those we interact with each day, suffering with others about their hurts and needs, and attending to those needs.

- God wills that Christians be *agents for the healthy growth of persons*, others as well as ourselves, with each person growing in accordance with their gifts and abilities.
- God wills that Christians be *agents for the flourishing of the natural creation*, by wise stewardship of natural resources and concern for a healthy physical and ecological environment.
- God wills that Christians be *agents for knowledge*, for greater understanding of all aspects of the created order, that we and others may live in proper relationship with that order.
- God wills that Christians be *agents for beauty*, showing appreciation for beauty both in God's creation and in the artistic creation of humans, and fostering the further creation of such beauty.

I still had a lot to learn about the meaning of some of these words. For example, what is an adequate full-orbed meaning of "justice"? Is "peace" more than the absence of conflict? Is there such a thing as "knowledge" that is informed by a Christian perspective? Some of these beliefs were only small seeds that would beg for elaboration later in my pilgrimage.

Christians sometimes refer to the values inherent in these beliefs as "kingdom values," for good reasons. The Bible makes repeated references to the "kingdom of God." Although Christians may disagree at to the nature of that kingdom, we all affirm its reality when we pray the Lord's Prayer that Jesus taught us to pray, saying, "Thy kingdom come, thy will be done on earth as it is in heaven." At a minimum, I believe these kingdom values refer to a state of affairs that will be fully realized some day. Although I cannot imagine how, a day will come when human conflict, injustice, oppression, domestic abuse, pollution, ignorance, and ugliness will be no more. God's good intentions for Creation will be fully accomplished. That which is broken by human sinfulness will be restored. In light of that hope for the future, I will hereafter refer to these values as restorative values. In the meantime, like a morning sunrise hints at the promise of a noonday sun, God intends for these restorative values to be realized in some measure on earth as intimations of eventual complete fulfillment.

There will be areas of agreement and disagreement between Christians and those holding to other worldview commitments relative to these restorative values. Many will not affirm a need for *reconciliation between persons and God,* nor the centrality of Jesus Christ for effecting such reconciliation. But the worldview commitments of many human beings who do not share the Christian faith will embrace, in some form, the values of peace and reconciliation between persons and groups in conflict, justice, the growth of persons, a healthy environment, knowledge, and beauty. In fact, many non-Christians put Christians to shame by their actions to foster such restorative values. To be sure, the exact meanings given to some of these restorative values and the means for fostering them may differ across worldviews. For example, we may agree on the value of the growth of persons, but disagree about the telltale signs of such growth and ideals toward which that growth should move. We then need to talk about such differences starting with our common commitment to personal growth. I claim that there should be enough common ground between Christians and those committed to other worldviews relative to most of these restorative values to enable such conversations to be productive (much more about that later).

I now refer to this set of my beliefs relative to restorative values as my first set of *lived beliefs*, since they are not beliefs that I hold to in the abstract, divorced from life; rather, they are beliefs that have emerged from my living and that directly inform my ongoing attempts to live well as a Christian.

For those who share my commitment to the Christian faith, you may find this expansive view of restorative values to be overwhelming. How can any one Christian be an agent for all of these values? Such an expectation is impossible for an individual Christian. The calling for Christians to be agents for restorative values is addressed to the collectivity of Christian believers. Consistent with I Corinthians 12, each Christian is to make his or her particular contribution to restorative values, without any judgment that one type of contribution is superior to any other. Therefore, each of these values is important in itself (intrinsic), not just useful (instrumental) toward the realization of some supposed higher value. For example, I should love others not only because I view this approach as a means to their reconciliation with God, although this could happen. Rather, I should love others because this is what Jesus calls me to do.

Note also that this summary of what I understand to be restorative values provides absolutely no direction for what I or any other Christian should be doing at any point in time. This summary list provides me with a framework of *background principles* that inform my daily decisions, but not in a determinative fashion. This is similar to the background rules for the game of chess allowing for a great variety of individual moves. My most profound insight into how I should use these background principles came to me because of a second experience I had while teaching at King's, a fleeting, very ordinary event that had extraordinary significance for me.

As indicated earlier, I was a mover and shaker on campus. In addition to my teaching and many institutional service assignments, I also had the opportunity to speak occasionally in our daily chapel service. I would receive commendations like "nice talk, Harold." In short, I was a "big man on campus," a "Christian big-shot," or so I thought. But then something happened one evening in our home.

By now Jonathan had been joined by sister Janice (born in December 1964) and brother Jeff (born in November 1967). In our family's division of responsibilities, I gave our three children their daily bath together, while Pat prepared dinner. One particular night, our three J's were unusually rambunctious. When we were finished there was more water on me and the floor than was left in the tub. I lost my cool, angrily shouting at my fun-loving kids.

The look of shock on my children's faces told me they didn't understand why I couldn't join in the fun of being young, regardless of age. Of course, my wet clothes sticking to my skin was not a big deal in the grand scheme of things. But it became a big deal for me because a life-changing thought came to me as I knelt there, soaking wet, next to the tub: my colleagues at the college should see me now; the "big-shot" Christian educator who received much praise for tireless work on behalf of his college and his students, in the private of his own home, ranting and raving at his kids. You see, there was no one in the bathroom to say "nice bath, Harold."

The thought that came to me at that moment became a fixed point in my emerging map of that which is important: wherever I am, whatever I am doing, I should be a certain kind of person, a person characterized by certain enduring attitudes (inner dispositions), like kindness, patience, humility, joy, peace, gentleness, and love. I have often fallen far short of that ideal. But I knew, from that moment on, that this was the ideal.

And the person who has most consistently exemplified this ideal for me these past forty five years is my wife Pat. In her quiet, unassuming way, without ever doing anything to call attention to herself, she has faithfully exhibited kindness, patience, humility, joy, peace, gentleness, and love in her day-to-day dealings with everyone she meets, starting with her own immediate family and extending to grandchildren (Stephanie, Lacey, Noah, Samuel, and John Thomas), great-granddaughter Averi, cousins, nieces and nephews, grand nieces and grand nephews, and all others who unexpectedly come into her life. More than anyone else, Pat has taught me that the real heroes of the Christian faith are not necessarily those on public display, but those who live faithfully as Christians in the everyday activities of life, including the mundane and ordinary.

Seeds: I now realized that my narrow view of God's redemptive purposes had to be expanded to a more comprehensive view, encompassing such restorative values as jus-

tice and peace. But I still had much to learn about the meanings of justice and peace, and how one can become an agent for their realization. I also needed to figure out what it means to talk about "knowledge from a Christian perspective."

7

Becoming Who I Am

o o o o o o o o o o o o o o o o o o o o o o o o o o o o o o o o o o o

The real goal is putting in good minutes one after the other.

My commitment to restorative values began to significantly shape who I was becoming, my "character." Arthur Holmes has proposed that "character development is the development of personal identity through the solidification of values in inner dispositions that define who I am and how I will therefore conduct myself in the various relationships in life" (Holmes 2003, p.120). Note especially the primacy of our inner dispositions as elements of a seamless web between our value commitments, inner dispositions, and actions. It became my hope that my life would emerge as an exemplification of that interconnectedness.

The writing of Nick Wolterstorff also helped me to better understand the relationship of my value commitments to who I was becoming. Wolterstorff's thinking on the distinctives of Christian higher education has converged on "educating for shalom." He defines "shalom" as that state of affairs "where everything exists in right relationship with everything else—God, humanity, nature" (Wolterstorff 2004, p.130). It appears to me that the word "shalom" succinctly summarizes most, if not all the restorative values to which I am committed, for they typically deal with one or more such relationships. I have been especially helped by Wolterstorff's suggestions as to the multiple, interconnected ways in which Christians should express their commitment to shalom. We should bear *witness* to the examples of shalom that we see around us. We should *delight* in and *celebrate* such manifestations. We should also *mourn* "the shortfall of shalom in our world." And, we should also be agents for fostering ongoing manifestations of shalom (Wolterstorff 2004, pp. 23, 24, 26, 33, 130, 144). Once again, there is here a seamless web of the multiple ways in which we should give expression to our commitment to shalom (or, to use my variation, commitment to restorative values).

Based on what I have learned from Holmes and Wolterstorff, I am now ready to state my overarching *lived belief,* my understanding of my calling as a Christian.

- I should be becoming the kind of person whose inner dispositions, witnessing, celebrating, delighting, and mourning reflect commitment to restorative values, and I should be an agent for fostering restorative values.

As with my first set of *lived beliefs* about restorative values, this statement of what I understand to be my overarching calling as a Christian does not present me with easy, cookbook-style rules for living, proscriptive or prescriptive. It doesn't answer the "how" question. God has granted me freedom to make those "how to" choices. This freedom is not license. I am not free to choose actions that contradict my understanding of restorative values, like inhibiting the growth of people with whom I engage, or fanning the flames of conflict between people, or sexual intimacy outside the context of a lifelong covenant relationship. But within this "boundary," I am free to choose ways to foster restorative values (God's redemptive purposes for creation) that are uniquely expressive of who I am.

My free choices may reflect elements of my personal biography, like my experiences with Mom, Pop, and the girls. They may also reflect my understanding of my gifts, like my perceived ability to teach. My free choices may also reflect my past engagements with those not committed to the Christian faith, like my interactions in graduate school and my early negative attempts at evangelism. They may also reflect the measure of faith that God grants me, like the times in my career when I have dared to believe that I could be an agent for improving Christian higher education (recognizing that at the moment of choice, before you see the results, there may be a fine line between faith and stupidity; and I was seldom sure about which side of the line I was walking). My free choices may also reflect the intuitive promptings that emerge from my inner dispositions, like my efforts at gaining knowledge and helping others to do likewise, that flow from my insatiable love for learning. In making such free choices, I should dare to be imaginative, envisioning creative possibilities for fostering restorative values. I have come to believe that all of these influences on my choices to promote restorative values may be manifestations of what Christians call the "leading of the Holy Spirit."

But, where to begin? There is a starting point as I seek to foster restorative values: begin with the persons whose paths you cross each day. This is strongly suggested by Jesus' parable of the good Samaritan, as recorded in Luke 10:25–37.

> Just then a lawyer stood up to test Jesus. "Teacher," he said, "what must I do to inherit eternal life?" He said to him, "What is written in the law? What do you read there?" He answered, "You shall love the Lord your God with all your heart, and with all your soul, and with all your strength, and with all your mind; and your neighbor as yourself." And he said to him, "You have given the right answer; do this, and you will live." But wanting to justify himself, he asked Jesus, "And who is my neighbor?" Jesus replied, "A man was going down from Jerusalem to Jericho, and fell into the hands of robbers, who stripped him, beat him, and went away, leaving him half dead. Now by chance a priest was going down that road; and when he saw him, he passed by on the other side. So likewise a Levite, when he came to the place and saw him, passed by on the other side. But a Samaritan while traveling came near him; and when he saw him, he was moved with pity. He went to him and bandaged his wounds, having poured oil and wine on them. Then he put him on his own animal, brought him to an inn, and took care of him. The next day he took out two denarii, gave them to the innkeeper, and said, 'Take care of him; and when I come back I will repay you whatever more you need to spend.' Which of these three, do you think, was a neighbor to the man who fell into the hands of the robbers?" He said, "The one who showed him mercy." Jesus said to him, "Go and do likewise."

In this story told by Jesus, it would appear that none of those who passed by the injured man, the priest, the Levite, or Samaritan, expected such an encounter on that day. They simply responded, albeit in different ways, to the needs of a person whose path they crossed. The priest, Levite, and Samaritan all saw the same things with their physical eyes, a man lying almost dead on the side of the road. But they didn't see the same thing within their whole beings, in terms of the significance of what they saw physically, so they were led to different responses. When the priest saw him, he passed by on the other side. When the Levite saw him, he passed by on the other side. When the Samaritan saw the injured man, he was moved with pity and bandaged his wounds.

If all three saw the same thing with their physical eyes, why did the Samaritan in this story respond differently? One can imagine various reasons, given the context in which Jesus spoke. They could include social and cultural factors like ethnic tensions, patterns of segregation, the assumed responsibilities of various offices, or religious taboos against contact with outsiders. I can also imagine there being differences in the enduring inner dispositions of the three passersby, possibly reinforced by social and cultural factors. Our inner dispositions shape the significance of what we see with our physical eyes. Possibly the priest and Levite had dispositions of indifference, which is the opposite of love, leading them to see the wounded man as an inconvenience, for whom stopping might interrupt their schedules. The Samaritan likely had a disposition of love and compassion, and this led him to see the wounded man as someone who needed his immediate help.

The inner dispositions that first became important for me as I was on my knees, soaking wet in the bathroom while giving my children a bath, are the ones that I aspire to exemplify, however imperfectly. The Bible refers to them as fruits of the Spirit, as recorded in Galatians 5:22–23: "The fruit of the Spirit is love, joy, peace, patience, kindness, generosity, faithfulness, gentleness and self-control. There is no law against such things."

But one cannot just muster up these attitudes. They are a gift of grace from God. Therefore, I often start my day with a simple prayer that God will grant me the enduring gift of these inner dispositions, the fruits of the Spirit, and then help me to have the eyes to see the needs of those whose paths I will cross today, and the grace to respond to those needs in a manner that will foster restorative values. Serving those around me is a good place to start. Of course, this service does not exhaust my Christian calling, which also encompasses my responsibility to those I will never meet.

By now, you may be feeling sorry for me because of the magnitude of the Christian calling that I have embraced, at least on paper. It appears overwhelming. But that is not at all how I have experienced my sense of calling because I have never thought of myself as called to be successful. Rather, I am called to be faithful, one minute at a time. This insight came home to me powerfully one day when I was reading Robert Pirsig's book *Zen and the Art of Motorcycle Maintenance.* Pirsig tells a story of a father and son on a cross-country motorcycle trip. As they take a break on the side of the road, they look far into the distance and see a snow-covered mountain, their eventual destination. The father tells his son that reaching the top of that mountain is not the real goal. The real goal is "putting in good minutes one after the other" (Pirsig 1974, p. 214)

Seeds: My emerging conviction that I am called to be faithful in attempting to foster restorative values, not necessarily successful, was easy to say. I had much to learn about how to live out that conviction.

8

God Did Not Make Me a Stone

o o o o o o o o o o o o o o o o o o o o o o o o o o o o o o

I have heard it suggested that to be a mature Christian, you have to give up your will. I disagree.

My emerging understanding of my Christian calling led me to rethink two ideas that were sometimes beneath the surface of teachings I was exposed to in my pietist upbringing. The first had to do with the nature of my will, and the relationship between my will and God's will.

At times I have heard Christians talking as if God wishes to obliterate my will, replacing my will with God's will. For example, I have heard it suggested that to be a mature Christian, you have to give up your will. I disagree. God did not make me a stone, an object without a will. God made me a person. And having a will is a God-given attribute of personality—the ability to formulate and execute purposes.

Rather than wishing to obliterate my will, God desires that my will be transformed. God wishes a metamorphosis of my will, away from "selfish will," which is the essence of sin, into the likeness of Christ (II Corinthians 3:18, 5:17). There should be a synergy of wills, God's and mine, as noted in Philippians 2:13: "for it is God who is at work in you, enabling you both to will and to work for his good pleasure." What God intends for my will is that I be so attuned to God's restorative purposes for creation that I choose to exercise my will in harmony with God's will. John Macmurray refers to such a harmony of two wills, God's and mine, as a "unity of persons in fellowship" (Macmurray 1957, p. 222).

This idea of a potential harmony between God's will and mine greatly expanded and enriched my understanding of the focus on "personal relationship with God" that was central in my pietist upbringing. Surely my relationship with God does include a sense of communion with God, often through times of prayer, and my experience of forgiveness by God when I acknowledge my sins (my falling short of the ideals I have embraced on paper). But to that dimension I have now added a sense of partnership with God, the possibility of my being so in touch with what God wills for creation that both God and I are working toward the realization of the same restorative values (see Fretheim 2005). An analogy may help here. My wife Pat and I often know what the other wants without having to ask. We simply know each other that well. Possibly, in some halting analogous way, my "partnership with God" includes knowing what each other wills enough to realize a harmony of wills. That such an analogy may be apt is hinted at in some biblical passages that suggest a likeness between the human marriage relationship and the relationship between Christ and the Church (see Ephesians 5:32).

A potential harmony between God's will and mine also greatly expanded and enriched the calling to holiness that was prominent in my pietist upbringing. To be sure, holiness does include the proscription of certain deeds that are destructive of God's redemptive purposes for creation. My boyhood proscriptions against activities like playing cards and going to movies are now displaced by proscriptions like that against silencing a person who disagrees with me or imposing my beliefs on those I have been entrusted to teach. But it is not enough to focus on appropriate proscriptions. I now view holiness as having a predominant positive dimension: doing deeds which contribute to the realization of restorative values. For example, the proscription against silencing another person has a deeper positive aspect: I should listen to someone who disagrees with me, providing a welcoming space for her to have a voice because that is an expression of love. To be sure, the ultimate realization of restorative values is God's task and will be fully accomplished some day in ways about which I have little understanding. Meanwhile, I am called to be a faithful partner with God.

The second idea I had to rethink because of my emerging understanding of my Christian calling was a static understanding of both God's will and my will that was prevalent in my pietist upbringing. The old blueprint for my life idea had to go, to be replaced by a more dynamic view.

I remember well how my teenage Christian friends and I were attracted by sermon topics like "How to Find the Will of God for Your Life." We listened intently, hoping to find easy formulas (no more than five steps) for determining who we should marry someday or that special vocation to which we should devote our lives. The premise behind all of this was that there was some predetermined, static plan that God had for each of our lives, and our job was to find out what it was as quickly as possible. This mentality led some of us to adopt a very static view of what we called "God's leading"—I sit around, not doing much of anything, waiting for God to grant me some special revelation of that unique blueprint for my entire life. As soon as I know that blueprint, then I'll get busy on behalf of God's restorative purposes for Creation.

I do believe in the possibility of such a special revelation, although I've never had one. I also believe that in some mysterious way that goes beyond my partial, finite understanding, God may indeed know my end from my beginning, and all the stops in-between. But, also mysteriously, God's knowing doesn't mean I don't get to choose. I no longer believe that there is in the mind of God a static predetermined plan for my life, and that God must reveal that plan to me in an extraordinary manner. Rather, I believe that my Christian pilgrimage is a dynamic process: *As I walk, faithful to my present level of understanding of how I should contribute to the realization of restorative values, that very process of walking will lead to further insights about how I should continue walking. In this dynamic process, my history of past decisions informs who I am becoming, which influences my ongoing decisions. As I live within my present set of beliefs, that very process of living will help me to appropriately refine those beliefs.*

A number of biblical passages point to this dynamic view of Christian living. Consider Isaiah 58:10–11. If you will pardon me for reverting back to my days of teaching mathematics, this passage is a conditional statement of the form "if p, then q." It doesn't make an outright assertion; there is a condition attached (the p clause): "*If* you offer your food to the hungry and satisfy the desire of the afflicted, *then* your light shall rise in the darkness and your gloom be like the noonday. The Lord will guide you continually" (italics mine). It is in the very process of attending to the needs of the hungry and afflicted that we gain greater understanding of how we should continue to address the needs of others in the future.

Seeds: I have slowly come to embrace a dynamic view of Christian living in which reflections on my ongoing experiences help me to refine my beliefs and to continue living faithful to my understanding of God's restorative purposes. I need to learn how to practice better that new way of looking at life. I am also beginning to understand better the prescriptive dimension of Christian ethics (what I ought to be doing). I still have a long way to go.

9

An Expanded Vision

o o o o o o o o o o o o o o o o o o o o o o o o o o o o o o o o o o o

No matter how good things are, Harold can always imagine them being better.

In retrospect, I feel as if I had a lifetime of educational experiences crammed into my twelve years at The King's College. However, the downside of loving your work is that you can spend too much time doing it. My time priorities were sometimes cockeyed. I allowed myself to be too busy with my work at King's, sometimes shortchanging my family. I believe that my commitment to fostering restorative values should inform my multiple responsibilities as husband, father, member of a church, citizen, and educator. It has been a challenge for me to maintain a proper balance between these various responsibilities, and there are no cookbook rules for maintaining balance. Since my days at King's, when I didn't meet this challenge very well, I've found it to be a matter of "having eyes to see" what is happening around me, being sensitive enough to detect imbalance and adjusting accordingly.

In the spring of 1975, David Wolfe, who was in his first year of teaching at Gordon College in Massachusetts, told me of a faculty opening in mathematics at Gordon. I was not dissatisfied at King's but decided I owed it to myself and my family to at least explore this new possibility. I liked what I heard in my interview and accepted a faculty position for the fall of 1975.

I suspect that part of my motivation for this change was my need for new challenges. If you haven't figured it out by now, I am a restless pilgrim. It proved to be an excellent move for our family. After twelve years of living in three faculty apartments at King's (in Ossining, Tarrytown, and Briarcliff Manor), we were able to purchase a modest home in Topsfield, despite our having a small down-payment. I remember the mortgage manager at our bank saying, "I have no business giving you this loan, but Gordon people have always been good at meeting their financial obligations." Professionally, my five years of teaching math at Gordon were a time of consolidating my past work and sowing important seeds for my future work. Here are some highlights.

Although Gordon, like King's, was a nondenominational Christian liberal arts college, most of the faculty were committed to the Reformed Christian theological tradition. The focus of this tradition on "Jesus Christ as Lord of all aspects of life" fit extremely well with my broad understanding of God's restorative purposes for creation that had emerged during my years at King's. I didn't realize then that I was being "Reformed." I still remember my exhilaration when I first heard of the large view of redemption that the Dutch statesman and theologian Abraham Kuyper expressed in his inaugural address as President of the Free University of Amsterdam: "There is not a square inch on the whole plain of human existence over which Christ, who is Lord of all, does not proclaim: 'This is Mine!'" (Kuyper 1880, p. 32). I wish I had said that. Although I could not have stated this belief as eloquently, it succinctly summarized the direction that my thinking had taken.

During my years at Gordon, I concentrated on further shaping my thinking about possible relationships between my developing biblical insights and my teaching discipline of mathematics. In ways I had never anticipated, my emerging understanding of the value commitments made by mathematicians began to fit well with my understanding of restorative values.

In addition to the instrumental role that mathematics plays in applications in many areas of life, as in my past applied mathematics work as an engineer, I came to see for the first time its oft neglected aesthetic dimension. Mathematicians committed to aesthetic values are free to create new forms of mathematics characterized by beauty and elegance, independent of the question of applicability. Providing room for such mathematical creativity fit well with one facet of my understanding of restorative values, the creation of objects of beauty.

When students asked me why anyone would want to create such beautiful new forms of mathematics, I countered with the question, "Why does an artist paint a landscape?" For those many students who were too pragmatic to accept that line of reasoning, I pointed out that in the history of mathematics, some forms of mathematics were developed with applications primarily in mind, while some forms were created primarily from an aesthetic impulse. In an unusual turn of events, some mathematics created primarily for aesthetic reasons eventually proved to have enormous applicability (e.g., what mathematicians call non-Euclidean Geometries—see Barker 1964, pp. 15–55).

This coherent connection between my biblical and academic insights relative to common aesthetic value commitments became the kernel for my maturing response to my long-standing question about the relationship between law and liberty. I now believe that all of life, including doing mathematics, is more like art than science and is characterized by "freedom to enhance restorative values, within bounds" (see Heie 1987 for elaboration).

At various times in my academic career, I have proposed, half tongue in cheek, that the mathematics department at a college should be located in the fine arts division, rather than in the natural science division. I have never convinced anyone else of the validity of that idea.

It was while at Gordon that I first became heavily invested in faculty development initiatives and served on a Faculty Development Committee that shaped a "growth contracting" approach to faculty development that gained some national prominence in the mid 70s. We traveled far and wide across the country consulting about this approach to faculty development at various colleges, universities, and professional organizations. This was a seed that blossomed into a prominent focus on faculty development initiatives in my work in later years.

It was also at Gordon that the initial seed was planted that would eventually grow into a passionate commitment to the importance of scholarship for faculty at Christian liberal arts colleges. The saner teaching load at Gordon compared to King's (three courses at any one time rather than four) created some space for Gordon faculty to flourish as scholars as well as teachers. I had never been able to do that, but such modeling on the part of a number of Gordon faculty piqued my interest.

While at Gordon, I had the privilege of getting to know Jim Skillen, now President of the Center for Public Justice, who came in 1975 (as I did) to teach political studies. By listening and talking to Jim, I came to the realization that I had given very little thought to the possibility of there being "Christian perspectives on politics," and the relationship of such political perspectives with the Christian calling to foster the restorative value of justice to which I was committed, at least on paper. In later years, I would devote considerable attention to trying to figure out what it means to do justice.

In the long run, the most profound influence on me during those five years at Gordon was my experience of Gordon as a welcoming space where persons who disagreed with each other were given the room to express their points of view, and where conversations between those who disagreed were typically characterized by respect and kindness. We could disagree vehemently about issues in a faculty meeting and then have coffee together as friends. Although that was often the case at The King's College, I found this ethos to be exceptional at Gordon. What a rare gift! This atmosphere made me feel as if I were a boy at home again sitting around the table with Mom, Pop, and the girls. And these were all invaluable seeds that came to full fruition when I came back to Gordon for a second time later in my pilgrimage.

I left teaching mathematics when I still loved it and, I think, was my best at it. In the fall of 1980, I assumed the position of Vice President for Academic Affairs at Northwestern College in Orange City, Iowa. Some of my friends questioned my sanity for deciding on academic administration. Why would I possibly want to do such a thing? My motivations were no doubt multifaceted.

My need for new challenges was probably a factor. Although I loved teaching calculus, the seventeenth time through calculus, I asked myself whether it was time to spread my wings and embark on a new type of educational responsibility. I had also been heavily involved in quasi-administrative responsibilities throughout my teaching career. I enjoyed and had a gift for such work. I am actually one of those rare academicians who enjoys a productive faculty committee meeting. So I was not overly concerned that my going into academic administration would be an exemplification of the Peter Principle, being promoted from an area of competence to an area of incompetence.

A colleague of mine at Gordon remembers my saying in the spring of 1980 that "I was tired of not being able to balance my checkbook." I don't remember saying that, but I don't doubt my friend's recollection. We lived on the financial edge throughout my seventeen years of teaching. Pat had decided to be a stay-at-home mom during my teaching career. To make ends meet, during the last seven to eight years of my teaching career I supplemented my income from my full-time teaching job with part-time teaching at neighboring schools. I remember vividly an incident late one evening after teaching an introductory algebra course for a local community college at an offsite campus near my home, as my second part-time job that semester. I was walking home because my car was in the shop for repairs. I was so tired I could hardly put one foot in front of the other. During that walk, I had a flashback to my days as a young engineer in southern California when I would put paychecks into a dresser drawer because I didn't need them. I had no regrets about the direction my career had taken. I still embraced that direction with enthusiasm. But I was very tired.

To be better able to balance my checkbook might have contributed to my accepting a new position at a higher salary in the Midwest, where the cost of living was so much lower than on the North Shore of Boston. But as far as I can recollect that was not a major factor in my decision. I like to think that the major factor emerged from my desire to take seriously my understanding of my Christian calling. Let me explain.

At this point in my teaching career, I believed that my commitment to teaching fit well with my understanding of restorative values that emerged during my years of teaching. My teaching enabled me to foster the value I attributed to the growth of other persons (my students) in accordance with their gifts. My teaching also fit my commitment to the value of knowledge that improves our understanding of all aspects of God's created order, with a special emphasis on that "integrated knowledge" that seeks to draw out relationships between biblical and academic insights.

My devotion to teaching also fit well with the vocational advice purportedly given by Jack Nicklaus, which I had embraced, but with an added dimension. I concluded that Nicklaus' advice, as good as it was, was incomplete. It was not enough to love doing something so much that you would do it for nothing. After all, I might have loved stealing hubcaps off cars on the streets of Brooklyn as a kid and selling them for a nice profit (not that we would have ever thought of doing that), but such loving would hardly justify this destructive act. My augmented version of Nicklaus' advice now became the following: Find something you love so much you would do it for nothing, something that enhances restorative values, and then find someone who will pay you to do it. More succinctly, the suggestion of Frederick Buechner is that "[t]he place God calls you to [is] … where your deep gladness and the world's deep hunger meet" (Buechner 1973, p. 95). In my seventeenth year of teaching, I believed that what I was doing fit well with this advice. Why would I even think about doing something else?

The change had to do with an expanded vision for the possibility of my contributing to the realization of restorative values. During my last year of teaching at Gordon, two wild ideas occurred to me. First, could my commitment to the growth of my students be expanded to the growth of the faculty who teach students? Second, and even more grandiose, since I had been working assiduously in my mathematics corner of two colleges, trying to draw out relationships between my biblical insights and my understanding of the nature of mathematics, was it conceivable that I could inspire, support and encourage a whole college faculty to seek for such integrated knowledge relative to their academic disciplines?

If you think these two dreams are too grandiose, you need to know something about me, as stated by a friend of mine, not knowing that her words would get back to me: "No matter how good things are, Harold can always imagine them being better." That's me! This attitude has been both my joy and my burden throughout my professional life. I have seen some good things happen because I dared to have some big dreams. However, what has happened has seldom measured up to the magnitude of my dreams. I have then embraced the following homemade adage regarding my expectations for change: "Hope for 10, expect 5, get 2, and 2 is better than nothing."

Seeds: It was an encouragement for me to find a place in the academy, Gordon College, where respectful conversations about disagreements were common. That initial seed planted around the dinner table in Brooklyn was growing. But I still had a lot more to learn about trying to make respectful conversation about disagreements the norm, and not the exception, in the academy. I also came to realize how little I had thought about a possible Christian perspective on politics, and how I needed to remedy that shortcoming. I also embraced a few big dreams while at Gordon as to how I could continue to be an agent for God's restorative purposes for Christian higher education. Time would tell whether such dreams could come true.

10

Learning Leadership in the Trenches

o o o o o o o o o o o o o o o o o o o o o o o o o o o o o o o

If you're thinking of becoming a college chief academic officer, take two aspirin, go to bed, and call me in the morning.

Being a chief academic officer at any college is a grueling job, if you wish to do it well. More accurately, it's a grueling two jobs. The first job is to manage the plethora of administrative details related to curriculum and faculty. That is a full-time job in itself. But I didn't become a Vice President for Academic Affairs to be only a manager, or for any perceived prestige that comes with that position. I became a VPAA for the second job, which was to pursue my expanded vision for Christian liberal arts education. During my time at Northwestern College, I was able to invest myself significantly in this second job. But this pursuit was always in addition to, not in place of, the first job. The challenge for me once again was to forge a proper balance between these two sets of responsibilities and still have a life outside of work.

Initially, I was like a duck out of water. I really missed teaching. One morning I was literally in tears as I drove to work. I remember my first few weeks of just reading files left by my predecessor (Uff da!). I didn't know where else to start. I thought I might fall victim to the Peter Principle after all. This was certainly on-the-job training. I then decided to have a face-to-face conversation with each of my faculty, over fifty in number. I came to their offices with no agenda. I simply wanted to listen to their perceptions of the status of the college and their dreams for the future of the college, including their own work as teachers and scholars. In these conversations I began to learn that you are a good listener when you can restate what the other has said to their satisfaction.

Providing such a welcoming space for all my faculty to have a voice turned out to be a great move. From these conversations, I not only got to know my faculty on a personal level, but I also developed an intuitive sense of what needed to be done at the college and how to go about doing it. For the next eight years, I learned a great deal about the meaning of leadership and forged some deep convictions about how a Christian should lead (which came back to bite me in my next job. But that is getting ahead of my story).

I first learned that most people, including faculty, don't want major change, at least initially. They say "if it ain't broke, don't fix it." My contrary adage was "even if it ain't broke, let's work together to make it better." This resistance to change often reflects a fear that the changes will be imposed by others, without those most affected having much say in the matter. I decided that the only way to effect major change at Northwestern College was to initiate processes where those who would be significantly affected by the change had an important role in shaping the nature of the change (I am process oriented, to a fault). I initiated such a process, using for the first time a rudimentary form of a strategy that I would eventually refine into an art form. My friends later called it "Harold getting his oar into the water."

The context at Northwestern in which I first tried this strategy can be best described as "curricular bloating." In my estimation, there was an excessive proliferation of courses in the curriculum, ranging from 1 credit to 4 credits, so that at any one time students were taking too many courses (as many as 6 or 7) and faculty were teaching too many courses (4 or 5). I decided I wanted to work with the faculty toward a major revision of both the curriculum and faculty teaching loads that would make most courses 4 credits, with allowance for some half-semester 2-credit courses, structured so that at any point in time each student was taking no more than four courses and each faculty member was teaching three courses. I believed that in-depth study in fewer courses would provide a higher quality educational experience for students. Having faculty teach at most three courses at one time was a very modest first step in my emerging desire to enable faculty to become more involved in scholarly work.

Needless to say, this overhaul was no small undertaking. I started by writing a grant proposal to the Bush Foundation in St. Paul, Minnesota, requesting funds for a multifaceted Planning Project focusing on the possibility of curricular restructuring, without prejudging what results would emerge from this planning process. Upon receiving a grant from Bush, the first step was for me to form an ad hoc faculty committee to undertake this task. I chose an interdisciplinary cohort of highly respected faculty for this committee. And then, I "put my oar into the water."

For any aspect of this multifaceted task that the committee was to consider, I always initially came to the committee with a first draft of my present thinking about the issue at hand. What I would then say to the committee was in effect the following: "Here is my present best thinking about this issue. It is now in your capable hands. I expect you to come up with a proposal for eventual faculty action that is better than what I have just given you, a proposal that reflects the best thinking of all of you, not just one person. If you come to the faculty with exactly my proposal, I will be disappointed."

Collectively, we then as a committee discussed a number of ensuing revisions of my initial draft, and the final proposal that went to the faculty for action might have been a 4th or 5th draft. And when a committee draft went to the whole faculty for discussion, it was in a series of "open hearings" in which the faculty at large could provide significant input, after each of which the committee went back to the drawing board, demonstrating that we had listened well by making revisions that reflected the best thinking of the entire faculty. When a final draft came to the faculty for a vote (and eventually to the administration and Board of Trustees since our proposal had significant financial implications), it was no longer my proposal. The faculty had shaped it and owned it. How could they vote against a proposal they had so much input into shaping? Of course, this process requires much time and patience, but the quality of the result justifies that commitment. To those readers of a more impatient bent, I leave you with a question we used to pose in the aerospace industry: "Why is there never time to do it right the first time, but always time to do it over again?"

One component of the plan that emerged from this project that fit well with my commitment to the restorative value of fostering the growth of persons in light of their particular gifts was a program for "individualization of faculty responsibilities" that gained some recognition beyond Northwestern. This program allowed a faculty member to sign a contract for the next year that stipulated one of four types of faculty assignments: a standard assignment (prescribed normal expectations in the major areas of teaching, scholarship, and institutional service); a teaching emphasis; a scholarship emphasis; or an institutional service emphasis. For the latter three categories, one contractually assumed an increased expectation in the chosen area of emphasis, with a corresponding decrease in assignment in one of the other two categories. The strength of this more individualized approach to faculty assignments is that it recognizes the differing gifts of faculty, creating the possibility for each faculty member to focus more on that area where she is most gifted.

As you can imagine, this approach to faculty assignments is not as easy to administer as the usual cookie-cutter approach. But these individualized contracts are still options at Northwestern more than twenty years after the program was instituted. I left Northwestern College the year after this individualized strategy was initiated (no cause and effect). I am told, however, that the college-wide plan for streamlining curriculum and faculty teaching loads that emerged from this comprehensive project has been significantly altered, with each academic department now having the option to elect, or not, a streamlined curricular structure (about a 6, rather than a 10 in my rating system for expectations).

My view of the meaning of leadership that emerged from my experience at Northwestern was that a leader starts with a vision; she trusts her followers to refine and improve that vision; and she then empowers her followers to implement that refined vision. This view is congruent with the following reflection by Parker Palmer, which takes Jesus as an exemplar of such leadership and suggests that it is only this approach to leadership that fosters true community between persons.

> Jesus exercises the only kind of leadership that can evoke authentic community—a leadership that risks failure (and even crucifixion) by making space for other people to act. When a leader takes up all the space and preempts all the action, he or she may make something happen, but the something is not community. Nor is it abundance, because the leader is only one person, and one person's resources invariably run out. But, when a leader is willing to trust the abundance that people have and can generate together, willing to take the risk of inviting people to share from that abundance, then and only then may true community emerge. (Palmer 1990, p. 138)

For me, this view and practice of leadership is a deep expression of what I understand to be my Christian calling. Giving faculty members such "room to move" and empowering them to maximize the use of their creative abilities is integral to what it means for me to love my faculty and to contribute to their own growth as persons in accordance with their particular gifts.

My leadership experience at Northwestern added a third dimension to the notion of providing welcoming spaces that was emerging as a central motif in my life and work. I previously saw the need to provide welcoming spaces that will enable those I live and work with to give voice to their points of view, and welcoming spaces that will enable those who learn with me to creatively pursue questions that are important to them. I now saw more clearly the need to *provide welcoming spaces for those I engage to creatively exercise their particular gifts.* Building on my leadership experiences at Northwestern, providing such welcoming spaces for college faculty became a major focus during the remainder of my career.

While at Northwestern, I made it known, more by attitude than announcement, that I was available for faculty to talk to at most any time. I was surprised at how many faculty members wanted to talk, or more accurately, wanted someone to listen to their concerns, mostly about professional matters, but sometimes about personal issues. The desire of faculty to engage me in conversation reflected the good measure of trust that had developed between my faculty and me. I was surprised by the level of interpersonal conflict that existed between some faculty members. Having no formal training in conflict resolution, I found that I could be most helpful by calling the two parties in conflict into my office and providing a welcoming space for them to talk about their disagreements and differences. I mostly listened, interjecting suggestions for resolution as I deemed appropriate. I had as many, if not more, failures as successes in these attempts to mediate strong disagreements. But I saw these attempts at reconciliation as an expression of my Christian calling. These experiences, good and bad, were important seeds that eventually blossomed into a focus later in my career on orchestrating respectful conversations between persons who disagree.

The most challenging and rewarding face-to-face conversations I had with the faculty revolved around periodic evaluations of faculty performance for purposes of promotion in rank and the awarding of tenure (a college commitment to a faculty member's long-term service at the college after six years of working on year-to-year contracts). When I was contemplating going to a VPAA position at Northwestern, a trusted Gordon colleague wondered out loud whether I was too easy going and gentle to "bite the bullet" and confront faculty when their performance was inadequate. Ironically, I came to look forward to my conversations with individual faculty members about their performance, even when we had to talk about some inadequacies in performance, but only because I initiated a process that was far removed from confrontation.

The procedure at Northwestern for these milestone faculty evaluations was for me, as VPAA, and the Faculty Rank & Status Committee to independently evaluate the performance of the faculty member, using the same input (e.g., student course evaluations, peer evaluations, classroom visits). We then made independent recommendations to the President, who then made a final recommendation to the Board of Trustees. After a final decision was made, I then wrote an extensive personal letter to the faculty member, summarizing the evaluation results. My letters always started with good news, commending the faculty member for strengths and special signs of giftedness. Then, whether the faculty member received promotion/tenure or not, I summarized the suggestions for continuing growth that emerged from the evaluation process. I then asked the faculty member to come to my office, and we had an extended conversation about the content of my letter.

Most faculty, not all, found these conversations to be congenial and helpful. I think they sensed that I was not judging them from a supposed perch of superiority. Rather, I was appreciative of their gifts and genuinely concerned about their ongoing growth, no matter how gifted they already were. I remember well the comments of one faculty member who had just received a promotion. At the end of our conversation he thanked me not only for his promotion and the positive comments in my letter, but especially for my suggestions for further growth. I surmised that this might have been the first time a supervisor had the courage to tell him where he could improve. I think I was able to provide constructive criticism because I did so in a context of affirmation, not confrontation. I had built up a storehouse of trust with most of my faculty that enabled us to talk respectfully and constructively about difficult evaluative issues. I was beginning to see the great value of first establishing personal relationships of mutual trust prior to talking about disagreements, a lesson that would prove to be invaluable in my later career.

The fulfillment I experienced at Northwestern in being able to help faculty, individually and collectively, to continue growing in accordance with their gifts led me to a conclusion that proved to be a major focus for the rest of my academic career: *What I do best is help others to do their best.*

Seeds: I experienced first hand that building relationships of mutual trust was a good first step toward resolving disagreements, even in the academy. I also learned that empowering others is a key component of effective leadership. I would soon find out, the hard way, that not everyone in Christian higher education would embrace that approach to being a leader.

11

On Being Evangelical

o o o o o o o o o o o o o o o o o o o o o o o o o o o o o o o o o

I aspire to be an "evangelical Christian." However, I personally disagree with many of the positions on contemporary issues proposed by those few evangelical spokespersons who are given a voice on most TV and radio talk shows.

In Orange City, Iowa in the 1980s, you could occasionally see a bumper sticker that read "You're not much if you're not Dutch." That line was typically said in jest. But the ethnic Dutch residents of the town were serious about their theological convictions, which, for most, were Calvinist, or Reformed. Since Northwestern College is affiliated with the Reformed Church in America (RCA), it was there that I was deeply immersed for the first time in the Reformed Christian tradition.

My in-depth exposure to the Reformed tradition was not a shock to me since my own theological inclinations had clearly moved in a Reformed direction without my being fully aware of that label. In fact, my intense immersion in the Reformed tradition at Northwestern deepened my appreciation for many of its central emphases. It was like a breath of fresh air to be immersed in a setting that so consistently valued the life of the mind—that viewed thinking deeply about important issues as an act of worship. The broad, comprehensive view of God's restorative purposes that was integral to this tradition affirmed the conviction I had embraced that Christ is Lord of all aspects of life. I would later elaborate on that conviction as I sought to discern how I could strive to be a transforming agent in society, including the political realm. I sought to find a way to foster restorative values in all areas of life while rejecting the view that I should impose my Christian beliefs on others in our pluralistic world.

There were other aspects of Reformed beliefs to which I was attracted. Drawing on a summary of Reformed beliefs presented by Nick Wolterstorff (2004, pp. 280–284), I embraced the Reformed teaching that God's Creation was good, intended for flourishing; that humankind's sinfulness had destructive effects on all aspects of this good Creation; that God wishes to renew all aspects of this "fallen" Creation; and that God's sovereignty over all of life will insure complete renewal some day, in ways I cannot comprehend. I did become troubled when some Reformed Christians, not all, tried to explain God's sovereignty to me in terms of a strong view of predestination, the idea that certain persons are already chosen by God for redemption and others are not so chosen. That doctrine seems like a sheer determinism that eliminates human choice.

My eyes used to glaze over when someone tried to explain predestination to me. If someone would tell me that you don't have to be a rocket scientist to understand predestination, I'd be inclined to say: "But I was a rocket scientist—of sorts." I have a vague recollection of once responding to an explanation of predestination by saying something like: "I don't know what 'predestination' means, but I know it doesn't mean that I don't get to choose." That quip proved to be a quick way to end the conversation, which was not my intention. I was interested in getting to the question of how that doctrine might affect how I live. That inquiry didn't seem to interest the person I was talking to. I know of no Christian, Reformed or otherwise, who lives as if she did not have freedom to make choices. But, despite this significant reservation, many Reformed teachings made good sense of my experience.

At the same time that I came to a deeper appreciation of the Reformed tradition in Orange City, I also saw that some in that tradition had a truncated view of Christian living, parallel to the truncated view of some pietists, but in the opposite direction. There is the ever present danger of some pietists emphasizing deeply felt religious experience so much that there is a relative neglect of thinking deeply. In its extreme form, this emphasis leads to anti-intellectualism and a mindless emotionalism. The danger in the Reformed tradition was to emphasize thinking deeply so much that deeply felt religious experience was suspect. In its extreme form this emphasis led to an arid intellectualism. From having been immersed in both traditions, I have come to the conviction that it is both/and not either/or. As a whole human being, I need both to think deeply and feel deeply. In his classic book *The Idea of a Christian College*, Arthur Holmes points to the integral relationship between thinking and experiences that may be deeply felt (Holmes 1975, pp. 87–97). In my own words, no one learns anything from experience. Experiences are not self-interpreting; they do not come to us with prepackaged meanings. Our experiences take on meaning only as we reflect on them in light of our beliefs, our interpretive framework of thought. Hence, deeply felt experience and thinking inevitably are two sides of the same coin.

The suspicion of a few of my Reformed friends about a focus on deeply felt religious experience surfaced most significantly in the guarded reception I received when I said that I was an "evangelical" Christian. I was surprised. Some in the Reformed tradition seemed to think that all evangelicals believe that to become a Christian you had to be able to point to a specific time and place, after you had "come of age," when you made a personal decision to accept Christ. Some evangelicals believe that. I don't. I could point to such a place and time in my life. But I don't believe that a pinpointed conversion experience is necessary for all Christians. However, I do believe that being a Christian involves personally appropriating the Christian faith, even if one has been baptized as an infant. This appropriation can take the form of growing into the faith commitment of parents and church congregation that was expressed at infant baptism. But, it can also take the form of raising your hand at an altar call in a tent with sawdust on the floor. We must be open to a variety of ways in which such personal appropriation takes place.

The cool reception that I received in some Reformed circles when I called myself an evangelical made me wonder whether this word has been so misunderstood and misused as to have outlived its usefulness. This feeling has since been multiplied many times by the pervasive tendency of the media to equate being an "evangelical Christian" with being a member of the political Christian Right. I reject this assumed association because I am an evangelical Christian who is not a member of the Christian Right.

Despite the fact that the word evangelical has fallen on hard times, or because of that fact, I want to salvage that word. But my exposure to the Reformed tradition had led me to develop some correctives to the extremes of the evangelical tradition, leading me to forge during my years at Northwestern what I have called elsewhere a "chastened evangelicalism" (Heie 1997). Drawing on the work of David Bebbington, I consider myself to be a "chastened evangelical" in the sense that I embrace three central emphases of most expressions of evangelicalism, but with addenda that incorporate my Reformed convictions as well as insights that I have gained from some other Christian traditions. My three "chastened" evangelical emphases constitute my second set of *lived beliefs*.

- *Biblical Centrality*—the biblical record is the primary source and ultimate authority for an understanding of the Christian faith and the implications of that faith for how Christians should live. *However,* the Bible is not self-interpreting. Its interpretation requires theological reflection and assistance from study in the academic disciplines and from the gifts of Christian tradition, reason, and experience.

- *Personal Commitment*—a Christian personally appropriates the gift of grace made possible through the person and work of Jesus Christ. *However*, the means for such commitment should not be prescribed and can be varied. Such commitment should be celebrated with other Christian believers and should be expressed in a personal integration of one's thinking, feeling, and acting.
- *Comprehensive Christian Activism*—the good news of God's gift of grace that needs to be witnessed to includes the message that persons can be restored to a proper relationship to God through Jesus Christ. *However,* it is also good news that the person and work of Jesus Christ are decisive for the restoration of all aspects of the created order, including the natural world and societal structures. Christians are called to act as faithful agents for such restoration.

Some evangelicals will argue that I have vitiated the evangelical emphases with my "however" addenda. On the other hand, some of my historian friends tell me that these addenda restore elements of evangelicalism that were vital in the nineteenth century—elements that were squashed by many twentieth century evangelicals and need to be reaffirmed. My chastened evangelicalism also seeks to blend the best of a populist stream of evangelicalism, which evidences fervor for personal commitment to Christ, and a scholarly stream, which emphasizes theology and scholarship (see Pearcey 2004, p. 256).

I aspire to be an evangelical Christian. However, as will become evident later in this book, I personally disagree with many of the positions on contemporary issues proposed by those few evangelical spokespersons who are given a voice on most TV and radio talk shows. Our citizens would be better served if the media would provide a welcoming space for a broader spectrum of evangelical voices (for a compelling alternative evangelical voice, see Balmer 2006).

A friend who read an earlier draft of this manuscript noted that my concern to get "my beliefs right" (as in my various lists of *lived beliefs*) is "oh so evangelical." She asked: "What if a Christian tradition emphasizes something other than beliefs? Is that necessarily a truncated faith? Is it possible to celebrate that each church tradition nurtures a particular part of the body of Christ [the collectivity of Christian believers] and we don't have to be striving toward consensus?" Good questions. My response is "yes" and "no." I appreciate the fact that different Christian traditions can be most helpful to certain sets of believers in light of their personal pilgrimages. But there can come a point, difficult to define, where a one-sided emphasis (on thinking, feeling, or acting) can be destructive of what it means to be a whole human being, which I believe God intends us to be. Another response that anticipates a later portion of this manuscript is that the reader should not be deceived by the prominence of my *lived beliefs* in my narrative. Remember that they are "background principles." You may eventually be surprised at the prominent role that I will give to non-cognitive factors as I seek to live out these principles.

My shaping of a "chastened" set of evangelical *lived beliefs* reinforced the belief I have had since my earliest days as a Christian that the Bible is the primary source of my understanding of my Christian faith and how I should live out that faith. But my understanding of what the Bible teaches has changed significantly since my teenage years. This change took place gradually, over many years. It was during my years at Northwestern when I was pressed to consider more carefully the meaning of "biblical centrality" that greater clarity emerged for me as to the nature of biblical teachings. I will now seek to summarize this change in my biblical understanding.

Seeds: As I gained more understanding of the way my Christian beliefs were increasingly Reformed in nature, as a complement to my pietist upbringing, I realized more fully that I needed to be open to the best insights of multiple Christian traditions. I would soon have a lot more to learn from a third Christian tradition. While embracing a more nuanced understanding of what it means to be an "evangelical Christian," I was beginning to see the danger of the erroneous view prominent in the media and popular culture that to be evangelical means to be conservative politically.

12

Knowing Enough About the Bible To Live

o o o o o o o o o o o o o o o o o o o o o o o o o o o o o o o

I can assert that the Bible is true in all that it affirms. But, what exactly does the Bible affirm?

"The Bible Says It; I Believe It; That Settles It." There is an element of truth in this bumper sticker adage. As an evangelical Christian who holds to the centrality of the biblical record, I can assert that I believe what the Bible says. In other words, relevant to the ongoing debate about biblical inerrancy, I can assert that the Bible is true in all that it affirms. But, there are some thorny prior questions. What exactly does the Bible say? What exactly does the Bible affirm?

An underlying assumption about the Bible that appeared to be operative in the Norwegian pietist church in which I was nurtured as a young Christian was that what the Bible says is absolutely clear. I don't recall much discussion about the possibility of there being alternative interpretations of biblical passages. In retrospect, I think we were generally presented with one interpretation of any given passage, without much acknowledgment that Christians in other traditions may interpret the same passage in different ways. As a result, it seemed to me that what the Bible taught was absolutely clear.

One version of the position that the Bible is absolutely clear is that everything you read in the Bible is meant to be taken literally. There are obvious counterexamples that make that position untenable. For example, Isaiah 55:12 says that "all the trees of the field shall clap their hands." No one I know would argue that this verse should be taken literally. Once you allow for even one obvious counterexample, you are left with the difficult problem of discernment: how can you tell when the biblical record is to be taken literally and when that is inappropriate?

The fact of the matter is that the Bible contains numerous genres of literature, ranging from poetry to historical account, and what the Bible says depends on the particular genre being used. To be sure, biblical scholars have written extensively on biblical hermeneutics, intended to help lay persons like me to interpret the various forms of literature found in the Bible (See, for example, Fee & Stuart 1983). Despite these helpful guides, the number of differing interpretations that Christians have gleaned from the same Bible is nothing less than mind boggling.

This multiplicity of interpretations of the same Bible was brought home to me in my reading of *Across the Spectrum* (Boyd & Eddy 2002). In this volume, the authors summarize differing positions that Christians who read the same Bible have taken relative to numerous doctrinal issues, such as Inspiration, Providence, God's Foreknowledge, Atonement, Sanctification, Eternal Security, the Destiny of the Unevangelized, Women in Ministry, the Millennium, and Hell.

Help! It all seems like "a big, blooming, buzzing confusion," to borrow a phrase from William James. How can a Christian lay person like me make sense of the Bible in light of this multiplicity of biblical interpretations? To begin with, I sought a reason for this multiplicity of interpretations. I eventually came to a belief that the Bible is not a revelation dictated by God to passive human scribes. Whatever the role of God in this revelation process, the humans who wrote the Bible brought themselves to the writing process, including their particular social locations. In ways I cannot comprehend there was a partnership between God and human authors in the writing of the Bible, the result of which I can only haltingly express in this way: The Bible is the Word of God, mediated, by God's choice, through human authors, thereby reflecting both teachings relevant to Christian faith and living and the social location of the authors.

Another way of putting this perspective is that, whatever the role of God in biblical revelation, the human authors brought an interpretive framework to their writing that influenced what they wrote. But it gets more complicated. In addition to the biblical authors bringing their interpretive frameworks to the writing of the Bible, we who read the Bible also bring our interpretive frameworks to our reading, including our particular social locations. To compound the difficulties further, the social locations of the ancient authors and contemporary readers are separated by thousands of years and vast cultural differences.

In light of this multiplicity of interpretive frameworks that were/are operating in both the writing and reading of the Bible, and the vast gaps in time and culture between writing and reading, it is not surprising that multiple biblical interpretations exist. Recognizing the reason for such a multiplicity of biblical interpretations was a first step in helping me sort through these various interpretations.

I eventually made two important distinctions, both of which may be controversial. The first was a distinction between those biblical teachings that appeared to be timeless and applicable across cultures (e.g., the teaching that humans should love one another) and those that appeared directed to a particular place and time (e.g., the teaching of Paul in I Timothy 2:9 that Christian women should not braid their hair). The second distinction was between those Christian beliefs that were most directly related to my experience, thereby directly affecting my choices on how to live well on a daily basis, (e.g., my belief that Jesus has called me to love others) and those beliefs that appeared to be further removed from my daily experience and decision-making (e.g., my understanding of the nature of the Trinity).

Those emerging beliefs of mine that appeared to me to be timeless and applicable across cultures, as well as most directly applicable to my daily experience and decision-making, I have called my *lived beliefs*. I have already identified two sets of my lived beliefs that reflect my understanding of the biblical record: the set of restorative values and the facets of what I believe to be a chastened evangelicalism. My third set of *lived beliefs* is comprised of what I understand to be the broad contours of the Christian story that emerge when I examine the biblical record as a totality.

- God created the world in accordance with a divine purpose for that creation, including the intention that human beings participate in the realization of that purpose.
- Humankind rejected God's invitation to participate in the realization of the divine purpose by choosing rather to serve self, thereby causing alienation from God and brokenness in all aspects of Creation.
- Jesus Christ embodied God's love and divine purpose for all of Creation, and by his life, death, and resurrection provides a means by which human beings and the rest of the created order may be restored.
- Guided in faith and practice by general and biblical revelation, the Christian Church keeps the vision of the divine purpose alive through the gifts of the Holy Spirit manifested in worship, fellowship, and serving toward the realization of God's purposes.
- God's divine purpose will be fully realized and God will render final judgment as to good and evil.

As was the case for my earlier sets of *lived beliefs*, the above set of *lived beliefs* is also conspicuous in what it does not say. I assert *that* God created, I say nothing about *how* God created. While asserting *that* Jesus Christ is a means for redemption, I say nothing about *how* that is made possible (I propose no "theory of atonement"). I assert *that* there will eventually be a judgment, but I say nothing about *how* (*or when*) that judgment will take place. I believe there is ample space for Christians to disagree about these "how" issues, and they surely do, as mapped out in *Across the Spectrum.*

Since my preoccupation with my *lived beliefs* may be viewed as highly unusual by some Christian readers, I must clarify further what I am not saying here. First, I am not suggesting that my *lived beliefs,* which focus on my understanding of my ethical responsibilities, comprise a full-blown theology. A comprehensive Christian theology needs to deal with those many doctrinal issues that go beyond my *lived beliefs*, such as those issues enumerated in *Across the Spectrum.* Rather, my *lived beliefs* comprise my "practical theology": those beliefs that most directly inform my daily attempts to live well as a Christian. At the same time, I deeply appreciate the work of Christian theologians who have embraced their Christian calling to shape comprehensive Christian theologies, and I do read the works of some of these theologians in an attempt to gain broader theological understanding.

However, I do venture out beyond my *lived beliefs* when I recite some of the early church creeds as an important part of my worship with other Christian believers. In contrast to the individualism that is a temptation in the pietist tradition, I view reciting such creeds as an expression of my worship of God and my communion and solidarity with all Christians everywhere, present and past. But I do not claim to know the meanings of all the words I recite, such as the affirmations in the Nicene Creed that Jesus is "of one substance with the Father," or that Jesus "was incarnate by the Holy Ghost of the Virgin Mary," or that the "Holy Ghost … proceedeth from the Father and the Son." In my finitude, these are mysteries for me. But I dare to utter the mysterious.

Secondly, I am not suggesting that my sets of *lived beliefs* are to be normative for all Christians. Other Christians may arrive at different sets of such beliefs that reflect their interpretations of the Bible. I am merely claiming that as a Christian lay person who is seeking to live well, I have found sufficient direction for living in the *lived beliefs* I have gleaned from my understanding of the Bible. And I am willing to say "I just don't know" about the many doctrinal issues that are not addressed by my *lived beliefs*. However, the background principles provided by my *lived beliefs* generally enable me to "know enough to live" as I aspire to be an agent for God's restorative purposes.

However, my focus on *lived beliefs* emerging from the Bible did not enable me to reconcile easily my understanding of God's restorative purposes with all that I read in the Bible, especially in the Old Testament. The practice of slavery in ancient Israel that seems to be condoned, or at least allowed, in the biblical record is to me a flagrant violation of God's redemptive purposes. And believing that God calls Christians to be agents for peace, how do I make sense of the many accounts in the Old Testament where it appears that God condones war as a means to preserve God's chosen people, the Jewish nation? These practices made no sense to me. I would eventually have to grapple with these apparent contradictions.

Despite my ongoing struggles with biblical interpretation, I am deeply appreciative of those colleagues at Northwestern College who helped me to shape a clearer understanding of the nature of my commitment as an evangelical Christian, which, in turn, helped me to gain greater insight into the nature of the biblical record and the additional *lived beliefs* that I could glean from its pages.

Further seeds for an eventual new direction in my career were sown while at Northwestern, building on an initial seed planted during my experience at Gordon College. I now gravitated strongly toward an emphasis in faculty responsibilities and faculty development that had not previously played a major role in either my teaching or academic administration: an emphasis on faculty scholarship. What emerged during these years was a deep commitment to the belief that faculty at Christian colleges should be both teachers and scholars. It took me a while to understand that dual responsibility, a topic to which I now turn.

Seeds: My earlier commitment, at least on paper, to being an agent for God's restorative value of peace has run into the difficulty of the pervasive violence I find recorded in the Old Testament. I would still need to do a lot of work to address this difficulty in a way that could harmonize the two testaments of the Bible. Also, I was beginning to develop a strong interest in promoting faculty scholarship at Christian colleges. I still had much to learn about how scholarship could be feasible at "teaching institutions."

13

Being a Teacher and Scholar

o o o o o o o o o o o o o o o o o o o o o o o o o o o o o o o o o o

If you want to ascertain a college's real priorities, it is better to read its annual budget than the first few pages of its catalog.

My scholarly life essentially dried up when I entered the arena of Christian higher education. Shortly after completing my doctoral dissertation, my advisor and I co-authored a brief article in an aerospace journal that summarized the results of my dissertation. That article was it! I was up to my ears in teaching and institutional service responsibilities, leaving little time for my own scholarly work.

As you will recall, I was also deeply immersed in a self-study program of liberal arts education to make up for the deficiencies in my formal schooling. Since I think best when I am writing, shortly after my sabbatical while at King's I wrote a book-length manuscript titled *My Star: Reflections on Being a Person*, in which I tried to capture the results emerging from my own program of study. I wrote it in a style that I thought would be accessible to the thinking Christian lay person, but with expansive end notes of a more scholarly nature. Although I wrote it primarily for my own edification, I did explore the possibility of it being published by a Christian publisher. The response I received was that I needed to target one audience, the popular or the scholarly, and not try to reach both in the same volume. That reality may well be true from a marketing standpoint, but I still think it ignored the enormous need to build bridges between the academy and the Church, between Christian scholars and Christian lay persons. Of course, I realize now that my manuscript probably was not good enough to build such a bridge. Nevertheless, I now believe more than ever that these bridges need to be built, for the mutual benefit of both Christian scholars and laity. The good news is that I made a cottage industry of sharing the content of this manuscript in adult Sunday School classes in three churches I attended in New York, Massachusetts, and Iowa, with the last stint starting as a six-to-eight week class that expanded into about three years, ending only because I left town.

This unpublished manuscript did not enhance my resume. But that gap was not problematic as I advanced through the faculty ranks from assistant professor to professor because my accomplishments in teaching and institutional service were judged to be exemplary, and scholarship was not as highly valued as these two other areas of service. After all, our colleges were "teaching institutions."

On the surface, to be a teaching institution is laudatory in light of some of the excesses that can occur at research institutions. Anyone who has studied in graduate school probably knows of at least one professor who has advanced through the faculty ranks because of exemplary scholarly work but has little commitment to teaching and to the well-being of students, with the possible exception of his dissertation advisees. An acquaintance of mine who taught at a research university was called into the office of his department chair one day shortly after students in one of his classes had completed course evaluation forms. Since the evaluations were excellent, he anticipated that the chair intended to commend him for his evident teaching ability. Rather, the chair cautioned him that such fine evaluations may indicate that he was committing too much time and energy to teaching, which could keep him from the scholarly work he needed to do for faculty advancement.

I do not wish to generalize concerning the commitment of faculty teaching at research universities. I have been exposed to a number of excellent teachers at such high quality universities, like Forman Acton at Princeton. I am simply pointing to some possible excesses at the research university end of the higher education spectrum.

While I am dwelling on excesses, let me tell you about the excesses at the teaching institution end of the spectrum, like at Christian liberal arts colleges. I have seen too many potentially productive Christian scholars dry up because they accepted appointments at Christian liberal arts colleges. The teaching loads and institutional service assignments are simply too heavy to allow much time for concentrated scholarly work. These colleges are not necessarily hostile to scholarly work. More often, the unspoken message is, "Scholarly work is fine, in your spare time, after you've done the really important work of teaching and serving the institution."

The secondary importance given to faculty scholarship at many Christian colleges reflects unambiguous value commitments that are prevalent in many Christian subcultures, especially those with an evangelical bent. We often highly value activities that promise immediacy of results that are, hopefully, easily measurable.

Therefore, many applaud church growth in terms of membership or the number of persons who have made a commitment to Christ in an evangelistic campaign. But scholarship doesn't fit that mold. It is arduous, long-term work, the results of which cannot be easily foreseen or measured. There is a cadre of Christian historians, including George Marsden, Nathan Hatch, Mark Noll, and Joel Carpenter, whose painstaking scholarly work over many years has literally transformed the way the larger academy views the role of religion in American history. If they had sold out to the lure of immediacy of results, they would have given up many years ago.

Don't be fooled by anyone who tells you that the reason many Christian colleges don't place high value on faculty scholarship is that they don't have the money to do so. Nonsense! Even struggling colleges manage to find the money for that which they consider to be most important. I remember sitting around a table with other chief academic officers trying to encourage each one to devote a total of $5000 (a pittance!) to support faculty scholarship for the next academic year. One CAO said that his college just didn't have the money to do that. It was only after the meeting that I found the words I should have said to him: "Show me your college's budget for next year, and I'll find $5000." It would only take relatively minor adjustments in a few line items.

Be assured that budgeting, in colleges and elsewhere, is always a matter of assigning value priorities. If you want to ascertain a college's real priorities, it is better to read its annual budget than the first few pages of its catalog. In a plenary session in a national meeting at Wheaton College (IL), I dared to propose that a substantial program for faculty scholarship (for summer research grants and some released time from teaching during the academic year) could be fully supported by the funds that even struggling colleges devoted to one major intercollegiate sport. That assertion raised more than a few eyebrows. It isn't that I'm against college athletics. I'm all for it. My point was that colleges do find funds for things they highly value, and too often faculty scholarship is not one of the high priority items.

By now, you have no doubt guessed that I have become passionate about the importance of supporting faculty scholarship. Although this passion evolved slowly and became most prominent during the latter years of my tenure at Northwestern College, the seed for it was always implicit in my understanding of my Christian calling. An important element of my calling was to be an agent for knowledge, for greater understanding of all aspects of the created order, and faculty scholarship expands the frontiers of such knowledge. In addition, the quest for new knowledge is important for all areas for which I understand God to have restorative purposes, such as the quest for peace, justice, a healthy physical environment, beauty, and the growth of persons.

In brief, the ideal that emerged during my time at Northwestern was that faculty at Christian liberal arts colleges should be both teachers and scholars. My main argument for this ideal was not that scholarship can contribute positively to effective teaching. That correlation is often evident, but that only relegates scholarship to an instrumental subordinate role as a means to a more highly valued end. Rather, my argument was that the scholarly work of Christian teacher/scholars that helps to foster God's restorative purposes for Creation is of great value, whether or not it contributes to effective teaching.

This rather major shift in my view of the role of faculty at Christian liberal arts colleges amounted to suggesting that the typical statement of mission for such colleges is truncated. My own succinct version of the typical Christian college mission statement is that such colleges intend to prepare students to be agents of redemption who are committed to fostering God's restorative purposes for all aspects of life. That is a marvelous mission as far as it goes. I started contending that in addition to, not in place of, this first time-honored aspect of mission, Christian colleges should embrace the mission of enabling its faculty to be agents of redemption through their scholarly work.

To be sure, I wasn't proposing something brand-new. A number of Christian colleges had already embraced a mission that encompassed the fostering of faculty scholarship (Calvin College in Michigan may be the most notable example). But it was a new idea for most colleges that were members of the Council for Christian Colleges & Universities (CCCU). By this time, I had become heavily involved in the many excellent faculty development activities (mostly national and regional workshops) sponsored by the CCCU for faculty at CCCU schools. I have the highest admiration for the CCCU and have enjoyed immensely my work with two very capable friends who have filled their position of Vice President for Faculty Development & Research—first Karen Longman, and more recently, Ron Mahurin. But, I think it is fair to say that the focus in CCCU faculty development activities in the mid 80s was more on teaching and institutional service than on promoting faculty scholarship. However, as my friends will tell you, I am persistent. So, I chipped away at promoting greater CCCU support for promoting faculty scholarship, with some eventual positive results. With the help of some friends, I shaped and continue to direct an endowed CCCU Initiative Grant program to network Christian scholars. This annual program provides grants to teams of Christian scholars for research on themes judged to be of keen interest to the larger academy. The purpose of this program is to enable Christian voices to gain a more prominent hearing in high-level academic conversations.

As I worked to encourage the CCCU to do more to promote faculty scholarship at CCCU institutions, I also sought ways to implement this new passion in my VPAA position at Northwestern. The enormous challenge, of course, was to create programs and structures that would give faculty members the time and resources needed to be both effective teachers and productive scholars. The streamlining of faculty teaching loads that I noted earlier was of some help. So was the program for individualization of faculty responsibilities, which enabled at least an interested subset of faculty to have more time for scholarly work by electing a scholarship emphasis contract for a given academic year. We were also able to award some stipends for summer research projects and some release time from teaching for scholarly projects during the academic year, all on a competitive application basis.

But I was getting restless again. I sensed that the extent to which I could pursue my new passion for promoting faculty scholarship at Northwestern was relatively limited due to lack of resources. In the winter of 1988 I was approached about my possible interest in a VPAA position at Messiah College in Grantham, Pennsylvania. Once again, I decided that I owed it to myself and my family to explore the possibility. In my interview, it was obvious to me that this larger school had the resources to support my vision for faculty scholarship and could do so if it had the will. I accepted Messiah's offer and assumed my new responsibilities in the summer of 1988.

Seeds: I gradually became a strong advocate for more scholarship at Christian colleges and universities. But I sensed that I needed to seek greater clarity as to the type of scholarship I should be promoting.

14

Fired

o o o o o o o o o o o o o o o o o o o o o o o o o o o o o o o o o o o o o o o o o o o o

I was devastated. I felt violated without any warning. One of my faculty members likened my dismissal to a drive-by shooting.

Messiah College wanted its faculty to be both teachers and scholars. I relished the opportunity to shape faculty development initiatives that supported scholarship. We were able to expand an existing program to provide generous summer stipends and some release time from teaching for both scholarly and curriculum development projects that were approved by a Faculty Development Committee on a competitive basis.

The most important contribution that Messiah made to my own growth was to expose me for the first time to the Anabaptist Christian theological tradition. Loosely affiliated with the Brethren in Christ Church, whose most famous parishioners were the Eisenhowers of Kansas, the college had multiple roots in the Anabaptist, Wesleyan Holiness, and Pietist traditions. But, it was my first in-depth exposure to the central tenets of the Anabaptist tradition that I found most helpful.

The Anabaptist insights that attracted me were not heavily theological in nature, for my new Anabaptist friends were not particularly interested in building theological systems in the abstract. An Anabaptist theological vision focuses on discipleship that translates into an ethic of peace and service and the importance of Christian community (Keim 2002, pp. 269–273; Roth 2005, pp. 19–26). What I found most appealing was the strong focus on living out on a daily basis that which you say you believe, individually and, especially in a community of believers committed to modeling a Christian way of life. Whereas my pietist upbringing primarily taught me the value of feeling deeply and my in-depth exposure to the Reformed tradition primarily taught me the value of thinking deeply, it was primarily my Anabaptist friends who taught me that what you feel and what you think about are hollow unless you put it all into practice. This was not a new idea for me, since the Christian calling that I had embraced was very much action-oriented, and my Reformed friends had already helped me to see the importance of my being a transforming agent in all aspects of life. This focus on practice also resonated with the teaching of Jesus that "[n]ot everyone who says to me, 'Lord, Lord,' will enter the Kingdom of Heaven, but only the one who does the will of my Father in Heaven" (Matthew 7:21). But the particular Anabaptist emphasis on being agents for peace and for reconciliation between persons and groups in conflict was a special inspiration to me since I had already been trying to do that in small ways. I found especially intriguing the pacifist position within this tradition—that the use of violence in any form is never morally justified.

The power of the Anabaptist focus on "doing" came home to me vividly during a faculty meeting at Messiah when we were discussing general education requirements (course requirements for all students—a perennial topic of debate at many colleges). One faculty member argued that the Anabaptist emphasis on preparing students to be agents for peace and reconciliation should surely inform our deliberations. In response, another faculty member said, "That is all well and good, but, after all, aren't we here to educate students?" Despite being at a college having Anabaptist roots, that second faculty member had a very narrow view of the meaning of education, which didn't fit with Anabaptist convictions. To him, education was focused exclusively on the development of the intellectual aspect of being a person, as if students were disembodied intellects without wills.

A more compelling view of the search for knowledge that is at the center of good education is the Hebraic view that "to 'know' [is] to 'do'" (Wilson 1989, p. 288). This view is beautifully supported by a number of passages from the Epistles of John that illuminate the nature of the "truth" that we seek after in our search for knowledge, like reference to "your faithfulness to the truth, namely how you walk in the truth" (III John 1:3), and the critique of those who "do not do what is true" (I John 1:6). My understanding of the Anabaptist vision is that it embraces the view that "to know is to do." I strongly agree.

My exposure to the Anabaptist Christian tradition rounded out my view of what it means to be a whole person, which can be viewed as the personal integration of the cognitive, affective, and volitional dimensions of personhood (or, in more colloquial terms, a wedding of the head, heart, and hands). This exposure also helped me to further clarify an intuition that had been emerging throughout my pilgrimage: I must carefully avoid the extremes of each of these three Christian traditions. Some extreme anti-intellectual expressions of pietism amount to a mindless emotionalism. Some extreme expressions of the Reformed faith are so concerned with "getting theology right" in the abstract, divorced from life, that a lifeless intellectualism can result. And some Anabaptist expressions of the Christian faith can be so wary of theological reflection as to result in activism that is not firmly rooted in that faith. To formulate an adequate view of what it means to be a whole Christian person, I had to draw deeply from the best insights of all three of these great Christian traditions while avoiding their extremes. I am sure that my view could be further enriched if I could be immersed in a few other Christian traditions, such as Anglicanism, Pentecostalism, Catholicism, or the Orthodox Church. Alas, life is too short.

My broad view of human wholeness helped me to expand the traditional meaning given to liberal arts education as those studies that liberate the mind from ignorance. That is a good start. But what about the intellectual giant who no longer marvels at the sight of a sunset or no longer weeps when a friend is hurting? He too must be liberated. And the person who thinks deeply and feels deeply but lives a life that belies his thoughts and feelings must also be liberated. Therefore, a liberal arts college should not be solely preoccupied with providing a strong curriculum—the academic courses available to students. Such courses need to be complemented by a rich array of out-of-class educational experiences (co-curricular activities) that foster integrated development of the cognitive, affective, and volitional dimensions of each student.

Relative to the volitional aspect of student development, my conviction is that many CCCU schools, not just those steeped in the Anabaptist tradition, should place more emphasis on preparing large cadres of students to be social activists on behalf of restorative values. In particular, more graduates of Christian colleges need to evidence strong commitments to being agents for peace and reconciliation; agents for the flourishing of the natural Creation; and agents for justice on behalf of the poor, the marginalized, and oppressed of the world.

A comprehensive perspective on human wholeness also calls into question some common Christian views of what it means to be "spiritual." Too often "spirituality" is defined exclusively in terms of spiritual disciplines, such as prayer and Bible reading. Again, that is a good start. But I now embrace a broader integrated view of spirituality that also includes expressions of the life of the mind and acts of the will that seek to foster God's restorative purposes for all Creation. When a student writes a good term paper or does volunteer work at a local hospice, she is giving expression to her spirituality as much as when she attends a church worship service.

I was not as much of a catalyst for curricular changes at Messiah as I was at Northwestern. A strong curriculum was already in place. One notable exception was my providing some guidance for the initiation of a new engineering major at Messiah, for which my own background in engineering was of some help. One experience related to initiating that major reinforced my conviction that the most important task for a Chief Academic Officer is to hire excellent faculty. As we were searching for engineering faculty, one college trustee suggested to me that I would never find good engineering faculty if I wouldn't offer them salaries that exceeded those called for by the existing faculty salary scale that applied to all other faculty. I think he forgot where I came from. I vaguely recall telling this trustee that I expect as much productivity from an art teacher as I do from an engineering teacher. So, if they have comparable credentials and experience, why should they be paid differently? Anyway, the trustee was wrong. I was able to hire a few engineering Ph.D.s who also had strong professional experience. They took huge cuts in salary. When I interviewed them, I could see the fire in their eyes for the cause of Christian higher education; salary was not their primary consideration. That vision was what I was primarily looking for. It brought back many memories.

My five years at Messiah College were good years, except for the end of the last one. On August 13, 1993, I was called into the office of the President, Dr. D. Ray Hostetter. The thought crossed my mind that I was going to receive a commendation and affirmation for the recent results of a faculty evaluation of my work, which were very laudatory. The first ominous sign was that the Chair and the Vice Chair of the Board of Trustees were also present. President Hostetter told me that I was being relieved of my responsibilities due to "lack of deference to the President and Board."

There surely are two sides to this story. Since no one in higher authority at the college ever expressed an interest in listening to my side of the story, before or after August 13, I will give a much abbreviated version here. Dr. Hostetter is a good man, deeply committed to the Christian faith, to the Brethren in Christ expression of that faith, and to the well-being of Messiah College. He retired a year or so after my dismissal, after over 30 years as President, during which time he built a very strong college from modest beginnings.

As I understand it, the major problem between President Hostetter and me was that we were committed to diametrically opposed leadership styles. As you have no doubt gathered by now, my approach to leadership was very collegial, working closely with faculty and providing a welcoming space that empowered faculty to do their best possible work in their designated areas of responsibility.

Therefore, I was very careful to protect designated faculty prerogatives for decision making. President Hostetter's leadership style leaned toward the traditional "command and control" model, in which the trustees, president, and administration make the important decisions, which the faculty then implement.

A complicating factor in this situation was that I inherited a situation at Messiah where there was great ambiguity as to "who at the college decides what" (the governance question). I initiated a multiyear project on governance to try to define carefully the decision-making responsibilities of the various segments of the college, with special attention given to the relationship between faculty decisions and administrative decisions (closure was brought to the project a year or two after my dismissal). However, even before this clear delineation of governance responsibilities was completed at Messiah, I proceeded in accordance with a time-honored practice at all colleges and universities that I am aware of—that it is the responsibility of the faculty to approve all new programs of study, and to design and approve the curriculum for such new programs. This context brings me to a concrete example of the conflict in leadership style between President Hostetter and me.

At the prompting, I have been told, of a college trustee or two who lived in Harrisburg, Pennsylvania (the state capital about 15 miles from Messiah College), President Hostetter decided that he wanted the college to offer a degree completion program for nontraditional students (usually older than the typical 18–22-year-old traditional students) who lived and worked in the Harrisburg area. I had no difficulty with that idea in principle, although I wasn't enthusiastic about it because I thought it would be best for the college to "stick to its knitting" of effectively serving traditional students. Consistent with my understanding of faculty decision-making prerogatives, I initiated a process (lengthy as usual) for faculty to consider this idea, possibly coming up with a proposal for a new program of study. Faculty opinion on the idea was very mixed, although after many conversations the faculty did eventually design and approve such a program. It is my judgment that my insistence on protecting the decision-making prerogatives of the faculty, and my working with them in a collegial manner as they exercised these prerogatives, contributed significantly to President Hostetter and some of the trustees dismissing me for lack of deference to the President and Board. In an ironic twist, the degree completion program the faculty approved and implemented was dropped a few years after I left Messiah, essentially because the faculty had developed a very rigorous academic program that didn't attract students who could enroll in much less demanding programs at other neighboring colleges.

There probably were other issues besides the degree completion matter that led to my dismissal, brought about by my consistent practice of attempting to carry out the decision-making prerogatives that I understood to have been delegated to me as Chief Academic Officer by the board and president. Such further issues were never articulated. So I had no opportunity to respond then, nor can I respond now.

To say that my dismissal left me in a state of shock is gross understatement. How could this have happened to me? My good friends from past jobs were equally perplexed, for they will tell you that I have been able to work well with most anyone over the years. Both rational and emotional responses surged within me.

With my head, I embraced the conclusion that "things will all work out." I would land on my feet. I had confidence in my abilities, and I had built up a considerable storehouse of respect and trust within Christian higher education circles that would enable me to find another position without much difficulty. Since the college and I had mutually agreed to a contract for the 1993–94 academic year, their reneging on that contract did not jeopardize my salary for that year, despite the fact that my services were no longer wanted (leading some of my faculty friends to refer to this year as the "Harold Heie sabbatical").

But at the level of feeling, I was devastated. I felt violated without any warning (one of my faculty likened my dismissal to a drive-by shooting) and believed that a great injustice had been done to me. I was never given a welcoming space to explain to anyone at the college why I felt this way. I am told that the college contracted the services of a mediator to seek to resolve the conflict between the faculty and president/board. Since this conflict focused on the nature of and reasons for my dismissal, I thought it strange, at best, that I was never given the opportunity to tell my side of the story.

The pain I experienced as a result of my dismissal was compounded many times over by the pain of having been silenced. My voice had been taken away. But I didn't wear my feelings on my sleeves. Like Pop and the proverbial Norwegian bachelor farmers that Garrison Keillor pokes fun at, I don't talk easily about the deep feelings I experience, and I seldom show much outward emotion. I do believe it is good for grown men (and women) to cry, but I seldom do so, except at the end of some sad movies (when I sit through the interminable credits so that it won't be too obvious to others that I have been bawling).

With the ever-present support of Pat and my son Jeff (who corresponded with the college's "powers that be," to no avail), the passage of time healed my painful feelings. What sustained me most was my reading of a response that Mikhail

Gorbachev was reported to have given when asked how he endured the difficult results of his commitment to glasnost and perestroika in the former Soviet Union: "I persevered because I know that what I did was right." Not to compare myself with Gorbachev in any way, I held my head up high because I had maintained my integrity, which was much more important to me than my job. I had faithfully done what I believed to be right, letting the personal chips fall where they may.

The circumstances surrounding my being fired at Messiah first led me to struggle with the tenets of peacemaking that I understood to be prominent in the college's roots. Many faculty were visibly upset by my dismissal, to the extent that a number of them boycotted the opening convocation for the fall semester. But I couldn't help but notice that some of the faculty members who chose to be silent in the wake of the apparent "injustice" were those who had the longest personal history of connections with the Brethren in Christ Church, including some who I perceived to be most steeped in the peacemaking emphasis of the Anabaptist tradition. I am not in a position to sort out the possible interplay of those two influences. And I am open to the real possibility that the reason for this silence was that they did not perceive my treatment to be unjust. However, I cannot shake from my mind the possibility that their silence represented a potential distortion of peacemaking, which could take one of two forms. The first is the reduction of peacemaking to passivity in the light of injustice, in the name of a perverted view of "peace" as the avoidance, at any cost, of any expression of deep-rooted disagreement or conflict. But, it is not even enough to commit to actions on behalf of the avoidance of conflict. A second potential distortion of peacemaking is to settle for an anemic negative view of peace as the absence of conflict. It appears to me that the positive biblical view of peace, an aspect of shalom, includes a focus on taking active steps to foster positive relationships in community.

In summary, the contradiction that I experienced at Messiah was that for all the rhetoric about the importance of Christian community within the Anabaptist tradition, the practiced sense of community at Messiah was not robust enough to create community between those who had strong disagreements. I perceived that decision-making was sometimes done behind-the-scenes, based on a few one-on-one conversations with those most likely to agree with the decision-maker, rather than on the basis of broad, open conversations with all those potentially affected by the decisions, especially those likely to disagree. As a result, at this early stage of my exploration of peacemaking I concluded that if I were ever to embrace its tenets it would be in a robust form that was also informed by my Reformed convictions. The small kernel of understanding that I embraced at that time was that

I should actively promote a broad spectrum of redemptive ends, including justice, but the means I choose should reflect a commitment to peacemaking. I recognized even then that this could be a very dangerous combination. If you actively oppose injustice with peacemaking, the perpetrators of injustice who reject peacemaking may crucify you.

Seeds: My embracing of Anabaptist insights, as complementary to my earlier pietist and Reformed insights, rounded out my view of the need to exercise cognitive, affective and volitional dimensions of being a person. I would eventually need to articulate how those dimensions could be translated into programming for "holistic education" at institutions of Christian higher education. My struggles with what it means to be a peacemaker received a substantial setback. I came to understand a few distortions of peacemaking. I still had a lot to learn about its most adequate meaning and practice.

15

Does a Bear Relieve Himself in the Woods?

o o o o o o o o o o o o o o o o o o o o o o o o o o o o o o o o o o

Dad, if you were running any slower, you'd be going backwards.

The week following August 13, 1993, I vacated my office at Messiah College, for it was clear to me that my dismissal was immediate. Others present at the August 13 meeting later claimed that I had been given the option of completing the 1993–1994 academic year. That side of the story was presented to the local Harrisburg newspaper by someone at the college, leading to a published assertion that the VPAA was deserting Messiah College a few weeks before the start of the fall semester. This newspaper report added insult to injury. But I know what I heard on August 13.

It was an unusual fall and winter for me. To help clear my head and relieve some of the tension resulting from my dismissal, I increased my jogging program, which I had begun 21 years earlier, from three miles three times a week to five miles four or five times a week. Running helped me to get in the best physical shape I had been in since my college days (lest you think that is a big deal, I share with you the words my son Jeff once said to me about my jogging: "Dad, if you were running any slower, you'd be going backwards"). I typically spent my mornings writing. My afternoons were divided between reading and doing this and that with Pat, who was, in her quiet way, so very supportive during those difficult days, as were many faculty and staff at the college, especially Shirley Groff and Jonathan and Cathy Lauer. In retrospect, it was good that I could slow down a bit. I also started thinking about what I would be doing after my "Harold Heie sabbatical" year.

In the late fall, I was provided with an opportunity that would prove to be providential. Joel Carpenter, then the director of the Religion program at the

Pew Charitable Trusts in Philadelphia, asked me to serve as a consultant for the Religious Scholarship segment of his program. In that capacity, I designed a program for instituting summer faculty research programs appropriate to "Christian Confessional Colleges," a program which was later implemented by Pew.

Around the Christmas season, Pat, Jeff, and I took a marvelous six-week, cross-country auto tour. One of the stranger things about me is that I love cross-country driving, sometimes covering up to 800 miles a day. We visited Jonathan and his family (wife Sheila and daughters Stephanie and Lacey), who had settled in Sioux Center, Iowa; Janice, who was living in Omaha; and my twin brother John and his wife Dorine in Alta Loma, California (John came to California in 1958 for a summer visit with me; he met Dorine and never left). I can't remember ever having had such a good time with loved ones. When we returned to Dillsburg in late January, it was time to get serious about job exploration.

As was my style, I was willing to explore any kind of new possibility. The wild idea occurred to me that I could possibly make the greatest contribution to fostering the restorative values I was committed to by serving as a college president. I made application for presidential positions at two Christian colleges and made it to the final four in each case. But my interviews can best be described as disastrous in light of what I think the presidential search committees were looking for. When asked about the future of Christian colleges, I focused on the need to maintain and strengthen the distinctives of Christian liberal arts education, such as the integration of faith, learning and living, a seamless web between the curriculum and co-curriculum, and an "integrated spirituality," rather than on the complexities of fund raising and constituency relations that typically take up most of the time of college presidents. Apparently, that answer is not what my questioners wanted to hear. However, going through this process was a good learning experience. It led to no presidential job offers, which, in retrospect, was fortunate since my accepting such a position would probably have meant that the Peter Principle finally caught up to me.

Sticking more to my knitting, I also applied for a Chief Academic Officer position at a small Christian college near Denver. Pat and I went out for an interview, and I was offered the position. While contemplating this offer, I received a phone call from my good friend Stan Gaede, then the Provost at Gordon College.

Stan relayed the fact that the faculty, administration, and board of trustees at Gordon had just approved a college long-range plan that included the establishment of a center that would promote "Christian thought and action." Would I be interested in serving as the founding director of that center? Would I be interested? Is the Pope Catholic? Does a bear relieve himself in the woods? My whole career had converged on a commitment to fostering faculty scholarship, and here was a golden opportunity to devote virtually all my time and energy to that focused passion.

Due to financial constraints, Gordon only had sufficient operational funds to pay me half a full-time salary and a modest operational budget to cover minimal administrative costs for the Center. I would be expected to raise extensive funds, through foundation grants and private donors, to cover the other half of my salary, the salaries of any other Center staff to be hired, and all programming costs. It was the best job offer I had ever received. After a rather perfunctory interview at Gordon, I was officially offered the position and accepted with enthusiasm. Pat and I returned to Gordon College in the summer of 1994.

I worked for six months on a half-salary, drawing from savings to get by financially. But in January of 1995, we received our first major foundation grant that provided funding to cover the other half of my salary and the salary of a 3/4 time secretary. That grant of $500,000 from the Pew Charitable Trusts was to implement the program for establishing summer faculty research programs at thirteen Christian colleges across the country, including Gordon, that I had designed as a Pew consultant.

I have often told people that I couldn't have written a better job description for myself than the one I had when I returned to Gordon College. I then hasten to add that "I did write my job description for myself," in consultation with Stan Gaede, a marvelous leader to whom I reported. Stan gave me much room to move—welcoming space to be creative. The beauty of this new Center was that it was defined so incompletely, barely one sentence in a long-range plan. All the blanks were to be filled in, and Stan and I did just that with vigor and enthusiasm.

The results of our initial work led to naming this new Gordon entity the *Center for Christian Studies* (CCS) with the stated mission "to facilitate Christian scholarship that will gain a hearing in the larger academy and have an impact on the Christian Church and the broader culture."

Two aspects of this CCS mission statement are pivotal. First, we were concerned not only with facilitating the doing of Christian scholarship. We were equally concerned with whether the results of such scholarship will make any difference. This focus emphasized "getting the word out." We wanted to identify the best ways to disseminate the results of Christian scholarship to insure that these results were given a fair hearing. Secondly, we embraced a broad view of the audiences who needed to hear about the results of this scholarly work. It was not just the academy, where Christian scholars could talk to other scholars. We were just as concerned that the results of Christian scholarship be translated in accessible terms that could have an influence on the general culture and the "persons in the pew" in the Christian church. These two emphases eventually led to the creation of forums for respectful conversation that involved, at different times and in differing ways, all three of these audiences.

As I sought to facilitate Christian scholarship at the CCS, I easily gravitated toward the "welcoming space" motif that is such a central aspect of who I now am. In this context, I tried to create a welcoming space for Gordon faculty to dream about their future scholarly pursuits, and then space to help them creatively pursue their dreams. My main strategy was listening. I invited any interested Gordon faculty member to sit down with me over coffee or lunch to tell me about their aspirations for scholarly work. Since I had no immediate funding to help make their dreams come true, I then worked at shaping their ideas into grant proposals for consideration by foundations or private philanthropists. Although I raised a reasonable amount of external funding for faculty scholarship over my nine years at the CCS, I had more failures than successes (you shouldn't venture into writing grant proposals for scholarly projects unless you can cope with significant doses of rejection). Although I typically started with the research interests of Gordon faculty, I also encouraged them to network with Christian scholars elsewhere who shared the same research interests. Because the research interests of Gordon faculty were quite varied, the research that has been addressed in CCS projects have been all over the map, including Global Stewardship, The Role of Religion in Politics and Society, Christian Apologetics, Civic Education, Christian Virtues in a Pluralistic Society, Evangelical Hermeneutics, and The Life and Legacy of the British Statesman William Wilberforce.

While shaping these various CCS projects, it became apparent to me that I needed a clearer Christian perspective on the restorative value of "knowledge" to which I had committed myself many years earlier while teaching at The King's College. In particular, I needed to develop a more nuanced understanding of the nature of Christian scholarship.

Seeds: Now that I had committed myself to directing a research center dedicated to facilitating Christian scholarship, I would have to give concentrated thought and study to seeking a clearer understanding of what it means for scholarship to be Christian. My desire to disseminate the results of Christian scholarship broadly—to the general public, the Christian church, and, especially to the academy—would require that I seek for greater clarity as to the optimum means for such dissemination.

16

Respectful Conversations

o o o o o o o o o o o o o o o o o o o o o o o o o o o o o o o o o o o

We all know that we can better say what is on our minds with friends we trust than with strangers. But, that has not been a dominant approach to public discourse.

It is by no means easy to hold beliefs for which you would be willing to die, and yet to remain open to new insights; but it is precisely such a combination of commitment and inquiry that constitutes religious maturity (Barbour 1974, p. 138).

All that I have said thus far in this book, starting with the tiny seed of good conversation that was sown around the dinner table in Brooklyn, now converges on my current focused passion, which my good friend at the CCCU, Ron Mahurin, has called Harold's Big Tuna. In the academy, the public square, and religious groups, *I want to create forums for respectful conversation, where those holding to different perspectives on important issues can have face-to-face dialogue, with each participant given a welcoming space to express freely her point of view.*

Such conversations will reject the anemic form of tolerance so prevalent today, which amounts to a stark form of relativism: "You have your beliefs, I have mine, end of conversation." Rather, I envision conversations that model a robust form of tolerance in which each participant is given room to express her particular truth claims on the issue at hand, while extending the same welcoming space for all participants. If such tolerance is practiced, all perspectives, Christian or otherwise, can gain a fair hearing. But such conversations should exemplify more than tolerance. They should model a desire on the part of those holding diverse views to enrich one another by learning from one another (see Sacks 2002, p. 200).

Who Should Be Invited to Talk?

My choice of invitees to a particular conversation will be based on two principles of *inclusion*. Drawing on the work of Jürgen Habermas (Habermas 1990), a first principle of inclusion is that in action-oriented situations, every group potentially affected by the results of the discussion is included in the conversation. My second principle of inclusion in facilitating any conversation is to invite as many people as possible who are both competent to address the issue at hand and who disagree with me relative to the issue, consistent with the purpose of the conversation. If we are to maximize the potential to learn from one another, then those around the table need to represent as wide a variety of competing perspectives as possible. Especially for conversations where one's views of the issue at hand are likely to be significantly shaped by one's religious or secular worldview commitments, I need to invite a diverse array of representatives of differing worldviews. This diversity will maximize the possibility of us learning from one another as we try to listen empathetically to the expressed beliefs that have emerged from our respective pilgrimages.

There may also be conversations where it is important for me to invite Christians and others living in portions of the United States and the world that do not provide the privileges I enjoy. My focus on "freedom to foster restorative values within bounds" surely reflects my social location characterized by a significant degree of "freedom to choose" and an opportunity to make choices that is not severely limited by a lack of resources. But there are many persons whose social location is characterized by severe governmental restrictions on freedom and/or by abject poverty that makes a farce of easy rhetoric about equal opportunity. I can learn much by listening to persons who struggle daily in the context of such debilitating social locations.

In addition to my two principles of inclusion for whom I invite to a given conversation, I would then make it clear in my letters of invitation that I will expect all those around the table to adhere to two minimal aspects of a respectful conversation, also inspired by the work of Jürgen Habermas. One is the principle of *reciprocity and mutual recognition*: each person takes into account the interests and viewpoints of all other conversationalists and gives them equal weight to his or her own interests and viewpoint. A second principle is that of *equal voice*: each person competent to speak is allowed to speak.

How Can I be a Good Conversation Partner?

Assuming that the invitees to a given conversation have been chosen well, and there is agreement to abide by the principles of *reciprocity and mutual recognition* and *equal voice,* how should I conduct myself as one partner in conversation? I will attempt to model the following ways of talking with others, which comprise my final set of *lived beliefs.*

- I should *listen* well, providing each person with a *welcoming space* to express her perspective on the issue at hand.
- I should present my perspective on the issue, with a non-coercive style that *invites further conversation* with those who disagree.
- I should seek to *understand* differing perspectives, religious or secular, by empathetically entering into the assumptions that distinguish other views and trying to grasp the rationales for those differences.
- I should seek some *common ground* with those who disagree with me, while also seeking to illuminate our differences.
- I should demonstrate *respect and concern* for the well being of all participants in the conversation, even when significant common ground is unattainable due to irreconcilable differences in perspective.

The presentation of one's perspective can include an explanation of its *genesis,* if judged to be pertinent, but must include a *public rationale.*

Genesis and Public Rationale

Blaise Pascal famously said, "The heart has its own reason, which reason does not know." He appeared to be allowing that the reason one may give for a particular perspective on the issue at hand can emerge from our exercising reasoning capacities or can originate from sources other than reasoning. I concur. But, this equivocation on the use of the word "reason" is confusing, at best. Therefore, I will avoid using this much misused word. Rather, I will use the words "genesis" and "public rationale," distinguished as follows.

I use "genesis" to refer to the source of a person's position on the issue being discussed. This source can surely be the product of exercising one's reasoning capacities. But I allow for other possible sources: deep feelings; experiences in one's pilgrimage; and worldview commitments, religious or secular.

This openness appears to be leading us into wild territory. A critical distinction must now be made between the genesis of a claim to knowledge, which can be a personal or private matter, and its evaluation in public discourse. The public evaluation of a claim to knowledge, whatever its source, must be based on the merits of a public rationale presented for the claim, expressed in terms accessible to everyone seated around the table, with the evaluation based on publicly accessible standards for evaluation (a complex matter to which I will return in Part II).

In the political realm, my openness to a variety of sources for knowledge claims suggests that a helpful model for deliberation known as "deliberative democracy" has limitations. Those arguing for deliberative democracy propose principles for "reasonable argument" that they believe will help to resolve disagreements relative to volatile contemporary moral issues, while helping us to live with disagreements that will inevitably persist (see Banhanib 1996 and Gutman & Thompson 1996).

Scholars who point to the limitations of deliberative democracy (see Young 1996 and Woodiwiss 2001) argue that this model is not inclusive enough. The proposed "norms of deliberation ... privilege speech that is dispassionate and disembodied" (Young 1996, p. 124). Since the focus is on "argument," "speech that is assertive and confrontational is ... valued more than speech that is tentative, exploratory, or conciliatory" (Young 1996, p. 123). Young proposes a "broadened theory," called "communicative democracy," that "requires in addition to critical argument: greeting, rhetoric, and storytelling."

By "greeting" Young means that "the parties in the dialogue recognize one another in their particularity," and their dialogue begins with "preliminaries in which the parties establish trust or respect." Young's appeal to "rhetoric" calls for going beyond "rational speech" that can too easily "denigrate emotion and figurative language," and that values speaking more highly than listening. By "storytelling," Young refers to the "narrative ('stories to tell') [that] reveals the particular experiences of those in social locations, experiences that cannot be shared by those situated differently but that they must understand in order to do justice to the others" (pp. 129–132).

My proposal on how to be a good conversation partner, on which I will elaborate further in Part II, resonates with Young's position. In the meantime, I can testify from my experience at the Center for Christian Studies at Gordon College as to the importance of that element of "greeting" that Young refers to as "preliminaries ... to establish trust or respect."

The Prior Need for Building Relationships of Mutual Trust

As I developed various initiatives during my tenure as director of the Center for Christian Studies, a focus on orchestrating respectful conversations emerged.

Many of our projects addressed topics that would be of interest primarily to scholars working out of religious traditions (e.g., a conversation on the Role of Religion in Politics and Society, cosponsored by the CCS and the Inter-Religious Affairs Department of the American Jewish Committee). But, some other projects dealt with projects that we hoped would be of interest to a broad array of scholars, religious or secular (e.g., a conversation on International Public Policy held at Faneuil Hall in Boston). For such events, we extended hardcopy and electronic invitations to scholars at the many excellent colleges and universities in the greater Boston area. Few, if any, came. Why?

Surely, one reason is that all scholars are very busy with their own teaching and research. Furthermore, one could attend an excellent academic conference most any night of the week in the Boston area, if so inclined. I gradually concluded that another reason could be that these scholars "didn't know us." Some may even have viewed us as "those strange Christian folks" up on the North Shore. We had not established the interpersonal relationships that could engender the mutual trust needed to motivate non-Christian scholars to want to know what a scholar friend who was a Christian thought about an important issue of common interest.

If that conjecture on my part is correct, then the ideals I proposed for being a good conversation partner may be necessary, but not sufficient. If Christians wish to attract non-Christians to their tables for conversations, an important prior step may need to be taken: *First, establish personal relationships of mutual trust with those with whom you wish to talk.* Such relationship-building has the potential to attract non-Christians to our table, thereby opening up the possibility for Christian perspectives on a given issue to gain a fair and respectful hearing, along with all other perspectives represented around the table.

Of course we have neither the time nor the energy to befriend everyone with whom we wish to talk. But, as circumstances allow, this interpersonal strategy is potent. Lest you think that claim is audacious wishful thinking, I will now summarize the results of a recently completed CCS project, titled *Christians Engaging Culture*, where this interpersonal strategy has proven to be very successful in enabling Christian perspectives to gain a fair and respectful hearing. This project focused on case studies in each of three areas of discourse: public policy practice, politics, and the academy (for essays that report on these case studies, go to www.gordon.edu/ccs). I report briefly here on two case studies, holding the academy case study for consideration in Part IV.

Public Policy Practice

The case study for the area of Public Policy Practice featured the work of Susan Emmerich on *Fostering Environmental Responsibility on the Part of the Watermen of Chesapeake Bay.* Dr. Emmerich, an environmental scientist at Trinity Christian College (IL), has completed an "action research" project focused on working with the colony of watermen on Tangiers Island in Chesapeake Bay. Her goal was to reverse their environmentally destructive practices perceived as necessary for economic survival. The watermen of Chesapeake Bay were deeply skeptical—even hostile—to solutions to environmental problems being proposed by certain environmental scientists without consultation with those whose livelihood could be adversely affected. In stark contrast to the impersonal approach taken by these environmental scientists, Dr. Emmerich moved in with the families of the watermen of Tangiers Island. She lived with them, socialized with them, and worshipped with those who were Christians. By getting to know them, she slowly developed the trust needed to engage in ongoing conversations that persuaded the watermen to address the environmental problems they were partially responsible for creating.

Politics

It is easy to sink into deep despair about the possibility of orchestrating respectful conversations in politics. Given the rampant partisanship and the pervasive influence of special interest groups and money, each politician's standard for evaluating his own legislative initiatives is often "will it get me reelected?" The idea of agreeing on standards for evaluation related to the promotion of a common good appears to be rare. And the idea of politicians on both sides of the aisle proceeding on the basis of building mutual trust seems ludicrous. But, there are notable exceptions, as modeled in a second case study, titled *Confrontational Politics Versus Finding Principled Common Ground.*

Dr. Paul Deweese is a former Republican member of the Michigan House of Representatives. While serving in the Michigan House, he was appalled by the dominant influence of special interest groups and, especially, the hyper-partisanship of contemporary politics. Swimming upstream, he sought to exemplify what he calls a "personalism in politics," which included seeking common ground with members of both parties concerning possible legislative initiatives that would foster "human dignity" (that being the standard for evaluating competing legislative proposals). His personalist approach also included his "getting to know" members of the other party (Democrats) on a more personal level, thereby helping to build bridges. His goal was to create bipartisan coalitions for supporting legislative initiatives that promote human dignity.

As a rich complement to Paul Deweese's experience, consider a reflection by Thomas Kean, former Governor of New Jersey, concerning his work on the 9/11 Commission: "We got to know each other personally ... If you just sit in meetings, you never get anywhere. But once you get to know the others, and their families, the D's and the R's start to disappear" (Moran 2005, pp. 21, 27).

A more recent example of the efficacy of a personalist approach to doing politics is the bipartisan proposal on immigration policy forged in May 2007. The ad hoc committee of Republican and Democrat senators who formulated the proposed legislation reported that they "overcame divisions and some level of distrust to produce the agreement ...," adding that "they forged bonds partly though the telling of personal stories about their own family roots, as well as long hours spent together ..." (Hulse and Pear 2007, p. A11). Unfortunately, debate on this proposal in the full Senate led to a stalemate. Hopefully, much needed legislation on immigration will emerge from the next session of Congress.

In brief, the formidable challenge to the bipartisan seeking for common ground is that it is contrary to the hyper-partisanship now rampant in politics. Laurence Tribe of Yale law School points to this challenge in his reflections on the candidacy of Barack Obama for president in 2008: "He brings to politics a desire to find common ground, which makes it impossible to predict exactly how he would line up on various people's litmus test issues." Obama "comes at things in a way that is perpendicular to the usual left-right axis" (Zeleny 2006, p. 1). Time will tell whether it is possible to do politics in this new way.

Church Education

Although not included in the CCS *Christians Engaging Culture* project, my own experience suggests that the interpersonal strategy of building mutual trust can also be helpful for educational initiatives within the Christian church. I have seen the positive results of such a strategy through my involvement in an evangelism initiative called the Alpha Program. This program originated in the Holy Trinity Brompton Anglican Parish in London and has rapidly spread worldwide.

When I was asked to provide leadership for this ten-session course at my local Evangelical Covenant Church in Peabody, Massachusetts, I was hesitant because of my disastrous boyhood efforts at evangelism. But I accepted the challenge, and Alpha was like a breath of fresh air.

We invited non-churchgoers, new Christians and some church regulars to attend Alpha. Each session started with a meal, followed by the viewing of a video produced by Holy Trinity Brampton that presented some aspect of the Christian faith in an engaging, winsome manner (albeit with a particular theological stance). We then broke into three groups of about 10 persons each to discuss the video. So far, nothing startling.

It was the ground rules that were different, and then the results. Everything was up for discussion. There were no prepackaged answers forced on anyone. No question was considered dumb or heretical. As mutual trust and friendships developed, we learned to be more open and honest with each other, sharing the ups and downs of our pilgrimages. We did a lot of listening. We created a welcoming space where participants felt free to share their struggles of faith and their doubts. Some of the lapsed churchgoers were dumbfounded, for they had previously experienced church as a coercive place where conversation was not encouraged and difficult questions could not be asked.

The truth claims of the Christian faith were presented through Alpha, but the mode of engagement was respectful conversation. As opportunity presented itself in the flow of conversation, I simply shared my experiences of the grace of God in my life, and witnessed to the ways in which my Christian faith helped me to find meaning in life and to make some sense of my experiences, inviting others to also share reflections on their various searches for meaning and sense. We then felt free to talk about our differing reflections. We didn't have altar calls, but some non-churchgoers made a commitment to the Christian faith. Others decided to become members of our church. The seeds of the gospel were sown in a caring, non-coercive manner.

The Homosexuality Debate

Current debates about homosexuality are particularly volatile within both the Christian church and the broader public arena. The raging debate within the Christian church is causing deep divisions in some Christian churches and denominations. My call for initiating respectful conversations on this issue by first building interpersonal relationships of mutual trust may seem like an impossible dream in such communities. But that is still my dream. I think that dream is realizable in some measure if Christians who disagree on this issue are willing to start with some elements of common ground.

First, we need to acknowledge that there are equally committed Christians who take opposing views on this issue (see the bibliography in "Further Recommended Reading"). It is not the case that all those on one side of this issue take a "high view of the Bible" while all those on the other side do not. There are persons who take diametrically opposed views on this issue who are equally committed to biblical authority. They disagree on how to interpret the relevant biblical passages. Therefore, a person's views on homosexuality should not be used as a litmus test as to whether that person is a Christian or for judging how good a Christian that person is.

Second, in light of our common Christian calling, we need to open our arms with a loving embrace toward those who disagree with us about this issue, especially those for whom this is not an abstraction but an issue that impacts their daily lives (for a compelling general description of the four elements in "The Drama of Embrace," see Volf 1996, pp. 140–147). Christian churches, at both the local congregational and denominational levels, should aspire to be places that welcome and create fellowship among Christians having diverse views on homosexuality. The Protestant tendency to run off to or start other churches or denominations where "all the people agree with me" on the issue of homosexuality should be avoided.

Third, those of us who are heterosexuals need to avoid the easy path of just talking *about* homosexuals. We need to talk *with* homosexuals. It appears audacious to me, at best, if church bodies debating whether homosexuals should have continuing membership in their communities do not give a voice to those they may wish to exclude. We need more face-to-face encounters, creating a welcoming space in which we listen to gay and lesbian persons telling us first hand about their experiences, commitments, and perspectives. If we end up with differing beliefs about this volatile issue, it should be after we have heard them speak and talked about our disagreements (see Heskins 2005, pp. 70, 71, 153). Marcus Smucker, a Mennonite pastor and educator who loves a daughter who is lesbian and has had in-depth conversations with Christians who are gay and lesbian, has presented a compelling account of the experiences of homosexuals within the Christian church and the larger society. Based on these conversations, he suggests some "Implications for the Church" (Smucker 2001). At the conclusion of his account, he proposes that "[w]e need to invest time and energy in learning to know gay and lesbian people and in beginning to understand their experiences" (Smucker 2001, p. 61).

Fourth, we need to agree that more patience is required as we seek to sort through differing viewpoints on homosexuality. Christians, especially those of an evangelical bent, are so prone to want quick and easy answers to complex issues. It is not likely that a "Christian consensus" about this highly contested issue will emerge in the near future. All of us can benefit from the insight of Mennonite theologian John Howard Yoder, who observes that the truth about a given matter often emerges slowly, as a gift, as we make ourselves vulnerable through ongoing conversation with one another (Yoder 1984). David Schroeder has made a proposal relative to the contentious question within the Mennonite Church as to church membership extending to same-sex partners living in a monogamous covenant relationship: "One alternative might be to declare that we are not yet ready to give a final answer to the problem of inclusion or exclusion of Christians who have made a same-sex covenant. We would declare this to be something we are working on and agree that people need to search together for what will have saving power for all" (Schroeder 2001, pp. 72–73). To paraphrase what another Mennonite educator once said to me: "We are committed to ongoing conversations as a community of believers, hoping and praying that as we listen and talk, collective discernment will emerge on the difficult issue of homosexuality." What a marvelous gift such collective discernment would be. But, the process will require much patience.

Finally, we need to agree to orchestrate conversations on homosexuality that start by identifying substantive common ground. In a marvelous essay on how to get such a respectful conversation started, the Mennonite scholar Mark Thiessen Nation notes no less than eight points on which "most within the Mennonite Church (and really the larger Church) would agree" (Nation 2001, p. 225). He then introduces "Glosses on Areas of Agreement" that "help us name the differences within the agreement so that, once named, they can perhaps be more accessible as points of discussion/debate" (p. 228). Such painstaking foundational work needs to be done if there is to be any hope for respectful conversation about this divisive issue.

As already alluded to in some of the works cited above, I believe that the Mennonite Christian community has much to teach all Christians about how to proceed in dealing with the homosexuality issue. As suggested by one Mennonite pastor, "If we avoid face-to-face conversation, debate, and discernment and use instead the politics of confrontation, then we, supposedly a historic peace church, will have no more a redemptive way forward than denominations seemingly ready to engage in Holy War" (Kaufmann 2001, p. 8).

Such interpersonal engagement has proven to be difficult and challenging because of strong disagreements on this issue within the Mennonite community (for one report, see King 2001). Nevertheless, the Mennonite Christian community has stated its commitment to "loving dialogue" and has published works that respectfully present a spectrum of competing views on this contentious issue as a basis for such ongoing dialogue (see Kraus 2001 and King 2006).

It should be noted, however, that one Mennonite educator who has been involved in a number of conversations with Mennonites about homosexuality suggests that "we may simply need to ... start over" because "we have built on a shoddy foundation ... *we simply have not built the necessary relationships*, and we are making decisions in anger and bitterness" (Schrock-Shenk 2001, p. 247, italics mine). To whatever extent her assessment is shared within the Mennonite community, it would lend support to my proposal that a necessary step prior to engaging others about contentious issues is to establish personal relationships of mutual trust with those with whom you wish to talk. The importance of this interpersonal emphasis is also highlighted in an edited volume that reports on discussions of homosexuality within some mainline Christian congregations, in which it is observed that the emotional responses to homosexuality are so powerful that before discussion will be possible it is necessary to establish "deepening interpersonal relationships" that will provide a safe space for persons to "come to terms with their guts," to prepare them "to use their heads" (Gaede, Beth Ann 1998, pp. 25, 30).

In my vision for respectful conversation about homosexuality, I propose that Christians need to take initiatives to extend the conversation about homosexuality beyond the Church to the broader public. For those who consider that to be an impossible dream, I point to one example where this dialogue has taken place.

A few years ago, Tufts University worked through a difficult situation in which a campus organization, the Tufts Christian Fellowship, lost its college support because it precluded homosexuals from holding leadership positions. As an aftermath of working through this situation, which led to the reinstatement of college support, the leadership of Tufts Christian Fellowship (TCF) and the Tufts Transgendered Lesbian Gay Bisexual Collective (TTLGBC) took the initiative to cosponsor a conversation, which they described as follows:

> Come join a discussion of relations between evangelical Christians and the homosexual community. The evening will be centered around presentations by two journalists who met while covering the 1999 Columbine High School shooting. Dave Cullen of Salon.com and Wendy Zoba of *Christianity Today* will be discussing their experiences as a homosexual and evangelical Christian forging a friendship despite their differences. It is hoped that this event will help lay the foundation for improved future relations and progress toward mutual respect and understanding within the Tufts community, and particularly between members of TCF and TTLGBC.

The goals may seem modest: "mutual respect and understanding" between persons having strong disagreements. But that is surely a rarity. Note especially that those leading this conversation were a homosexual and evangelical Christian who "[forged] a friendship despite their differences." This example exemplifies my claim that respectful conversations are best initiated by first building interpersonal relationships of mutual trust.

Preconditions for Respectful Conversation

My aspiration to model lofty ideals for respectful conversation that will enable me to be a good conversation partner will seem totally unrealistic to many in our times. But they are rooted in three enduring dispositions that I understand to be central to my Christian faith commitment. The first is humility.

> Humility—the conviction that as a finite, fallible human being, I do not fully understand Truth as God knows it, and I can therefore learn from conversation with others, Christians or non-Christians, who disagree with me.

Such humility distinguishes between capital T "Truth" and lower case t "truth," with Truth referring to the actual nature of things, and truth referring to the partial glimpse that a finite, fallible human being can grasp of the Truth. At the same time that I believe there is Truth, I don't believe I typically have direct, unmediated access to that Truth. At best, I can aspire to grasp a partial glimpse, for an aspect of the human condition is that "we see through a glass darkly" (I Corinthians 13:12). It is my experience that such humility is in short supply in the intellectual community. As David Claerbault has dared to propose: "There is something about being intelligent that seems to breed a sense of superiority" (Claerbault 2004, p. 165).

Such humility is not compromise. In respectful conversations, I will seek to express my *commitment* to certain "truths" with clarity. At the same time, I must be characterized by *openness* to the possibility that I am all wrongheaded about some of my present beliefs and need correction from others. In the process of give-and-take with those who disagree with me, I will hold more firmly to some of my beliefs—those *lived beliefs* that are at the core of my Christian faith commitment and that reflect my lived experience. I will hold less firmly to my present limited understanding about a number of issues of Christian doctrine, such as the nature of the Trinity, the nature of Christ's atonement, and the nature of the end times. But I must be open to the possibility that any aspect of my partial understanding of the Truth needs refinement. And humility needs to be complemented by patience.

> Patience—the hope that through ongoing respectful conversations, greater understanding will gradually emerge as a gift.

Chris K. Huebner beautifully captures the essence of such patience in his observations about the "nonviolent epistemology" of the late, distinguished Mennonite theologian John Howard Yoder. Huebner suggests that "theology operates according to a violent logic of speed whenever it is unwilling to risk the possibility that truthfulness is the outcome of ongoing, timeful, 'open conversation'" (Huebner 2004, p. 67). In contrast "Yoder's nonviolent epistemology ... assumes that truthfulness is an utterly contingent gift that can only be given and received and that it emerges at the site of vulnerable interchange with the other" (Huebner 2004, p. 66). We must overcome our propensity to want quick answers to complex questions. Patience and humility need to be further complemented by love.

> Love—that enduring disposition of caring deeply for other persons, which includes providing a welcoming space for them to freely express their points of view.

As I Corinthians 13:2 states, "If I have prophetic powers, and understand all mysteries and knowledge, and if I have all faith, so as to remove mountains, but do not have love, I am nothing." Jesus Christ has called all Christians to love others. My commitment to orchestrating respectful conversation with others is my deep-rooted response to that call.

Despite our rhetoric about the centrality of these Christian virtues that underlie the call to respectful conversation, there is compelling historical evidence that many Christians have not been interested in such conversation about different perspectives. They are more interested in imposing their particular perspectives, with their pseudo-invitation to conversation amounting to "I have the Truth; you don't, let's talk." There is a lot of historical baggage to overcome. To overcome that baggage, Christians need to create various forums for conversation with non-Christians, in which they model respectful conversations that exemplify these central Christian virtues.

Contra Fish

The above reflections on the role of religious people in public discourse present an alternative to a position taken by the eminent scholar Stanley Fish. I enjoy reading Stanley Fish. Never one to mince words, his writing is engaging and provocative. In his book *The Trouble with Principle* (Fish 1999), he calls into question the liberal ideology that the state or the academy stands above the fray in an impartial space that is neutral toward competing claims of what is true and good. Liberalism has its own commitment to what it considers to be true and good. I resonate with this assertion because it comports with my own claim that everyone has a worldview commitment of some kind, even the staunchest secularist.

But when Fish expounds on the possible role of religious people in the academy and public square, I find his generalizations inadequate. His generalizations don't describe me, and I consider myself to be a religious person. Consider, for example, how Fish envisions the conversation at "liberalism's table":

> Someone will now turn and ask, "Well what does religion have to say about this question?" And when, as often will be the case, religion's answer is doctrinaire (what else could it be?), the moderator (a title deeply revealing) will nod politely and turn to someone who is presumed to be more reasonable. To put the matter badly, a person of religious conviction should not want to enter the marketplace of ideas but to shut it down, at least insofar as it presumes to determine matters that he believes have been determined by God and faith. The religious person should not seek an accommodation with liberalism; he should seek to rout it from the field (Fish 1999, p. 250).

I respectfully disagree with Fish's portrayal of religious people. I do not want to shut down the marketplace of ideas, even on matters where I will make a claim to truth based on my faith commitment.

In a later passage, Fish suggests that "fairness is not what the strong religious believer wants." Rather, "what he wants is a world ordered in accordance with the faith he lives by and would die for" (Fish 1999, p. 298). Well, yes and no. I do live with hope as a Christian that the Kingdom of God will one day reign. But that is not a hope that I want or expect to happen by coercion. The Christian calling to love others precludes coercion.

Although Fish may capture the intent of some, possibly many, Christians, he misses me and many other Christians when he equates being religious with having "doctrinaire agendas" and suggests that our purpose is "to win … to occupy … be sovereign over, the discursive space, and expel others from it" (Fish 1999, p. 40). It is not my purpose to win. My purpose is to be faithful, witnessing to the truth as I presently understand it, and open to new insights and correction that can emerge from listening to and talking respectfully with those who disagree with me. The ultimate outcome of faithfulness I entrust to God. And my commitment to respectful conversation is not peripheral to my Christian faith. It is central to my Christian calling to love others.

Seeds: I have developed a strong conviction that the strategy of establishing personal relationships of mutual trust can enable Christian perspectives to gain a fair hearing in public discourse. I still need to think more about possible means for implementing this interpersonal strategy in the academy. I have come to see that there can be a variety of sources of knowledge claims. I need to eventually struggle with the nature of public rationales for such claims and how one can then evaluate competing claims.

17

Jesus and Me Again

o o o o o o o o o o o o o o o o o o o o o o o o o o o o o o o o o o o o o o

I could no sooner not pray than exit the moving train.

I love the novels of Chaim Potok, especially *The Chosen, My Name is Asher Lev*, and *The Gift of Asher Lev* (Potok 1967, 1972, 1990). Potok eloquently portrays the struggles of young Jewish kids from Brooklyn who cannot accept the Jewish faith as handed down to them. But, neither can they reject their religious tradition. They need to forge their own expressions of the Jewish faith that they can live by.

I relate to these marvelous stories because I was a Norwegian American kid from Brooklyn who couldn't accept in total the Christian faith as handed down to me. I needed to forge a more expansive expression of Christian faith that drew from the best insights of other Christian traditions. I have tried to tell my story in a way that highlights both the process of my Christian pilgrimage and the framework of Christian *lived beliefs* that have evolved during my pilgrimage, beliefs that have informed, however imperfectly, my attempt to live well as a Christian one minute at a time. I have found that being on a Christian pilgrimage cannot be thought of in static terms. It is a dynamic, lifelong process with twists and turns that cannot be foreseen, to which I must respond in creative ways that are informed by my evolving background framework of *lived beliefs*. It is my hope that you will find my story to be an extended illustration of this dynamic process.

I dare to suggest that my experience of this dynamic process is not idiosyncratic. Its contours are applicable to each Christian. In whatever way you have come to embrace the Christian faith, you are immediately embedded in a given Christian tradition, which invariably has its own doctrinal and lifestyle emphases. You have no choice but to start with these emphases as you seek to discern how to live well as a Christian. As you seek to live well, you must be open to the possibility that some of your Christian beliefs may evolve, perhaps even in unexpected directions, as you seek to make sense of your experience in light of the biblical record and your engagement with both Christians and non-Christians. That is a lifelong, dynamic process, and it is in the very process of seeking to live well in light of your current set of beliefs that you can gain greater insight into how to continue living well and how you may choose to modify your current set of beliefs to create greater congruence between your beliefs and the way in which you live out your beliefs. For example, consider the following question that may have been on your mind since chapter 3: If at the time I decided to become an engineer, I had already developed the broader view of God's restorative purposes that only emerged later in my Christian pilgrimage, would I have decided to become an engineer? That is a bad question. It has no defensible answer since at that time of decision I could only proceed on the basis of my current understanding of God's restorative purposes, even if that understanding eventually proved to be too narrow. Such is the dynamism of Christian living.

I will even go so far as to claim that the dynamic contours of a pilgrimage that I have outlined above for those committed to the Christian faith are applicable to any life pilgrimage, whatever the tradition may be, religious or secular, into which you were initially socialized. To make that point, consider the following question: If I had been nurtured in a series of Muslim communities, instead of Christian communities, would I be a Muslim today, with a different set of *lived beliefs* based primarily on my reading of the Koran? Or, if I had been raised in an atheistic community, would I be an atheist today, with a set of lived beliefs that reflected the prevalent worldview within that community? These are also bad questions. They have no defensible answers. I can't possibly know who I would be today and what I would now believe if I were raised in a Muslim or an atheistic community since I was not raised in either of these communities. We do not choose the communities into which we are socialized. They are initially chosen for us by others, and each of us must go on from where we started. This is the dynamic nature of living for all human beings.

It should be apparent from my story that an important dimension of the dynamic nature of my Christian pilgrimage is that the best insights from the various Christian traditions in which I have been immersed have remained dear to me, but they have gradually taken on expanded or deeper meaning. I am Evangelical, albeit in a "chastened" form that does not get much media exposure. I am Reformed in my commitment to fostering ends defined by a broad view of God's restorative purposes. I am Anabaptist in my commitment to use peacemaking means to foster what God intends for Creation. And, I am Pietist in the importance I attach to a deeply felt experience of the presence of God in my life.

The manner in which my exposure to other Christian traditions has maintained but also enriched my original pietist commitments can be illustrated by my ending Part I of this book by coming full circle back to the "Jesus and me" motif. This focus, which was dear to me as a teenage Christian, now has a much deeper meaning. My present "Jesus and me" motif still includes the deeply felt sense of communion with Jesus epitomized in the old hymn "In the Garden." But that is not all it means to me now. I can best lead up to describing the added meaning by telling you about the day when I came to a radical new understanding as to "who initiates prayer."

I had just agreed to sell my 1972 Ford Grand Torino station wagon to a boyhood friend, Ken Jensen, who lives on Long Island. That car was a real dog, getting about 8 miles per gallon, downhill. After driving it for about a year, I couldn't afford to keep it in gas, and Ken, being mechanically inclined, unlike me, said he could work on improving the gas mileage. So, I drove the car from my residence in Briarcliff Manor, New York to Ken's home in Huntington Station. After completing our transaction, Ken graciously drove me to Grand Central Station in Manhattan, where I boarded a New York Central train headed for Briarcliff Manor late that afternoon.

As I sat quietly on the train, reveling in the spectacular sunset over the New Jersey Palisades, I started thinking about one of the challenging institutional projects I was involved with at The King's College, a project on which I was making little progress. I was overwhelmed with an uncontrollable urge to pray about this project. It wasn't a matter of my praying because it was a time of day set aside for me to initiate prayer. Rather, praying seemed like the only natural (or is it supernatural?) thing to do. I could no sooner not pray than exit the moving train. In that moment, a radical thought occurred to me that revolutionized my thinking about prayer: in some mysterious way that I do not understand, God initiates my prayer. It is God who prompts me to pray, possibly through the situation in which I find myself, like marveling at the beauty of a sunset after unloading a dog of a car.

Since that experience on a fast-moving train, I have often wondered whether what transpired was a manifestation of what we Christians refer to as the "illumination of the Holy Spirit." We talked a lot about that during my pietist upbringing, but I never had much clarity then as to what such talk might mean, nor do I now. Some might argue that God performed some type of "cerebral miracle" in my head, causing me to think something I wouldn't think otherwise. I see no need for such an explanation, although I cannot rule it out. As a natural scientist, I do believe in the possibility of miracles, since science can only investigate what "typically" happens under given antecedent conditions and must remain mute as to the possibility or impossibility of miracles, which are atypicalities. But I think that what happened on that train was much more ordinary. The sight of a beautiful sunset reminded me of the restorative work to which God had called me, and it was quite normal for me to commit that work to God once again. If the "work of the Holy Spirit" includes bearing witness to God's restorative intentions for all of Creation made possible through Jesus Christ, then this situational prompting to commit to God the modest restorative work entrusted to me as I sat on that train qualifies as one possible manifestation of the illumination of the Holy Spirit.

Fast forward now to the spring of 2002 when, after a long day of work at the Center for Christian Studies, I walked Wingaersheek Beach in Gloucester, Massachusetts, accompanied by our late Australian terrier Thumper, who had come to be family. As I walk the beach, God initiates within me a prayer. I must pray. I cannot do otherwise. My prayer does include my pietist elements of "Jesus and me," for it includes an expression of gratitude to God for the grace that has been granted to me through Jesus Christ and a deeply felt sense of communion with Christ. In addition, my prayer flows out of my later understanding that a major aspect of my being in personal relationship with God includes the idea of "partnering with God" by seeking to conform my will to God's restorative purposes using peacemaking means. So my prayer now includes my committing into the hands of God, once again, the restorative work to which God has called me. I have been prompted by God to say this prayer so many times that I can share it with you word for word: "God, thank you for the restorative work to which you have called me. I pray that from the seeds I am able to sow, you will bring about a fruitful restorative harvest beyond what I can ask for or even imagine; that your Kingdom may come and your will may be done on earth as it is in heaven" (Matthew 13:31, 32). My conception of "Jesus and me" now embraces my deep conviction that God has called me to be an agent for the restoration that Jesus has made possible. And my response to that calling is not that of a lone ranger. I am part of a great community of Christians, past and present, who are responding to this call.

I hope the above account of my many prayers on the sands of Wingaersheek Beach will dispel your thinking that my story reveals me to be a frenetic do-gooder. Since more than one good friend of mine has accused me of being too modest, let me dispel that myth by immodestly sharing with you one of the nicest things that anyone has ever said about me—words penned by a Gordon faculty colleague on the occasion of my retirement from my position as director of The Center for Christian Studies in May of 2003: "Quiet, deliberate, unflappable, serene, smiling enigmatically as the Cheshire cat—while doing the work of ten ... How did you accomplish so much so inconspicuously? Is that what our Lord means by 'leaven' perhaps?"

If you will pardon this braggadocio, I think that despite a bit of hyperbole, this is an apt description of me. I do work like a beaver, not to earn God's favor, but as an expression of gratitude for God's love for me. God has granted me the gift of believing that my "partnership" with God is starkly asymmetrical. In a way that I do not understand, as I seek to bring my intentions into conformity with my understanding of God's restorative purposes, I rest assured that God's purposes will be realized, whether or not I contribute. Meanwhile, I believe God has called me to faithfully live what I am learning.

Introduction to Parts II–IV

The story of my pilgrimage reveals some of what I have learned in the process of living. But, much of what I learned at various stages of my life was in rudimentary form begging for further elaboration in more nuanced ways.

In particular, I needed to gain better understanding of:

- How to evaluate competing claims to knowledge (so that the conversations I call for do not hit dead ends).
- The meaning of justice, and the role of politics in fostering justice.
- How to be a peacemaker in various contexts of conflict.
- The meaning of "Christian scholarship" and strategies for disseminating such scholarship to the larger academy by means of respectful conversations.
- How to more adequately put into practice the two primary distinctives of Christian higher education: the *integration of faith, learning, and living*, and *holistic education*.

The chapters that follow in Parts II-IV present progress reports on my more nuanced understandings relative to these particular issues.

PART II

On What Basis Can We Talk If We Disagree?

My invitation to respectful conversation is spurious if there is no basis on which to talk about disagreements. The only way to get beyond the stark relativism of "you have your claims to knowledge, I have mine" is to invoke appropriate standards for evaluating competing claims to knowledge. This quest is complicated by my belief that there can be a wide variety of sources of knowledge claims.

Whether there are such standards for evaluation, what their nature might be, and how conclusive (or not) they may be in an actual conversation is addressed in the next two chapters. These chapters should be read as a whole. Chapter 18 proposes the existence of standards for evaluating competing claims to knowledge in various areas of discourse, with these standards emerging from an agreed-upon purpose for a given conversation. Chapter 19 proposes that chapter 18 presents too simple a picture, noting factors that contribute to open-endedness in conversation and calling for that rare combination of openness and commitment when talking with those who disagree with you.

18

Evaluating Competing Claims To Knowledge

o o o o o o o o o o o o o o o o o o o o o o o o o o o o o o o

Christians wishing to engage publicly in respectful conversation should not play the "Bible trump card," quickly ending the conversation by asserting "here is what the Bible says."

Imagine trying to hold a conversation with someone who makes a certain claim ("all Norwegian Americans like weak coffee"), and then in the next breath makes a contradictory claim ("all Norwegian Americans like strong coffee"). Or, how do you respond to a person claiming that all Norwegian Americans like weak coffee who will not rethink his claim when you report the empirical fact that there is at least one Norwegian American (Harold Heie) who likes his coffee strong? Or, worse yet, how do you talk to someone who believes that either of these two claims is as good as the competing claim?

While recognizing that one's position on this issue will not alter the course of history, this trivial example illustrates that my proposal for orchestrating respectful conversation between those who disagree with one another may be fruitless if there are absolutely no ground rules for discussion. Having learned to listen is not sufficient to sustain a fruitful conversation about a substantive issue on which those around the table disagree. One is not fully ready to talk about what has been heard unless there is some measure of agreement on how to sort through disagreements—how to evaluate conflicting claims.

I am not suggesting that those in conversation need to first agree on some universal standards for evaluating competing knowledge claims. In his marvelous book *Unapologetic Theology*, William Placher presents a model for pluralistic conversation that seeks a middle-ground between the unacceptable extremes of a stark "relativism" (each claim to knowledge is as good as any other) and what I will call "universal rationality" (those in conversation need to share prior agreement on universal standards for evaluation) (Placher 1989). I, like Placher, seek for that middle ground. I will argue, in this chapter and the next, that for conversation on issues about which those around the table disagree, the conversation will have the best chance of being fruitful if a "local rationality" emerges in the form of some agreement as to appropriate standards for evaluating competing claims in light of the purpose of the conversation.

Before proceeding, I recommend that this chapter and the next should be read as two sides of the same coin. By itself, this chapter will sound too formulaic (the kind of thing a mathematician might write). The next chapter, by itself, will sound too open-ended. The middle ground I seek will hold these two aspects in tension.

In the remainder of this chapter, I will consider the vexing question of whether in a given conversation one can hope for "local rationality" in the form of some agreement as to appropriate standards for evaluating competing claims in light of the purpose of the conversation. Considering the nature of such standards, if they exist, takes one deep into that area of philosophy that deals with the study of knowledge, formally called epistemology. Christian philosophers have written a great deal about epistemology (for two brief volumes that should be accessible to non-philosophers, see Wolfe 1982 and Wood 1998). I do not have the professional expertise to sort out all the competing claims as to the nature of knowledge. But for the sake of the conversation project I have proposed, I need to risk exposing my amateurish status by making some forays into this complex and hotly disputed area.

One approach to evaluating competing knowledge claims is to consider the sources of such claims. Is a particular claim to knowledge produced by human mental (cognitive) faculties that are functioning properly? For example, when observing some phenomenon that begs for explanation, are the person's perceptual processes reliable? Does she see adequately the phenomenon that is occurring? It may be reasonable to question a report about the number of geese on my front lawn given by a person suffering from double vision.

Or, when a person with normal vision is reporting on something she saw six months ago (like the number of geese on my front lawn), is her memory reliable? It is reasonable to argue that if physiological and psychological processes such as visual perception and memory are functioning properly, the resulting claims are credible.

While not denying the benefits of examining the source of a claim, this approach will not be sufficient for my respectful conversation project. As suggested by David Wolfe, "It would be a mistake ... to rule out beliefs because how we come to hold them can be explained psychologically, sociologically, or historically" (Wolfe 1982, p. 56). In addition to the processes of perception and memory, a sociological source of a knowledge claim could be the particular perspectives of the intellectual tradition, Christian or otherwise, out of which one is working. A historical source could be elements of an individual's personal biography, including, for a Christian, one's history of walking faithful to a sense of Christian calling. An extremely unusual physiological source could be a dream while sleeping. I would not prematurely rule out knowledge claims just because the source is highly unusual. As I have already stated, I wish to allow for a rich variety in possible sources of a person's claims to knowledge, including deep feelings, life experiences, religious or secular worldview commitments, and even products of a very active conscious or subconscious imagination.

Isn't this latitude introducing a scary subjective element into making claims, especially claims to knowledge? I used to worry about that when I believed that our knowledge of things is simply discovered by a passive knower based solely on the nature of those things, thereby enabling one to claim that such knowledge is "objective." I no longer believe that premise. I now believe that many claims to knowledge emerge from "interaction" between the knower and the known, thereby reflecting both a reality external to the knower and what the knower brings to the process of knowing. In fact, there may be situations where elements of a person's social location, such as her personal biography, enables her to see and understand things that others will miss. In such cases, the resulting claim to knowledge is neither strictly objective nor strictly subjective, as these two words are commonly used. I see no way for anyone to make judgments as to the extent of either "objective" or "subjective" elements in the knowledge claim.

Does this open-ended variety of potential sources of claims open wide the flood gates to all kinds of apparently bizarre claims in public discourse? Possibly. But once any claim is made, it needs to be supported by a public rationale, independent of its supposed source. No claim is self-evidently true (self-authenticating) based on a proclaimed unimpeachable source, even if the supposed source is the Bible or some special type of "revelation from God." Some Christians, claiming such sources, have made blatantly false claims, such as claiming the superiority of the white race. And some Christians have performed egregious acts destructive of God's restorative purposes for Creation in the name of special claims to knowledge, from the Crusades to Waco. Appeal to a particular source of knowledge will not suffice in public discourse. Rather, one needs to present a rationale for one's knowledge claim that can be understood by partners in conversation and can be evaluated using publicly accessible standards for evaluation.

This distinction between genesis and evaluation of a claim to knowledge means that Christians wanting to engage publicly in respectful conversation should not play the "Bible trump card," quickly ending the conversation by asserting "here is what the Bible says." Please note that I am not saying that what you believe about the issue at hand should not be informed by your understanding of the Bible. The biblical record should certainly inform your thinking. But as Duane Litfin has argued, "we must keep distinct the issues of Christian thinking and Christian communication in a secular setting" (Litfin 2004, p. 137). Appealing directly to what the Bible says may be convincing in an adult Sunday School class in a Christian church. But it carries no weight, nor should it, when few, if any, of the persons involved in the given conversation share a commitment to the Christian faith and its belief in biblical authority. Even if the source of the claim is my understanding of biblical teachings, it must be evaluated, along with competing claims, using appropriate publicly accessible standards for evaluation.

What could possibly be the content of the standards for evaluating competing claims? It depends on an agreed upon purpose that brings people to the table for conversation. Such purposes will vary, depending on whether the conversation takes place among scholars in the academy, politicians or public policy practitioners in the public square, or clergy and laity in a church. Allow me to illustrate by imagining some hypothetical conversations that could take place within these three areas of discourse relative to a perceived problem of homelessness.

One type of conversation relative to homelessness can be envisioned in the political realm. The purpose of a city council meeting may be to pass a local ordinance designed to provide humane services to the homeless in the immediate community. For example, one proposal for council consideration may be to establish tax incentives for local businesses to create job training and employment opportunities for those in the community who are currently homeless. Concrete proposals for such ordinances may be informed by the views of council members relative to issues that sociologists debate, such as the effects of social ties on "finding a home," or issues that philosophers debate, such as the "ultimate causes" of homelessness. But the surest way for council deliberation to go nowhere may be to drive the conversation "up" to such levels of scholarly discourse. I am guessing that persons holding to a variety of opinions on matters about which philosophers and sociologists debate will still be able to find some common ground on the need to provide some humane services, like job opportunities, to the homeless in their midst. Therefore, council members should present public rationales that are relevant to this pragmatic purpose. And the standards for evaluating alternative proposals for providing such humane services will be the extent to which each proposal is judged to have the potential to assist the homeless, drawing heavily on the personal experiences of homeless persons in the community, who should be given a voice in the council deliberations. Council members can also draw on available empirical data on how effective certain strategies have been in the past in other similar communities facing the same problem. The same kind of standards for evaluation would be appropriate for public policy practitioners in the community responsible for implementing whatever ordinances are passed by the council.

A different type of conversation about homelessness can be imagined in a meeting of sociologists. Before giving a hypothetical example, a crucial ground rule must be established. The standards for evaluating competing claims to knowledge within any academic discipline, such as sociology, are not given by God, or any other supposed authority outside the discipline. They are not external standards that lie outside the actual practice of scholarship within the discipline. Rather, to paraphrase Nick Wolterstorff, a scholar working in a given discipline is socialized into certain "epistemic practices" that include the current consensus of scholars within the discipline as to appropriate standards for evaluating competing knowledge claims. Such standards are not set in cement. Rather, they can change as actual practice changes in the particular academic discipline (Wolterstorff 2004, pp. 82–83, 117–118, 187–197).

With this ground rule in mind, imagine a group of sociologists attending a conference devoted to the purpose of exploring the effect of a homeless person's social connections, or lack thereof, on the ability to "find a home." Conference participants may be proposing competing "empirical theories" (expectations about regularities or typicalities in human experiences) relative to this stated purpose. For example, one proposed theory may be that forming a strong friendship with one or more members of the immediate community is a good way to radically alter the life of a homeless person. This theory may be informed by the participant's philosophical views about the "ultimate causes" of homelessness. Certain views about ultimate causation may rule out certain empirical theories relative to the effect of friendships. But certain empirical theories may also be compatible with differing views of ultimate causation. In any case, the purpose of this conference is not to get to the bottom of ultimate causes of homelessness. That question can be set aside in this conference. Whereas theories proposed at this conference may or may not be related to views about ultimate causation, any proposed theory must do justice to the testimonies of past and present homeless persons who have been given a voice at the conference and measure up to whatever consensus standards for evaluation of competing empirical theories are currently operative within the guild of sociologists, which should be the focus of the public rationales that are presented. Leaving that judgment up to those having expertise in sociology, let me merely suggest that such standards for evaluation may include explanatory power, simplicity, and fruitfulness for ongoing research.

Another possible conversation in the academy relative to homelessness could take place in a conference of philosophers working in the area of metaphysics, which deals with the most comprehensive of all human questions about the nature of reality and the place of humans within that reality (Hasker 1983, pp. 13–17). The stated purpose of this conference is to explore the "ultimate causes" of homelessness. In this context, each conference participant will likely be situating her view of ultimate causation in a broad view of the nature of human nature and the world in which humans live. For example, one participant may propose that the ultimate cause of homelessness is the lack of fit between a need that all humans have to engage in productive work and the opportunities available for such work within existing societal structures, such as a free-market economy. Another participant may argue that homelessness is ultimately caused by human irresponsibility, either on the part of the homeless or on the part of members of communities where homelessness is rampant, or some of both. Once again, the voices of the homeless must be heard at this conference. In any case, whatever knowledge claim is made, it is embedded in a broad worldview of the nature of reality since it is attempting to get at ultimate causes. A knowledge claim that is embedded in a worldview cannot be evaluated piecemeal. It can only be evaluated indirectly by evaluating the worldview that contains it.

How does one evaluate competing worldviews? A number of Christian philosophers have made proposals. William Hasker suggests the evaluative standards of "factual adequacy, logical consistency, and explanatory power" (Hasker 1983, pp. 25–28). David Wolfe has suggested the standards of consistency, coherence, comprehensiveness, and congruity (Wolfe 1982, pp. 50–55). Other philosophers may propose different standards for evaluation. In any case, competing claims as to the ultimate causes of homelessness need to be evaluated using whatever consensus standards for evaluating competing worldviews may be currently operative.

Finally, what might a conversation about homelessness look like in a church community? Once again, it depends on the desired purpose for talking. For example, the purpose may be to formulate concrete means to address the needs of the homeless, as in my hypothetical city council scenario. In the context of an adult Sunday School session, the purpose may be to gain better theological clarity relative to the more scholarly issues about which philosophers and sociologists debate. In light of that purpose, the second educational step should be to hear from such professional scholars, asking them to translate their work into terms that are accessible to the church's clergy and laity (the first step should be to attend to the voices of homeless persons invited to the conversation). Then, whatever the intended purpose, the standards for evaluating competing claims to knowledge should be congruent with that purpose.

Up to this point, I have suggested that the project I will be proposing for orchestrating respectful conversation between those who disagree with one another will be possible only if there are some standards for evaluating competing claims to knowledge or desirable courses of action. Furthermore, it is the content of such competing claims, not their supposed sources, that need to be evaluated. The nature of the standards for evaluation and the ensuing conversations will depend on the type of group that has been invited to talk about the issue at hand and an agreed-upon purpose for talking.

But this scenario is too simple. Let us assume that those gathered for conversation agree that there must be some standards for evaluating competing claims. If they can then reach consensus as to what those standards are, their conversation has the potential to be fruitful. But what if they can't agree on such consensus standards? For example, the current epistemic practices in a given academic discipline may be in such a state of flux that there is little hope that the scholars gathered for a particular conversation will find any common ground relative to standards for evaluation, thereby bringing that conversation to an abrupt halt. I will now turn to that potential problem, adding reflections on ways in which the respectful conversations I envision may be quite open and fluid.

19

Commitment and Openness in Conversation

o o o o o o o o o o o o o o o o o o o o o o o o o o o o o o o o o

One cannot predict beforehand the results of a respectful conversation.

A prominent Christian educator once told me that he prefers not to talk to Christians who take the "other side" in the homosexuality debate because what they have to say could influence his present views on this thorny issue. His comment hints at the risk involved in engaging others in conversation: talking to others who disagree with me may require that I rethink some of my present beliefs. One cannot predict beforehand the results of a respectful conversation.

In this chapter I will first elaborate on some of the factors that contribute to a significant degree of open-endedness in respectful conversation, resulting in unpredictability of results. I will then address the formidable obstacle to conversation presented if those around the table cannot agree on standards for evaluating competing claims.

Starting with the most unexpected factor contributing to open-endedness in respectful conversation, the initial stages of a conversation may reveal that there are more important things to talk about than agreements or disagreements about the announced topic of conversation. As we introduce ourselves to each other, it may become apparent that someone has an unexpected personal need about which others could provide helpful insight. Or, it may be apparent that we need more time to get to know and trust one another better before laying bare our disagreements. So we just go with the flow of conversation that emerges, taking us on a journey we could never have predicted. Good conversations that have nothing to do with sorting through agreements and disagreements should be welcomed and valued. The announced topic can wait for another day.

A second open-ended factor that could make the results of conversation unpredictable is that the persuasiveness of the views that I, or you, present is not dependent solely on the content of what we say. As suggested by David Cunningham, the persuasiveness of one's expressed views depend not only on their content, but also on the nature of the audience (others sitting around the table) and, in particular, the perceptions of those around the table as to the "characters" of the persons talking (Cunningham 1990). With respect to the perceived character of the speaker, Cunningham suggests that "[t]he speaker's character will affect the degree of confidence with which a speech is received" (Cunningham 1990, p. 98). He then proposes that the "clues" by which an audience constructs the speaker's character includes her associations ("the individual or group with whom a speaker is identified"), her attitudes (which are expressed, at least in part, by "the tone with which an argument is pursued"), and her actions ("in what activities is he or she involved, aside from the construction of persuasive arguments?") (Cunningham 1990, pp. 127, 132, 139). A case in point for the latter assessment is Martin Luther King, Jr. The persuasiveness of his arguments for civil rights for all peoples was surely enhanced by his putting his life on the line, and ultimately sacrificing his life, in ways that were congruent with his rhetoric. These influences related to attributes of persons sitting around the table, including perceptions of their "characters," surely point to a degree of unpredictability in the outcome of any conversation.

Such influences also suggest a potential connection between the source of a speaker's claim to knowledge in public discourse and the evaluation of that claim on the part of listeners. Whereas the speaker's claim should be evaluated in light of the merits of the "public rationale" that is presented, the listeners may be more inclined to give a fair hearing to the speaker's claim if they judge that she leads an exemplary life, the source of which could be her particular worldview commitments, religious or secular.

Cunningham's insights into how an audience's perceptions of the character of a speaker can influence their assessment of what the speaker says provides an important perspective on my invitation to Christians to engage in respectful conversation. If we Christians want those who do not share our faith commitment to give our views a fair hearing, it is not sufficient for us to have beliefs that are thought out well and articulated clearly. Those who do not share our religious beliefs may be looking to see if we actually live out that which we say we believe. They may even be attracted to our Christian way of life and thinking if they observe that the way in which we live aspires to follow the teachings and example of the Christ we claim to follow.

The results of a respectful conversation are also open-ended because even if there is agreement as to appropriate standards for evaluating competing claims, the application of these standards may not yield conclusive results. Especially in the realms of discourse inhabited by scholars, as in the hypothetical sociology and philosophy conferences imagined in the last chapter, the standards for evaluation I suggested will not enable anyone around the table to prove definitively that his claim is clearly superior to all competing claims. For example, as noted by David Wolfe relative to the standards for evaluation of worldviews that he has proposed, the application of such standards to a given worldview (what Wolfe calls an "interpretive scheme") "may result in its elimination or falsification, but it cannot result in final verification" (Wolfe 1982, p. 64). In other words, conversation may be able to weed out grossly inadequate worldviews, but it will not be able to conclusively prove any one worldview to be true. Consistent with the philosophical thought of Karl Popper (1963), a given worldview may be considered "plausible" if it has been able to withstand "continued criticism" in ongoing conversations (Wolfe 1982, p. 65). This approach to criticism leaves the outcomes of any one such "metaphysical conversation" far from conclusive.

As a result of this typical impossibility of conclusively proving a given claim to be true, even when standards for evaluation are agreed upon, persons sitting around the table may favor a particular claim that has not yet been falsified for reasons unrelated to the standards for evaluation, such as elements of personal biography, feelings, intuitions, and the perceived "characters" of those around the table. This possibility contributes further to the unpredictability of the results of a respectful conversation.

Good conversation partners should be open to the possibility of their discussion going in unpredictable directions and improvise accordingly. But where does one start a conversation on an issue about which those around the table have significant disagreements?

William Placher suggests that "particular conversations could start with whatever their participants happened to share and go from there" (Placher 1989, p. 12). In a similar vein, Kwame Anthony Appiah suggests that for "cross-cultural conversations," "the points of entry ... are things that are shared by those who are in the conversation. They do not need to be universal; all they need to be is what these particular people have in common" (Appiah 2006, p. 97). I would like to be a bit more directive, without, hopefully, being too formulaic or wooden. At some point in the conversation, preferably sooner rather than later, if the purpose of the conversation is not clear, that needs to be discussed. In light of a purpose that is agreed upon (explicitly or implicitly), those around the table need to talk about the standards to be used for evaluating competing claims. But what if no consensus emerges as to appropriate standards for evaluation? Is the conversation doomed to an abrupt end?

Alasdair MacIntyre answers "no." In his influential work *Whose Justice? Which Rationality?,* MacIntyre recognizes this potential problem, noting that it is not just one's claims to knowledge about a given issue that are socially situated or embedded in a particular tradition of thought (Christian or otherwise). The standards for evaluating such a claim are also embedded in that tradition (MacIntyre 1988, p. 350). So, if those gathered around the table represent different traditions, there may well be fundamental disagreements as to appropriate standards for evaluating competing claims. For the sake of elaboration, consider a conversation involving two traditions, with those in each tradition holding to standards for evaluation that are not accepted by those in the second tradition. How can conversation proceed?

William J. Cahoy has succinctly summarized MacIntyre's proposal for proceeding (Cahoy 2002, p. 99). Paraphrasing, one must empathetically seek to understand the other tradition *on its own terms.* In that light, one can explore in conversation with those embedded in the other tradition the extent to which their claims to knowledge measure up to *their own* standards for evaluation. In the other direction, one must be willing to expose one's own knowledge claims to the best critiques of the other tradition, to see oneself from its perspective, and then construct a response for ongoing discussion. By means of these strategies, mutual learning may take place even without first reaching consensus regarding standards for evaluating competing claims to knowledge. Therefore, I hold out hope for potentially fruitful conversation even when those around the table cannot reach consensus as to appropriate standards for evaluating competing claims.

To summarize my reflections in these last two chapters, those gathered for conversation about issues where competing claims to knowledge can be expected should first seek consensus on standards for evaluating competing claims, starting with discussion of the purpose of the conversation. Even when such consensus cannot be reached, the conversation can still be fruitful. One should enter into conversation aware of the factors that can contribute to open-endedness and improvise accordingly, exhibiting that rare combination of being both committed to one's own beliefs and open to serious consideration of the differing beliefs of others. One cannot predict beforehand the final destination of a good conversation.

PART III

Can We Talk about Justice and Peace?

A marvelous example of the respectful conversation to which I invite you is provided in the book *Let's Talk: An Honest Conversation on Critical Issues* (Koop & Johnson 1992). In this slim volume, Dr. C. Everett Koop, former Surgeon General of the United States, and Dr. Timothy Johnson, ABC News Medical Editor, dialogue about complex issues in medical ethics that have led to much strident public debate: abortion, euthanasia, AIDS, and health care. They demonstrate the "convicted civility" that Richard Mouw calls for, in which they "hold onto strongly felt convictions while still nurturing a spirit that is authentically kind and gentle" (Mouw 1992, p. 12, 15); See also Gaede, S. D. 1993). They proclaim commitment to a learning model for public discourse, in contrast to a fixed positions model:

> We have come to respect and love each other even as we have learned that we disagree on many specific subjects relating to medical ethics. However, we both acknowledge that we have learned from each other, and that we have grown in our understanding of the human condition because of each other. We also agree that too often persons of opposing viewpoints conclude that there is room in God's love for only one of them. We write this book to demonstrate otherwise; to suggest that it is possible to disagree, sometimes vigor-

> ously, and yet acknowledge that God loves us all even while we are less than perfect in this human pilgrimage. (Koop & Johnson 1992, pp. 7–8)

Before embarking on their dialogue, Drs. Koop & Johnson extend this invitation for respectful conversation to all their readers: "We hope that if you disagree, you will learn from each other's viewpoints, and respect those who differ with you. Let's talk" (Koop & Johnson 1992, p. 9).

My reading of this book by Koop and Johnson convinced me that respectful conversations can be modeled in written form, not just in face-to-face talking (for another good example, see Audi & Wolterstorff 1997). As a result, the next two chapters are presented in written form as reports on "simulated face-to-face conversations" in which I have embedded my present views about two challenging contemporary issues for which the restorative values of justice and peace are relevant: the role of Christians and other religious persons in politics; and alternative views on war, from just war theory to strategies for peacemaking. It is my hope that this attempt at modeling will help to initiate many respectful conversations about these issues around many tables that will include those who believe that my present views are all wrong.

20

Should Religious People Do Politics? If So, With What Agenda?

o o o o o o o o o o o o o o o o o o o o o o o o o o o o o o o o o

I was essentially apolitical through young adulthood. I voted for Eisenhower when casting my first presidential ballot in 1956. But, I have little recollection as to why ... Being Republican was typically who we were as children of Norwegian immigrants in Brooklyn.

Imagine a group of people sitting around the same table, invited by a moderator to have a conversation about the topic, "Should religious people do politics? If so, with what agenda?" Christians from various theological traditions, representatives from other religions, and some who consider themselves "non-religious" have accepted the invitation to talk. The moderator first asks each of us to introduce ourselves, focusing on those aspects of our pilgrimages that have prompted a keen interest in this topic.

We then talk about the purpose of our conversation, agreeing that it is primarily to help each of us to understand better how persons from a variety of worldview traditions, religious and secular, view the role of religious people in politics. Recognizing that each person will speak from his or her experience within a given tradition, we agree that it will be appropriate for listeners to discuss what is said based on different sets of experiences within different traditions.

We express the collective hope that at the end of our day together, the gift of some common ground will have emerged. We hope to uncover some common insights that ring true to our collective experience, insights that will help each of us as we return to our respective communities. We also reaffirm our individual and collective commitment to the principles of *reciprocity and mutual recognition* and *equal voice* that the moderator made clear in his letters of invitation.

Having agreed to some ground rules for our conversation, the moderator now asks each of us to give a five-minute opening statement on the topic at hand. My opening statement would be as follows.

◆ ◆ ◆

I need to first make it clear that I am speaking as one who is committed to the Christian faith. Therefore, my initial comments will address just one facet of our overarching question. I will share my reflections on the question of whether Christians should do politics, and, if so, with what agenda. Hopefully, after we all have had the opportunity to share initial reflections from within our respective traditions, our ensuing conversation will help us to gain collective insights relative to the broader issue of whether people embedded in any religious tradition should do politics.

Although I made a commitment to the Christian faith at the early age of 13, it was only much later in my life that I realized such a commitment could have political implications. I was essentially apolitical through young adulthood. I voted for Eisenhower when casting my first presidential ballot in 1956, but I have little recollection as to why. It certainly wasn't based on a well-thought-out political perspective. Being Republican was typically who we were as children of Norwegian immigrants in Brooklyn.

It was much later in my pilgrimage, in 1975, when I developed a friendship with Jim Skillen, a political studies faculty colleague at Gordon College, that I first began searching for a coherent Christian perspective on politics. The perspective I gradually developed was informed by the principles embraced by the organization Jim directs, the Center for Public Justice (CPJ), supplemented by the writings of Ron Sider, President of Evangelicals for Social Action (ESA). The core of the Christian perspective I gradually developed was the value of justice.

But, what exactly does justice mean? In its broadest sense, justice means "fair treatment." Of course, the meaning of "fair" can be debated endlessly. Although I cannot give a fool-proof definition of "fair," it is often possible to intuit when treatment is "unfair." Justice, as fairness, has multiple aspects. Commutative justice "requires fairness in agreements and exchanges between private parties" (e.g., "contracts should be kept").

Procedural justice defines the procedures and processes that must be fair if justice is to prevail (e.g., "unbiased courts") (see Sider 2005, p. 165).

A third aspect is distributive justice, which refers to a "fair" distribution of goods and rights among persons. At a minimum, the Bible clearly teaches that commitment to distributive justice calls Christians to be agents for a better distribution of goods and rights to the poor, the marginalized, and the oppressed of the world. In fact, the Bible says much more about meeting the needs of these most vulnerable people than it does about the "personal morality" issues about which many Christians in politics seem to be currently preoccupied.

A fourth aspect is retributive justice, sometimes called "corrective justice," which deals with how to treat persons who have done wrong, in a manner that is fair to all who are affected. Wrongdoers should receive an appropriate punishment. I happen to believe that such punishment can be administered in ways that focus on restoration, not retribution (which we can discuss in our ensuing conversation). Therefore, I refer to this aspect as restorative justice.

Persons committed to these four aspects of justice may well disagree as to who should be "doing such justice" in which contexts. Is it the role of government to do justice? Is it the role of the family? Or the school? Or the church? Or the business organization? Or the voluntary club? I believe it is the obligation of all such institutions to practice justice, within an appropriate understanding of their respective jurisdictions and responsibilities.

For example, in a school, it is a violation of distributive justice for a teacher to give one student an "A" and another student a "C" for term papers of approximately equal quality. In the family, it is a parental responsibility to decide on appropriate forms of punishment for erring children (within limits I will hint at later).

What, then, is the proper role of the institution of government? As has been elaborated by Jim Skillen, it is to promote justice in the public realm—to seek "public justice" (see Skillen 1990, 1994, 2004). This execution will also have commutative, procedural, distributive, and restorative elements. For example, it is appropriate for government to administer a penal system for restorative justice purposes. One component of the distributive element is for government to treat other institutions fairly. In other words, government must recognize the rightful existence of other non-governmental institutions of society and make room for them to flourish. For example, a government's laws should encourage (and not hinder) the ability of schools to educate, church congregations to worship, and parents to nurture their children. Public Justice requires the state, with its law-making power, to recognize the limits of its own authority so other institutions can carry out their distinct purposes. In CPJ parlance, this is referred to as "structural pluralism."

While structural pluralism militates against an over-reaching government, it also calls for government actions when such are appropriate to foster a "common good." For example, it is appropriate for government to legislate minimum educational standards, even for "private" schools, to insure an educated citizenry. It is appropriate for government to pass laws punishing child abuse or other forms of domestic abuse within the family, for the protection of powerless, abused individuals and the potential flourishing of all citizens. It is appropriate for government to provide national infrastructure, such as interstate highways and national parks, that can be good for all citizens.

Another component of the proper role of government to foster distributive justice is to treat fairly the adherents to each religious or secular worldview their due. Government should recognize the broadly diverse worldview commitments of its citizens, both religious and secular, and should provide a "level playing field" for its citizens to express such commitments. No preferential treatment should be given to adherents of any one particular worldview. CPJ refers to this principle as "confessional pluralism."

I affirm the role of government to promote public justice. I believe it is appropriate for me and other Christians to enter the political arena as responsible citizens to contribute to this governmental role by advocacy of legislation judged to serve the public good. This affirmation provides only background principles for me. It does not dictate potential legislative initiatives. Desirable and workable legislative initiatives can only emerge from the interaction of the legitimate role of government with the concrete circumstances in a given place and time. To give you further insight into the type of legislative initiatives these background principles could lead to, let me briefly mention two more examples.

The principle of structural pluralism recognizes that it is the ultimate responsibility of parents, not government, to decide on who educates their children. Parents should be allowed to choose any form of schooling, whether "public" or "private" (provided it meets acceptable educational standards), that best fits their own worldview commitments. However, the thorny question remains as to who should pay for whatever form of education is decided upon by parents. Specifically, should "public" funding be made available for "private" education? We can return to this complex issue in our later discussion.

A second example is related to the much debated issue of government funding of faith-based initiatives for providing social services. The principle of confessional pluralism suggests that there should be a level playing field that enables all social service organizations, religious or secular, to receive such public funding, provided any social service recipient can freely choose from a wide array of providers representing various worldview commitments, and that the service is provided in a way that does not coerce the recipient into embracing the worldview represented by the provider.

There is another thorny question relative to the appropriate scope of governmental legislation. To what extent, if any, should government legislate a particular morality? On this question, Christians having equally strong commitments to political involvement have some major disagreements.

Some Christians take the position that it is appropriate for government to legislate morality, by which they mean Christian moral principles, as they have come to understand such principles. They will argue that such laws should include bans on gay marriage and making certain forms (or all forms) of abortion illegal. Based on my principle of confessional pluralism, I don't believe it is generally appropriate for government to pass laws that coerce everyone into behaving in conformity with the moral commitments of any one worldview, Christian or otherwise, relative to consensual behavior between adults, or what appears to be strictly private behavior. However, I believe there is one category of exceptions to this general rule. If it can be persuasively argued that the behavior in question, if not proscribed or limited, has a high probability of leading to significant detrimental public consequences, then legislation could be appropriate.

Because we are dealing in probabilities, the challenge of determining what kind of exceptions this test of public consequences may allow is no easy task. Political space must be provided for well-meaning Christians and others to disagree as to what exceptions are allowed.

Does this test of public consequences call for gun control laws that limit the sale of assault weapons? I think so. Does it call for laws limiting what you can do publicly (like driving a car) after drinking too much in the privacy of your home? I think so. Does it call for legislation that takes away your freedom to not wear a helmet when driving a motorcycle? I think so. Does this test allow for legislation prohibiting the sale of pornographic videos in all video stores? I don't think so, even though I believe that such videos are destructive of the humanity of both the actors and the viewers. Does this test call for a total legal ban on abortion? I don't think so, even though I believe that abortion can be justified only in certain tragic situations, as when the life of the mother is endangered if the pregnancy is allowed to continue.

The debatable issue in each of these examples should be whether the behavior in question, if not proscribed or limited legislatively, has a high probability of leading to significant detrimental public consequences. Others will surely disagree with me on the conclusions I have reached in each of these examples, which

I have not defended here (we can talk further about the public rationale for my conclusions in our ensuing conversation). But, workable answers to such questions can only emerge though the political process, hopefully by means of respectful conversation between those who disagree.

There is an oft neglected category of potential legislative initiatives for which Christians in politics should be advocates. A proper view of Christian morality must deal with social morality, not just personal morality. Christians should be advocates for legislation that addresses problems of poverty, environmental degradation, an ailing non-restorative criminal justice system, inadequate schooling opportunities for many children, domestic abuse, and other social and economic justice issues. To be sure, this assertion reflects my commitments as a Christian. But these are not just concerns that Christians should have. They are human concerns. If Christian politicians will bring such issues to the forefront, there is political hope for finding sufficient common ground with those politicians who do not share a Christian faith commitment to enable the United States to adequately address these weighty issues that affect the general welfare of all citizens.

◆ ◆ ◆

Having had the opportunity to present my opening comments, I will listen attentively to the opening comments of all others around the table. In this conversation concocted in my mind, I assume the moderator will then encourage all participants to comment on the various opening statements and ask questions of each other. I can imagine the following questions being directed to me, after each of which I will indicate how I might respond, often posing follow-up questions intended to continue the conversation. (All questions are italicized.)

◆ ◆ ◆

Our culture is so morally bankrupt that I can't conceive of improving it much by political means. Society can be improved morally only if citizens will "get right with God." You can't legislate morality. You can only change people "from the inside out." What are your reflections on that perspective?

I agree with you that there is a lot of brokenness in our world, including no small amount of moral corruption. I also share your commitment to the importance of trying to help people to be transformed in their "inner beings," with the hope that they will then act in transformed ways. But, *is it necessary to create a rift between that important task and political involvement?* It appears to me that in certain circumstances, morality can be legislated. There are some notable examples where first changing laws has eventually led to a changing of hearts. If the civil rights legislation of the 1960s had waited until all human hearts were ready for it, such legislation would likely never have been passed. In other words, whereas correcting personal evil is often the best way to correct systemic evil, there is always the possibility that first addressing systemic evil can ameliorate personal evil. *Can't we be committed to both strategies?*

Wouldn't Christians have a more positive influence in our world if they would effectively model the living out of their beliefs about morality, hoping others will sit up and take notice, rather than getting involved in politics?

I agree with you wholeheartedly that it is imperative for Christians to live out what they say they believe. Much mischief and destruction has been wrought by Christians who do not "walk the talk." In contrast, many Christian communities are to be commended for their modeling of Christian moral convictions, and others should be encouraged to do likewise. I agree with you that such witnessing to alternative ways of living can have a positive impact on other communities. But *is it necessary to create a bifurcation between such positive modeling and political involvement? Do you preclude the possibility of some Christians believing that their particular calling is to help to ameliorate social ills through active involvement in the political process?* For me, it is not either/or. It is both/and.

I grant that Christians should heed the biblical call to work for greater justice in the world, especially addressing the needs of the poor, the marginalized, and oppressed of the world. However, I have a problem with your proposed means of political involvement. Shouldn't attempts of Christians to address injustice be strictly voluntary, through the charitable efforts of individual Christians, churches, and Christian relief and social service organizations? Doesn't your call for Christian political involvement introduce a coercive element that is foreign to the freedom Christians have been given? For example, isn't it a form of governmental coercion when Christians and all others are required to pay taxes to fund government welfare programs to assist the poor?

I am pleased that we agree that Christians are called to work for greater justice in the world. We obviously need to talk further about our differences regarding means toward that end. I agree with you that voluntary, charitable efforts on the part of Christians are a good place to start. Christians should continue their splendid efforts to address the needs of others through charitable means. But, *is that enough?* It appears to me that the magnitude of the injustices are simply too great to be met by the charitable contributions of Christians and others. I view it as appropriate for people of good will, from all worldview traditions, to agree through the political process to seek a common good by joining together to address the needs of the most vulnerable in society.

You raise an important issue concerning the relationship between freedom and coercion, about which we need to seek for better mutual understanding. I agree with your observation that Christians have been granted freedom. But, *what is the nature of "Christian freedom"?* A biblical passage we Christians usually appeal to in this regard is Galatians 5:13–14, which reads: "For you were called to freedom ... Only do not use your freedom as an opportunity for self-indulgence, but through love become slaves to one another. For the whole law is summed up in a single commandment: You shall love your neighbor as yourself." Although the initial portion of this passage calls for Christians to address the needs of other Christians, the latter portion extends the calling to all persons in need (for that is the biblical teaching on who our neighbor is). In either case, the freedom spoken of is not license to do as you please. In fact, it is a freedom that is accompanied by an obligation: a responsibility to use that freedom in ways that assist those in need.

As you correctly note, for Christians to carry out this social responsibility through political means does introduce an element of coercion. Those who do not share the majority view that emerges in legislation through the political process are still obliged to abide by the law. For example, a portion of the taxes I pay go to support a war in Iraq that I do not support. That is the nature of the political process. You express your perspective, Christian or otherwise, on the legislative issue at hand, and you don't always get what you argue for. Nevertheless, your responsibility is to present the most persuasive argument you can from within your worldview commitment and then let the majority chips fall where they may. At least that is how politics is structured in our present day in the United States.

Can you envision another way of doing politics that may be less coercive? I happen to think that the present way of doing politics in the United States leaves much to be desired. Its "winner-take-all" approach needs fixing. For example, CPJ has long been an advocate of a proportional representation system for election where legislative representation is proportional to the percentage of voters that each of a number of parties (not necessarily just two) receives. We can talk about the feasibility of that electoral approach, or lack thereof, in our later discussion. My closing point here is that while Christians are involved in doing politics under present ground rules, it is also appropriate for them to be involved in bold efforts to vastly improve current ways of doing politics.

The way that we who are not Christians perceive the intent of Christians who are politically active is that they are "triumphalistic." They wish to dominate public discourse for the purpose of making "Christian values" prominent in American society. To do so, they seek to wield power in the political process. Is our perception correct?

You are correct in your observation that many Christians in politics, notably those the media likes to tell you about, are triumphalistic in the ways that you describe. But many are not. I personally reject such triumphalism, and the pluralist political perspective that I have embraced rejects such striving for dominance. That rejection is not to deny that the exercise of power is inherent in the political process, and such political power is often exercised in brutish, destructive ways. Christians in politics need to exemplify unusual forms of power that are consistent with their faith commitment. Allow me to explain briefly.

If one thinks of power as the ability to influence others, then I am suggesting that Christians in politics need to exercise a type of power. Christians in politics ought to model respect in political discourse, working hard to create venues for conversation about legislative issues that welcome diverse points of view, where each participant is given room to express her viewpoint and the public rationale for it, with no preferential voice given to any participant. In such a context, the "power of a good public rationale" will be evident. Hopefully, Christians involved in such political discourse will give evidence of the Christian virtues of humility, patience, and love, and will model that rare combination of commitment to their own Christian beliefs and openness to learning from others by empathetically seeking to understand differing points of view. By creating such a welcoming space, Christian politicians will provide a good opportunity for Christian perspectives to gain a fair hearing on a level playing field with all other perspectives. In the corridors of power, the power that Christian politicians may thereby be exercising can be thought of as the power of love, for creating welcoming spaces for those you disagree with is a deep expression of loving others. That way of exercising power is surely a utopian ideal given our current political climate. But Christians in politics must aspire to that ideal.

There is another kind of legitimate power that we often overlook in public life, the power of moral influence. The role of Martin Luther King Jr. in the American civil rights movement is a compelling example of the efficacy of such power. King did not initially seek for political power by traditional means, such as winning elections. Rather, deeply motivated by his religious values, he initiated a moral movement, arguing that all Americans, whatever their race or religious or secular commitments, should embrace the moral principle of justice for all. To be sure, political initiatives eventually came. But the political influence of the civil rights movement flowed from the moral influence of King and those who shared his vision.

As pointed out by Jim Wallis in his compelling book *God's Politics: Why the Right Gets It Wrong and the Left Doesn't Get It*, the civil rights movement is only one example of the power of moral influence that has been exerted by religious communities as a precursor to eventual political influence. In Wallis' words: "Other great social causes led by religious communities—abolition of slavery, child labor reform, women's suffrage …—all followed the same strategy" (Wallis 2005, p. 64).

Although I cannot elaborate here, I believe that a primary focus for exercising the power of love in politics should be on building and nurturing caring personal relationships of mutual trust with those with whom we disagree. A marvelous example of the efficacy of this interpersonal focus is that of William Wilberforce, the British statesman who devoted his entire political career to eventually eliminating the slave trade in England. In words reported to have been said by Mark Hatfield, former Senator from Oregon: "One of the most compelling and encouraging characteristics I find in Wilberforce's life was the early resolve to focus his legislative and personal agenda on building relationships.… This took the place of power manipulation and legal machinations.… He sought to continue the incarnation of the Word in loving acts of mercy, justice and charity to those around him—even if they were his adversaries" (see Belmonte 2002 for an engaging biography of Wilberforce).

Since media coverage of Christians does not typically extend beyond those who are strongly triumphalistic, the non-triumphalistic approach to doing politics that I describe may sound foreign, and utopian. *Can you envision Christians, and others, doing politics in this way?*

You affirmed the right of parents to choose a form of education for their children that comports with their worldview commitment, but left open the thorny question of whether public funding should be made available if parents choose private education. Can you address that question?

Let me begin by summarizing what I understand to be the CPJ position, before outlining my variation on that position. The CPJ would argue that the choice of parents for public or private education for their children should be made without incurring a financial penalty. Currently, they are incurring a financial penalty if they choose and pay for private education, in addition to the taxes they already pay to support local public education. The remedy is for public funds to be made available to parents even if they choose private education. One possible mechanism for doing so would be for government to provide school vouchers for all parents, which can then be "cashed in" at schools chosen by parents.

To those who argue that such a school voucher system would, in effect, allow for using public funds to promote private education that may be religious in nature, the CPJ would have two responses. First, it is a false distinction to say that public education is neutral relative to worldview commitments, while private religious education espouses a particular worldview. All forms of education are informed by worldview commitments, whether such commitments are religious or secular. Public funding should not give preferential treatment to any particular worldview commitment. Secondly, granting that public funding should only be available for ventures that promote a "common good," all schools, public or private, can contribute to the common good if they build into their respective curricula the educating of students for responsible civic involvement as citizens.

I accept the general contours of the CPJ argument, including the potential use of school vouchers, but with some important qualifications based on other justice considerations and my understanding of the nature of "diversity" and the need for all citizens to engage those who are different from them. First, while the idea of school vouchers may look good on paper, its implementation can lead to gross injustices, especially against poor parents. Many who argue for school vouchers claim that it will enable poor parents to send their children to better schools. In reality, the funds that such vouchers typically provide are not sufficient to enable poor parents to pay for "better" education, and giving vouchers of equal value to richer parents who can already afford "better" education amounts to the government subsidizing the tuition that wealthier Americans are already paying to better schools. As has been suggested by Randall Balmer in his book *Thy Kingdom Come,* "[o]ne way to test the sincerity of those arguing for school vouchers on the basis of social justice would be to limit vouchers to children in households earning, say, less than $35,000" (Balmer 2006, p. 84). Therefore, great care must be taken to insure that the design and implementation of a school voucher system in a given place and time does not treat poor parents unjustly.

My primary qualification relative to the use of school vouchers is the danger of tribalism, creating a situation where adherents to any particular worldview, religious or secular, can be insulated from significant engagement with others who do not share their worldview commitments. My concern here goes deep down to my understanding of the nature of diversity in our pluralistic society. Diverse populations in our society should not just coexist. The public good that can result from diversity is enhanced if diverse populations engage one another, enabling each group to learn from and benefit from the best insights and practices of all other groups. In terms of my own commitment to the Christian faith, this rich view of diversity comports with my understanding that Christians are called to be "salt and light" in the world by engaging those who do not share their particular faith commitment, rather than withdrawing into insular communities.

In light of this second qualification, I have argued elsewhere (Heie 1992) that public funding should be made available for education under any auspices, "public" or "private," only if each educational institution makes a commitment to engage in public dialogue with those at other schools about alternative viewpoints on issues affecting the public good, and to collaborate with other schools in initiatives that enable their respective students to join together in service projects that foster the common good. It could be a logistical nightmare to try to implement such a strategy. Mine is surely a minority viewpoint for those who embrace the structural pluralism advocated by CPJ. Nevertheless, I think it is an ideal worth striving for. *Given your own experience in either public or private education, can you envision the possibility of such a collaborative model?*

You suggest that it may be appropriate for governments to pass laws that limit consensual behavior between adults or what appears to be strictly private behavior if it can be persuasively shown that the behavior in question has a high probability of leading to significant detrimental public consequences. I am struck by the "fuzziness" of that test. Can you clarify?

You are insightful in observing that my test involving public consequences is "fuzzy," and I find it difficult to clarify this point much, in the abstract. This test is fuzzy because there are no exact formulas for determining when a probability is high, or when an anticipated detrimental public consequence is significant. The measures to be given to such fuzzy words can only emerge out of conversations between politicians on a case-by-case basis. Such conversations will have to draw heavily on available, reliable empirical evidence pertinent to the case at hand. Allow me to illustrate by elaborating somewhat on one of the examples I simply noted in my initial remarks: possible legislation requiring motorcyclists to wear helmets.

As noted by Stephen Monsma relative to an actual legislative case debated a number of years ago in the Michigan legislature, when he was a member of that legislature, some motorcyclists argued against requiring helmets. They argued, in part, "on the basis of justice and freedom: the state should not interfere with their freedom of choice because even if helmets do add to safety, they add to the safety not of society but of the one who wears the helmet" (Monsma 1984, p. 33). On the other hand, it can be argued that "when a cyclist dies or is seriously and permanently injured because he wasn't wearing a helmet, all of society is affected. Insurance rates for all of us increase; surviving spouses or children may need to go on welfare; medical bills for long-term hospitalization, rehabilitation therapy, and nursing-home care are borne by all of us" (34). Such an argument would have to be supported by empirical evidence that such detrimental public consequences actually occur to a significant degree. As is usually the case, in politics and elsewhere, there are two sides to this debate. There is hope that wise legislative action will be taken if politicians on both sides of the issue are committed to listening to one another and to respectfully talking through the pros and cons of each position, being sure to first hear extensive testimony from those who will be most affected by their legislative action.

In brief, I am suggesting that the fuzziness relative to the public consequences test can only be sorted out through the political process. This is messy. But I don't see another way for politicians to proceed. *Do you? Is it possible that the public consequences test should be scrapped?* This test seems necessary to me if a role of government is to promote justice that is "public." But, I may be wrong about that.

If you allow Christians, or other persons having religious value convictions, into the political process, won't you be destroying the "neutrality" that is called for in politics?

As we seek for possible common ground relative to your question, it is important that we first strive for adequate understanding of the much misused and maligned "values" word. In our day, many persons think of values as only expressing private, personal preferences, which, therefore, should not be introduced into public discourse. I disagree. The values I am committed to do reflect deep personal commitments. They also reflect my understanding of the nature of a reality that is external to my personal preferences. Therefore, my values are relevant to public discourse, as are the values of all other persons. Since this may currently be a minority opinion relative to the status of values, you may wish to disagree.

Given my understanding of the status of value commitments, the political arena is not a neutral area of discourse relative to values. The prevalent myth of value neutrality goes something like this: Those holding to a secular worldview come to the public square without value commitments; they are neutral. Religious people, on the other hand, violate the ideal of neutrality by bringing their religious value commitments to the political process. Part of this line of thinking is true. Religious people do bring their value commitments to politics. But, so do all secularists. No human being is value neutral. Everyone has particular value commitments, religious or secular, that he or she brings to the public square. Members of Congress do not check in their values when they enter the doors of Congress.

If everyone brings their value commitments to the political process, then there is no compelling logical reason why giving expression to any particular set of value commitments ought to be precluded from political discourse. There should be a "level playing field," where a diversity of value commitments can gain a respectful hearing.

Isn't the expression of religious value commitments in politics a violation of the separation of church and state that is expressed in the First Amendment to the U.S. Constitution?

I take it from your question that you are committed to the inviolability of the First Amendment to the U.S. Constitution, which states that "Congress shall make no law respecting an establishment of religion [the establishment clause] nor prohibiting the free exercise thereof [the free exercise clause]." I share that commitment.

The thorny issue that is much debated is how to interpret and implement the First Amendment. We can possibly start navigating this morass by seeking agreement as to the overarching purpose of the First Amendment. It appears to me that our founders wanted to insure that there would be no state-sponsored religion in the new nation or state interference in the diverse religious practices of its citizens. *Isn't this to say that their overarching purpose was to protect religious freedom? Do you have a different understanding?* If we are in agreement about this overarching purpose, then the question to be debated is how best to protect religious freedom. The prevailing judicial paradigm assumes that the best way to protect religious freedom is to eliminate expressions of religious conviction from public life. Therefore, the practice of religion is essentially relegated to private life (with some accommodational exceptions, such as allowing government support of some activities of religious organizations deemed as not being narrowly sectarian). The form of religion that this paradigm protects is very narrow. This paradigm does not do justice to the belief of many religious people, like me, that religious commitment is pertinent to all areas of life, including the public domain. In other words, the prevailing paradigm may serve the establishment clause well by avoiding the establishment of any religion. But it hardly does justice to the free exercise clause, which should allow for freedom of religious expression in the public square.

A new judicial paradigm that is slowly emerging interprets the First Amendment as providing a level playing field for all religions, without giving preferred treatment to any religion or to secular perspectives. Such nonpreferential treatment does not relegate religion to a private sphere. Rather, it promotes a robust form of religious freedom that will enable religion to make a valuable contribution to public life. The Center for Public Justice is currently providing leadership for a Coalition to Preserve Religious Freedom, comprised of a variety of Christian and non-Christian organizations committed to articulating and promoting such a new paradigm. I strongly support this effort.

Two excellent books that elaborate on the position I have summarized are *Positive Neutrality: Let Religious Freedom Ring* by Stephen Monsma and *Equal Treatment of Religion in a Pluralistic Society* by Stephen Monsma and Christopher Soper. I recommend them for your consideration. In the meantime, I welcome your reflections on this paradigm for understanding the First Amendment.

Getting back to the possible role of values in politics and other public discourse, it appears that a significant factor contributing to President Bush's reelection in 2004 was his firm stance on moral values. Can you comment on that perception?

Based on media reports on exit interviews conducted after votes were cast, I think your perception is accurate. In fact, Northwest Iowa, where I now live, has been cited as one area of the country where this factor was particularly strong. However, I am concerned that the moral issues cited in these reports appear to be related primarily to the issues of gay marriage and abortion. I believe that these are important moral issues. As I have already suggested, I believe it is appropriate for such issues to be addressed in the political process, with a focus on discerning the public consequences of competing views.

But, *are moral values pertinent only to the issues of gay marriage and abortion that are prominent for many evangelical Christians?* I don't think so. Moral values also come into play when politicians address the following questions: What is an appropriate tax structure in light of the growing gap between the rich and poor? What are the implications of a huge federal deficit for our grandchildren? Can one ever justify a preemptive war? How can the United States best collaborate with other nations to ameliorate the environmental problems associated with greenhouse gases? What steps can be taken to improve an ailing criminal justice system? How can the basic education provided by our schools be improved? How can decent housing become a reality for everyone? What are the best ways to reduce high rates of unemployment? How can everyone be guaranteed basic health care?

It appears to me that these are all moral questions. And the response anyone gives to any one of these questions reflects a commitment to certain moral values. Therefore, I believe it is wrong to think that politicians who struggle with this set of moral questions bring no moral values to their deliberations.

Relative to the 2004 presidential contest, it cannot be argued that supporters of President Bush were devoted exclusively to addressing moral questions related to issues such as gay marriage and abortion. Nor can it be argued that Democratic supporters of John Kerry were devoted exclusively to the second set of moral questions I have enumerated. But I think it can be argued that the rhetoric of the Republicans so emphasized the first set of moral issues, apparently because that platform is what most energizes a large block of evangelical Christian voters, that they did not pay adequate attention to the second set of moral issues. The Democrats were not able to counter this one-sidedness because of a lack of an appropriate moral vocabulary to talk about these other moral issues in terms of value commitments. More Democrats need to learn to say publicly that the causes about which they are most passionate also reflect strong commitment to certain moral values. In the words of Ellen Goodman shortly after the 2004 elections: "This is the time for the losers to go back to basics, to restate their views into a basic simple, straightforward language of values and morals" (*Boston Globe* "Ideas" Section, November 7, 2004, P. D11). This call for moral discussion will require getting beyond the truncated view that values only express private, personal preferences.

What I have just said has strong implications for the post-2004 election task that both President Bush and Senator Kerry embraced, at least on paper: seeking for "unity" in the midst of differences. Such unity will remain elusive if the myth of value neutrality is maintained. Politicians on both sides of the aisle, and citizens reflecting a variety of worldview commitments, must be willing to articulate the value commitments that underlie their respective aspirations for public life and must be willing to engage in respectful conversations with those with whom they disagree, both about the underlying values and their implications for our common life together. Since I am guessing that there are both Republicans and Democrats seated around this table, I welcome your responses to my views on the potential role of "values" in future political discourse.

The call of President Bush and Senator Kerry for "unity" in the midst of differences sounds good. But isn't "the devil in the details"? What concrete things can Democrats and Republicans do to actually work toward such unity?

For a thorough answer to your question, I highly recommend that you read the book by Jim Wallis, *God's Politics*, to which I previously referred. My own response, which is informed by Wallis' position, is as follows.

First, members of both parties need to defuse the volatile rhetoric by more carefully distinguishing between "means" and "ends." For example, politicians on both sides of the aisle may share the view that it is good to alleviate extreme poverty, while disagreeing vehemently as to whether government programs, tax cuts, private charity, or some combination thereof are the best means toward that worthy end. So, the conversation should begin with the search for common ground relative to worthy ends.

Along the same lines, members of both parties need to express more sympathy and support for the values embraced by the other party that reflect common human values, independent of political affiliation. For example, all Americans should be appalled by the proliferation of sex and violence in the media, the prevalence of teenage pregnancy outside of marriage, and the erosion of marital fidelity and commitment. These are not just the concerns of Republicans. Democrats should also embrace the family values that underlie these common concerns and be quicker to say so publicly.

For an example on the other side of the coin, all Americans should be appalled by environmental degradation, loss of jobs, and the growth of poverty in our country. These are not just the concerns of Democrats. There are many Republicans who share these concerns. To be sure, Republicans and Democrats may argue for different means to address these shared concerns. But the place to start deliberating about alternative means is to publicly acknowledge that there is some common ground relative to the values that inform these common concerns. In light of examples like these, Jim Wallis insightfully points out how both Republicans and Democrats have some things right and some things wrong: "The Republican definition of family values, which properly stresses moral laxness but ignores the growing economic pressures on all families, simply doesn't go deep enough. Similarly, the Democrats are right when they focus on economic security for working families, but wrong when they are reluctant to make moral judgments about the cultural trends and values that are undermining family life" (Wallis 2005, p. 326).

A second strategy for working toward greater unity between Democrats and Republicans is to convince people on both sides of the political aisle (as well as people divided on controversial social issues, independent of their political affiliation) that "half-a-loaf is better than none." The nature of politics is that you seldom, if ever, get everything you want. Political discourse will often reveal irreconcilable differences, requiring bargaining and compromise. A politician is not compromising her integrity or worldview commitments when she settles for half-a-loaf in political legislation, as long as she argued faithfully for the full loaf and respectfully engaged those who disagreed with her before a vote was taken. It is also appropriate to engage in "coalition building" by creating alliances with those persons or organizations who agree with you on the legislative issue at hand, even if they disagree with you on other matters (see Monsma & Rodgers 2005, pp. 334–336). Let me give a controversial example.

In the raging debates about abortion, pro-lifers who argue for a total ban of all abortions, under any circumstances, will probably never get their full loaf in the legislative process. Likewise, those from the pro-choice movement who argue for a woman's right to choose an abortion at any time during a pregnancy and under any circumstances will probably never get their full loaf legislatively. Stalemate? Only if each group will settle for nothing less than their full loaf. But there is so much common ground that both groups could agree upon if they would make more effort to engage each other respectfully. *Couldn't both groups work together, on both sides of the political aisle, to address the problem of excessive teen age pregnancy outside of marriage, to improve on current options for adoption, and to offer support to those women who live in circumstances that present greater risks for unwanted pregnancies*? I think so. And the former President of Planned Parenthood, Gloria Feldt, appears to agree when she stated that "[the pro-choice movement] must focus on the prevention agenda. It is the morally right thing to do. It is a place where the majority of Americans can agree" (*Newsweek Online* excerpt, February 7, 2005, p. 4).

However, we all know that calls for greater unity between Democrats and Republicans immediately after major elections seldom lead to unity. The hyper-partisanship of American politics returned with a vengeance shortly after the 2004 presidential election, leading to greater disunity. True to form, Democrats and Republicans have again called for unity after the 2006 congressional elections. Only time will tell whether politicians on both sides of the aisle have the courage to actually take concrete steps toward such unity, such as those I have proposed.

In summary, we could find more unity across both sides of the political aisle if we would respectfully engage each other in the search for common ground, rather than writing each other off because of differences that may not be resolvable.

As you made clear up front, your initial remarks and your responses to our questions are all based on your commitment to the Christian faith. Would you extend your proposal that "Christians should do politics" to a claim that "religious people should do politics," whatever the nature of their religious commitment?

I can't presume to speak for other religions. Others seated around this table can speak to whether adherents to their respective religions are called to active involvement in politics. From my particular Christian perspective, the healthiest way for government to fulfill its task of doing public justice is for all citizens committed to religious freedom to become actively involved in politics, whatever their religions or secular worldview commitments. Such religious freedom includes the opportunity to choose allegiance to any expression of religion or any non-religious worldview, provided that such expression is not judged in the political process to be harmful to others or to be destructive of the public good. And the ideal political process will provide a level playing field for all citizens to participate, whatever their religious or secular worldview commitments. No religious or secular worldview perspective should be given preferential treatment.

My response leaves unanswered the issue of political involvement of citizens who understand their religious or secular worldview commitments to preclude religious freedom. For example, some may believe that if their religious party comes to power, all citizens should be required by law to pledge allegiance to the teachings of their party. I would argue that such persons should have the freedom to express that point of view in the political realm, hoping that the vast majority of U.S. citizens will continue to have the sense to reject that viewpoint through political means.

◆ ◆ ◆

Since this conversation exists only in my mind, I suppose I can end it any way I like. I will conclude by summarizing my fondest hopes for all of us around this imaginary table. I hope that by the end of the day we understand each other's perspectives a lot better than when we started. I hope we have gotten to know each other better as persons, leaving the table with greater respect for one another and with mutual concern for each other's well-being. I hope we have been able to clarify those differences in viewpoint on which we agree to disagree. Finally, I hope we have found some common ground on the thorny issue of whether religious people should do politics, and we are prepared to go back to our respective communities committed to exploring potential implications of that common ground.

21

Tragedy, Just War, and Peacemaking

o o o o o o o o o o o o o o o o o o o o o o o o o o o o o o o

John Howard Yoder ... convinced me [Stanley Hauerwas] that if there is anything to this Christian "stuff," it must surely involve the conviction that the Son [Jesus] would rather die on the cross than have the world to be redeemed by violence. (Hauerwas 2004, p. 203)

Do not be overcome by evil, but overcome evil with good. (Romans 12:21)

Imagine with me once again a group of people sitting around a table. This time they are invited to have a conversation about alternative views on war. In the interest of inclusiveness, the moderator has invited both Christians and those committed to other religious or secular worldviews. Participants also represent a wide spectrum of views about war, including a pacifist and a few just war theorists, at least one of whom will argue that just war principles can, under certain circumstances, be invoked to justify a preemptive war. I suspect I have been invited because my own pilgrimage has taken me from a just war position to a commitment to peacemaking, and the story of how that shift took place could be helpful to others around the table. After appropriate introductions, we all agree that our main purpose in gathering is for each of us to gain greater understanding of a diversity of perspectives on war. We also agree on the need to test our various perspectives against the realities we perceive in our conflict-ridden world. Each participant is given the opportunity to give a five-minute opening statement. I am encouraged by the moderator to focus on how my thinking about war has changed during the course of my pilgrimage. My story about this change follows.

◆ ◆ ◆

My initial thinking about war was shaped as I considered a broader ethical question in my informal studies in philosophy while I was teaching mathematics at The King's College in New York. What is the nature of moral choice for finite, fallible human beings (what I will call "finite moral choice"), and are there any conceivable situations where such a choice will be "tragic"?

Every moral choice is a finite moral choice in the sense that my finitude makes it impossible for me to foresee all the consequences of my choice, some of which may eventually prove to enhance the values I am committed to (as intended), and some of which may actually prove to be destructive of these same values. For example, I may choose to support financially the college education of Joe Smith, instead of Bill Brown, because of my present judgment, based on what I now know, that Joe has more potential than Bill to exert a positive influence in society. But for reasons I don't know about at the time of decision, Bill could actually turn out to be a solid citizen, while Joe turns out to be a criminal.

In this context, a pressing question is whether there is a subcategory of finite moral choices for which I know that whatever course of action I choose will be destructive of a value to which I am committed, and I have no other choice but to sacrifice one value for the sake of what I take to be a higher value. If there are such choices, and the sacrificed value is judged to be of sufficient import (such as life or physical well-being), philosophers refer to these choices as tragic moral choices. Allow me to illustrate with a hypothetical situation, after noting a problem with dealing with hypothetical situations.

A major school of thought in the area of moral development, typically associated with the work of Lawrence Kohlberg, proposes that a person's level of moral maturity can be assessed on how she responds, in paper and pencil tests, to hypothetical situations of tragic moral choice. Without denying that Kohlberg's work has provided many valuable insights relative to the existence and nature of differing stages of moral development, a fundamental flaw of this approach, in my estimation, is that in real life actual moral dilemmas are not dealt with in the abstract, as hypothetical situations. Rather, they are experienced in the flow of life, and the response of any one person to such a situation flows from the same multiplicity of personal factors that inform all of our decisions, such as elements of personal biography, and especially, our inner dispositions, those enduring attitudes that have been shaped over a lifetime of decision-making. In light of this, it is impossible to deal adequately with hypothetical moral choices in the abstract.

However, it is possible to at least point to one or more sub-issues that would be relevant in hypothetical cases of tragic moral choice (recognizing that other sub-issues can only be identified in a concrete situation). I will illustrate by posing a hypothetical situation relative to the much contested issue of abortion.

Since this is not a conversation about abortion, I will only give a summary statement about this thorny issue that is relevant to the point I wish to make, recognizing that a full discussion of abortion would require much more elaboration and defense of my position. In a nutshell, whatever one decides about the question of whether the fetus can be considered a person, I believe that a fetus is at least a form of "potential human life" that is of great value. Therefore, I do not believe in a general policy of abortion on demand since it allows the destruction of potential or actual human life when nondestructive alternatives may be available, such as adoption.

However, I also believe there can be genuine cases of tragic moral choice relative to a possible abortion, where one has no other option but to knowingly sacrifice one value for the sake of what one judges to be a higher value. One such tragic case is "save the mother or save the child." If my wife were pregnant and medical experts told me that if the pregnancy was not terminated, it was almost certain that my wife would die, then that would be one factor pointing to the choice of an abortion (noting again that it is impossible to point to all other possible factors for or against choosing an abortion in such a hypothetical situation divorced from real life). My reason for this factor pointing toward the choice of abortion is that my wife has established loving personal relationships that the fetus has not. Therefore, I would be sacrificing one value (the life of the fetus) for what I have judged to be a higher value (the life of my wife).

As illustrated by this hypothetical situation, I came to the conclusion early in my pilgrimage that I could not preclude the possibility of finding myself in a situation where I would have to make a tragic moral choice. However, I also believed that it would be highly unlikely for me to be in such a situation. And if I was, I would need to be careful not to make a premature appeal to unavoidably having to sacrifice a value, without having exhaustively explored the possibility of creatively finding a nondestructive alternative that sacrificed no values. Making a tragic moral choice would always be a last resort.

It is in the context of my position that there can be cases of tragic moral choice, albeit very rare, that I formulated my early position about war, which I now think can be viewed as a variation of just war theory.

According to just war theorists, a war can be justified if it satisfies certain necessary conditions for "going to war" and other conditions for "conducting a war."

For example, two necessary conditions that must be satisfied prior to going to war are *just intention*—"the only legitimate intention is to secure a just peace for all involved," and *last resort*—"war may only be entered upon when all negotiations and compromise have been tried and failed." Two necessary conditions for then conducting a war are *proportionate means*—"the weaponry and force used should be limited to what is needed to … secure a just peace," and *noncombatant immunity*—"only those who are official agents of government may fight, and individuals not actively contributing to the conflicts … should be immune from attack" (Holmes 1981, pp. 120–121; see also Walzer 1977 and Ramsey 1983).

There is much debate about the applicability, or lack-thereof, of just war principles to modern warfare. In particular, a difficult question has been asked as to whether modern means of conducting war, including the use of weapons of mass destruction such as nuclear arsenals, could conceivably satisfy the conditions of proportionate means or noncombatant immunity. I doubt it. While allowing for differences in opinion about that issue, it was the principle of *last resort* that resonated most closely with the position I had adopted relative to tragic moral choice. In brief, I could be comfortable holding to a just war position at that point in my life if, assuming the other just war principles can actually be satisfied in a given present-day conflict, the principle of *last resort* could be satisfied. In other words, all nondestructive alternatives to war have been tried and have failed. Although war is judged by everyone to have significant destructive consequences, going to war is judged to be the least destructive alternative.

In my earlier years, my position on war could be described as a just war position. But I gradually moved away from that position. Why? My movement away from just war theory resulted from struggling with the problem of not having complete knowledge of the consequences of my taking any course of action, including an action that I perceive to be a tragic moral choice.

If one is in a situation perceived to be a genuine tragic moral choice, where all available courses of action are destructive in some way, then attempting to make a responsible moral choice requires that one project the likely consequences of each possible action. However, a finite human being cannot typically foresee the consequences of each action being considered. A given action may have destructive consequences that were not intended at the moment of decision. Reaching a decision is further complicated by the fact that you are often typically dealing with "probable" consequences, not having certainty that a given action will lead to a projected consequence. What is one to do in light of these limitations on present knowledge relative to consequences?

One can only do whatever is possible to close this knowledge gap in the time that is available before a decision must be made. In certain cases calling for moral choice, the time available for such reflection may be severely limited. But as time allows, one projects the likelihood of various consequences, drawing on two resources. One is the resource of other persons with whom you can talk through the possible consequences. The second resource is the body of available empirical data that reflects the past experience of others relative to possible consequence in similar situations, especially data relative to long-term unforeseen and unintended consequences that actually occurred in these comparable situations.

Eventually, it was the history of long-term unforeseen and unintended consequences of going to war that became the major stumbling block to my earlier view of justifying war as a tragic moral choice, choosing for higher values in a given situation of apparently irresolvable conflict. There appears to me to be irrefutable historical evidence that typically *violence begets violence*, often in unforeseen and unintended ways, and that the only way to break out of this spiral of violence is to say "no" to violence. Therefore, I now operate according to what I will awkwardly call a "presumption for peacemaking." Because violence typically begets further violence, in ways I cannot foresee or predict, I must typically say "no" to violence, devoting myself to being a peacemaker. As you will soon hear me say (to the consternation of some of my pacifist friends), my presumption for peacemaking does not mean that I absolutely preclude the possibility of my having to resort to violence as an "irrefutable last resort" in a tragic moral choice. But this possible rare situation, which I suspect I will never experience, does not diminish my aspiration and efforts to always be a peacemaker.

As I was moving toward my presumption for peacemaking, I struggled with apparent mixed messages in the Bible relative to whether violence, or, more specifically, going to war, is ever justifiable for a Christian. Some Christians appeal to the many accounts in the Old Testament where it appears that God condones war as a means to preserve God's chosen people, the Jewish nation. For those, like me, who believe that such accounts are not meant to be normative under the New Covenant inaugurated by Jesus Christ, the ambiguity is still not solved. For if one goes to the New Testament, some Christians will appeal to the teaching in Romans 13:1–7 that human government is ordained by God to preserve order in society, and this mandate entails punishing those who do evil, even to the point of drawing the sword. On the other hand, other Christians will point to Jesus' rejection of the use of the sword by his disciple Peter (Matthew 26:51–52) and to those portions of Jesus' Sermon on the Mount (see Matthew 5) that reject the use of the sword or any form of violence by Christians.

As is to be expected, each group of Christians provides explanations for the biblical passages that appear to be inconsistent with its position. Those who hold that Romans 13 allows for Christians going to war may take the position that the Sermon on the Mount is only applicable to one-on-one relationships between persons; it does not tell Christians how to respond to violence perpetrated against innocent third parties. On the other hand, those Christians who hold that the Sermon on the Mount precludes the use of violence by Christians under any circumstances may hold that Romans 13 is a teaching of the Apostle Paul that must be superseded by the teachings of Jesus. What is a Christian to do in light of these conflicting interpretations of what the Bible says?

My attempt to bridge the apparent gap between Romans 13 and the Sermon on the Mount is to interpret Romans 13 as pointing to an appropriate role for government toward the good end of maintaining order in society, including the punishment of those who transgress the established law, and to interpret the Sermon on the Mount as pointing to an extraordinary means for carrying out this governmental function. Jesus hinted at this combination when he said, "Do not think that I have come to abolish the Law of the Prophets; I have not come to abolish them but to fulfill them" (Matthew 5:17). Such fulfillment of the law suggests a deeper meaning to its dictates. One aspect of this deeper meaning, which I will not develop here, is that adherence to the law must be judged by the attitudes that motivate behavior and not just by our outward actions. Jesus illustrates this point with various examples, such as "You have heard it was said to the people long ago, 'Do not murder and anyone who murders will be subject to judgment.' But I tell you that anyone who is angry with a brother or sister will be subject to judgment" (Matthew 5:21–22). I propose that another aspect of such deeper meaning, which is pertinent here, is commitment to an extraordinary means for implementing the codified law. The nature of such an approach can be illustrated by the work my son Jeff has done in the area of restorative justice.

Jeff worked for a number of years for the Restorative Justice Initiative at the Community Mediation Center in Harrisonburg, Virginia. Under the rubric of victim/offender conferencing, Jeff was assigned cases by the Virginia Judicial System where the criminal sentence for a juvenile offender included face-to-face conversations, mediated by Jeff, between the offender and the victim. The purpose of these conversations was to go far beyond the prevalent truncated view of criminal justice, which suggests that such justice is accomplished when the offender is given suitable retribution by government. The vision of restorative justice is broader in scope than punishment. It focuses on meeting the needs of all persons affected by the crime, including the victim and offender, and the communities in which the offender and victim live. Steps are taken to hold the offender accountable to the victim, possibly leading to some form of restitution, or, if possible, even reconciliation (two good books about the restorative justice movement are *Changing Lenses* by Howard Zehr, and *Beyond Retribution* by Christopher Marshall). To be sure, Romans 13 calls for the judicial system to punish criminal offenders. But the deeper meaning of the Sermon on the Mount suggests that even in the punishment of criminals, the ultimate purpose, however difficult it may be to attain, is accountability, reconciliation, and restoration of the offender. That is surely a utopian ideal, but the Sermon on the Mount calls for nothing less.

Jeff was indeed committed to upholding the law, in the spirit of Romans 13. But his extraordinary means was that of peacemaking, in the broadest sense. Such peacemaking was not passivity or a lack of response to injustice. Nor was it settling for a truncated view of peace as merely the absence of conflict. Rather, his peacemaking was a robust response to injustice that embraced the biblical ideal of *shalom*: the restoration and flourishing of positive relationships. It was Jeff's example that helped me to solidify my commitment to be a peacemaker.

Are there viable options for a peacemaker in a world torn by conflict? In particular, were there peacemaking options in response to the horrific events of September 11, 2001, and was there a peacemaking alternative to the waging of war on Iraq by the United States? It helps me to think in terms of appropriate responses to terrorism and regime brutality by the community of peacemakers as a whole rather than in terms of the possible responses of individual peacemakers. Individual Christians may sense differing Christian callings in light of the differing elements of their social locations. In that light, here is my present understanding of various options that individual or collective peacemakers might consider.

The options for September 10 are fairly clear to me. There is little hope for peace without justice. Peacemakers should be working to eradicate those unaddressed elements of injustice that can contribute significantly to the outbreak of terrorism and war. But, what was a peacemaker to do on September 12 as a vigorous nonviolent response to terrorism? What was a peacemaker to do when the United States was on the brink of going to war against Iraq?

A few responses come to mind. First, it is appropriate for peacemakers who are educators to provide educational experiences for students that promote peacemaking strategies in the face of horrific events. Secondly, it is appropriate for some peacemakers to protest publicly any violent responses of the United States to these dire situations. However, if these responses are all that the community of peacemakers enact, then they are insufficient. They only protest the violent response of others without proposing alternative nonviolent responses intended to hold terrorists and brutal dictators accountable for their destructive deeds. So, other peacemakers must respond in more proactive ways.

An appropriate proactive response for some peacemakers will be to vigorously support and participate in channels for diplomacy and negotiation. This suggestion flies in the face of the received wisdom that "we do not negotiate with terrorists." Why not? Is it because we fear that this dialogue will be interpreted as a sign of weakness? Is it possible that a call for conversations is, rather, a sign of strength? Do we dare to embrace the ludicrous sounding proverbial wisdom that "[a] soft answer turns away wrath, but a harsh word stirs up anger" (Proverbs 15:1), not just in our personal relationships (which I can attest to be true), but in the public realm? If one responds that diplomacy and negotiation will never work in the war against terrorism, I respond by asking whether there is sufficient empirical evidence that responding to violence with violence is more likely to end a cycle of violence.

Another possible course of action that some peacemakers could deem appropriate is to respond to these atrocities by vigorously supporting multilateral use of appropriate means to bring terrorists to justice in accordance with principles of international law, for these atrocities are surely criminal acts against humankind. In *God's Politics,* Jim Wallis suggests that this approach to peacemaking could include the establishment of an "international police force acting with the multinational authorization of international law" (Wallis 2005, p. 166).

The obstacles to large scale implementation of this international law approach are enormous, to say the least. For starters, it will require that many nations, most notably the United States, will have to moderate their claims to national sovereignty in the interest of seeking a more peaceful world community. If the United Nations is viewed as playing a central role in administering international criminal law, this approach may require significant rethinking of current UN structures and the current ground rule that each participating nation can maintain its own absolute national sovereignty. I know of some mature peacemakers who are championing this international law approach. This approach has the potential, in the long run, to be the most adequate response of peacemakers to ongoing acts of terrorism.

Finally, for some peacemakers, a vigorous response to terrorism will mean putting oneself in harm's way, as a lamb in the midst of wolves, such as volunteering to join a peacemaking team in the midst of violent conflict. This risk could lead to a cross. For if I vigorously oppose injustice and other evils nonviolently, those I oppose who are willing to resort to violence may well crucify me. Ghandi and

Martin Luther King Jr. found that to be the case. Neither sought suffering. Rather, they suffered and sacrificed their lives as a result of faithfully living out their commitments to overcoming evil by nonviolent means.

The peacemaking options enumerated above preclude justification of the United States going to war against Iraq. Even if one accepts the logic of tragic moral choice, it cannot be argued that the United States was in a situation where all the available options were destructive and the "lesser of values" had to be sacrificed. First, there was no compelling evidence that the United States was in danger of imminent attack by Iraq. Iraq did not have a stockpile of weapons of mass destruction, and there is no compelling evidence of there having been a collaborative connection between Saddam Hussein and Al Qaeda. Secondly, available nondestructive alternatives were not exhausted, such as channels for diplomacy and negotiation and bringing terrorists to justice in accordance with principles of international law. Therefore, even for those holding to a just war position, the principle of *last resort* was not satisfied.

I have still hedged on the question of whether there can be any conceivable circumstances under which a Christian can justifiably go to war or resort to any form of physical violence. I cannot, in the abstract, preclude that possibility. Therefore, although I consider myself a peacemaker, the community of Christians embedded in the pacifist tradition may not consider me to be a pacifist because I do not preclude a resort to violence in extraordinary circumstances. Since being a peacemaker and being a pacifist are generally considered to be equivalent, this position will take some explaining. I start by considering Dietrich Bonhoeffer.

Toward the end of World War II, Bonhoeffer was a member of Abwehr, a group that conspired to overthrow Hitler, involving at least one attempt at assassination. Yet, Bonhoeffer had been a lifelong pacifist. How does one explain that apparent inconsistency? Since the secrecy required by this conspiracy precluded the existence of substantial written documentation concerning Bonhoeffer's exact role, one can only conjecture.

The easiest and most commonly accepted conjecture is that toward the end of World War II, Bonhoeffer rejected his lifelong commitment to pacifism, realizing the necessity of violence to eliminate the scourge of Hitler. If that is the case, a related conjecture is that Bonhoeffer viewed this necessity as a tragic moral choice. After a lifetime of teaching and practicing nonviolent resistance to evil, he realized that all the options now open to him were destructive, and he saw the destructive option of assassinating Hitler as a way to bring the war to a close with less violence.

But some pacifist scholars reject the view that Bonhoeffer rejected his pacifism when he became involved with Abwehr. Rather, he was a consistent pacifist unto death (see Nation 1999). How can that be? Again, one can only conjecture. Possibly he was outvoted when members of Abwehr decided to try to assassinate Hitler. Or, even if Bonhoeffer favored "pulling the trigger on Hitler," is it possible that this decision did not nullify his pacifism since he devoted his life to peacemaking? To generalize, is it possible that whether a Christian can be considered a pacifist should be judged on whether one has devoted an entire life to peacemaking efforts, rather than on conjectures as to what one would do in dire, extremely rare circumstances, like the situation in which Bonhoeffer found himself?

It is possible that further research by Bonhoeffer scholars will help me to sort through these conjectures. In the meantime, I am attracted to the possibility that I can be considered to be a pacifist if the ebb and flow of my daily life is devoted to peacemaking efforts and my character reflects an ongoing predisposition toward peacemaking, even if I cannot, in the abstract, preclude the possibility of resorting to violence in an unusual circumstance that I consider to be a tragic moral choice. It just seems reasonable to me that whether I am a pacifist should be based on my entire life and not on conjectures as to what I might do in a circumstance in which I will probably never find myself. If that is not the case, then I am content to aspire to be a peacemaker.

◆ ◆ ◆

I am guessing that should this imaginary conversation be taking place, others around the table would articulate significant objections to my opening remarks. I can imagine at least the following comments and questions, to be followed by my possible responses to them, which will often include follow-up questions intended to continue the conversation.

As a Christian working out of the pacifist Mennonite tradition, I do not agree with your suggestion that there may be situations where one has no choice other than the tragic choice of sacrificing a lesser value for the sake of a higher value. Your position reflects a lack of moral imagination. In any given case of apparent tragic moral choice, if one is creative enough, one should be able to identify a nondestructive course of action that sacrifices no values. Even if you can't identify such a nondestructive action, isn't it better to take no course of action, entrusting the situation to God, who can intervene, or not, in light of complete knowledge of unforeseen and unintended consequences?

As you can tell from my opening remarks, I am very sympathetic to the particular Mennonite perspective you embrace. But I cannot take that perspective as far as you wish to. First, in any given case of apparent tragic moral choice, it is impossible to "take no course of action." To decide to "do nothing" is a course of action. For example, relative to the hypothetical abortion case of "save the mother or save the child" that I referred to, it has been suggested to me by others that the only proper Christian response is to prayerfully entrust the situation to God and tell the doctors to just "let happen what happens." I do not minimize the importance of prayer. I believe that God can miraculously intervene in such a situation in ways that I cannot comprehend. But I also believe that for me as a finite human being to count on such divine intervention in the face of compelling empirical evidence that to just let happen what happens will almost certainly lead to the death of the mother, if not the fetus, would be morally irresponsible on my part. *Does this reflect a lack of faith in God on my part?* Possibly so. Some day, the two of us should sit down and discuss Søren Kierkegaard's provocative book *Fear and Trembling* in which he discusses the difficult case of Abraham deciding that it would be appropriate for him to kill his son Isaac (Genesis 22). Kierkegaard suggests that the justification of Abraham's decision is that as a "knight of faith," he is "suspending the ethical" for the sake of a higher "religious calling." *Can you help me to understand better what Kierkegaard is suggesting?* I am inclined to say that as a finite, fallible human being, I should not make decisions that contradict my understanding of ethical Christian behavior by appealing to a supposed higher religious calling. I believe my religious calling is to live well in light of my understanding of Christian ethical principles. But, I could be wrong.

You suggested that the many accounts in the Old Testament where it appears that God condones war are not meant to be normative under the "New Covenant" inaugurated by Jesus Christ. Would you please elaborate on that?

I have struggled with this issue for years, so I will give you a progress report. It is not only the wars that are apparently condoned in the Old Testament that cause me consternation in light of my understanding of God's redemptive purposes. I am also perplexed by the condoning, or at least allowing, of the practice of slavery that I read about in the Old Testament (and into the New Testament). *How can we who hold to biblical authority make sense of that acceptance?*

Let me start with the practice of slavery in ancient Israel, which I take to be a flagrant violation of God's redemptive purposes. Relative to this issue, I have been helped by a Redemptive-Movement Hermeneutic proposed by William Webb (Webb 2001, pp. 30–66). In brief, the cultural context in and around ancient Israel was characterized by "slavery with many abuses" (p. 37). In this context, the Bible portrays a "redemptive movement" toward "slavery with better conditions and fewer abuses" (p. 37). For example, Leviticus 25:39–43 calls for "seventh-day release for Hebrew slaves" (p. 44). Deuteronomy 24:7 and Exodus 21:16 call for the "denouncement of slave traders" (p.44). In Webb's view, and mine, this redemptive movement is toward the "ultimate ethic" of "slavery eliminated" (p. 37).

This idea of redemptive movement informs my understanding of progressive revelation in the Bible. As summarized by Douglas Jacobsen and Rodney Sawatsky, "The Bible as a whole recounts the story of God's interactions with humanity, and that historical narrative has a progressive tone. Ideas develop. The plot thickens. The story line becomes more complex. God did not change in the process, but humanity's perception of God did" (Jacobsen & Sawatsky 2006, p. 106). Therefore, there is progression in humanity's understanding of how God's purposes for Creation will be accomplished. For example, "At one point, the rule of justice is an eye for an eye and a tooth for a tooth—no one is to exact more damage than they themselves have received—but later the standard is redefined in terms of forgiveness and nonretaliation" (Jacobsen & Sawatsky 2006, p. 107).

This view also helps me to begin to make sense of the record of violent wars recorded in the Old Testament in light of my lived belief that God wills that Christians be agents for peace. It appears to me that the redemptive movement is away from an understanding that God's purposes are to be accomplished through violent means. Rather, the New Covenant, inaugurated by the Incarnation of God in Jesus, reveals the peaceful means God intends for accomplishing God's redemptive purposes, as reflected in the understanding of God and God's ways recorded by the New Testament authors.

As you already suggested, there is even ambiguity in the New Testament, between Romans 13 and Jesus' Sermon on the Mount, relative to whether violence is ever justifiable for a Christian. You have attempted to reconcile these biblical passages by creating a synthesis of "ends" (the desired end of preserving order in society pointed to in Romans 13) and "means" (a methodology of peacemaking pointed to in the words of Jesus recorded in the Sermon on the Mount). Is such a synthesis necessary? It is my understanding that in the Lutheran Christian tradition in which you were raised, it is taught that there are two distinct realms, one being the secular realm, where a Christian's behavior is governed by Romans 13, and the other being a sacred realm, in which a Christian is guided by Jesus' teachings in the Sermon on the Mount. Isn't that another viable way to reconcile these two passages?

Thank you for bringing up this alternative approach to reconciling Romans 13 and the Sermon on the Mount. The distinction you point to is often referred to as the "two-kingdoms" distinction. I am told by theologians that there is disagreement as to how firmly Martin Luther, the founder of Lutheranism, held to this distinction. I have read an essay by Martin Luther on the Sermon on the Mount supporting such a distinction (Luther, in O'Donovan 1999, pp. 596, 600). Let me quote portions of this essay that concern me:

> What does it mean then to be meek [as Jesus exhorts Christians to be in Matthew 5:5]? ... Here you must realize that Christ is not speaking at all about the government and its work ... he is only talking about how individuals are to live in relation to others, apart from official positions and authority ... [w]e must sharply distinguish between these two, the office and the person. The man who is called Hans or Martin is a man quite different than the one who is called Elector or Doctor or Preacher. Here we have two different persons in one man.... Thus, when a Christian goes to war or when he sits on a judge's bench, punishing his neighbor, ... he is not doing this as a Christian, but as a soldier or judge ... (pp. 596, 600).

Uff da! (A Norwegian expression of dismay). Despite my indebtedness to my Lutheran upbringing, I can think of few things with which I disagree more than the above words penned by Martin Luther. I am not "two different persons in one man." I am one person! As one person, I cannot separate out some of my actions as secular and some as sacred (an insight I gained from my later exposure to the Reformed Christian tradition). I must create the kind of synthesis I proposed between Romans 13 and the Sermon on the Mount that helps me in my attempts to live well, as one Christian person, in all areas of life. It's possible that my strong emotional response blinds me to an important point that this distinction makes. *Can you help me to understand better the nature of this distinction and its concrete implications?*

You suggested that the options for peacemakers prior to September 11 were clear to you. They should be working to eradicate those injustices and oppressions that can contribute significantly to the outbreak of terrorism and war. That cryptic assertion begs for elaboration.

I appreciate your giving me the opportunity to elaborate somewhat. First, one could take what Willard Swartley has called the "small-step approach to peace" (in his book *Covenant of Peace,* p. 426). Such small-steps can "create environments that build peace," such as "teaching conflict resolution in elementary schools, providing peace-building activities for junior high and high school youth, and even offering gun buy-back programs" (pp. 427–428).

For a more elaborate response, I refer you to two books by Glen Stassen: *Just Peacemaking: Ten Practices for Abolishing War* and *Just Peacemaking: Transforming Initiatives for Justice and Peace.* By "just peacemaking," Stassen is referring to steps that need to be taken to prevent war. He states elsewhere that "just peacemaking" theory does not try to answer the question that pacifism and just war theory answer: if just peacemaking fails, is it right to make war, or should we be committed to nonviolence? (Stassen 2005, p. 306).

Allow me to mention just a few of the ten peacemaking practices that Stassen proposes: reduce offensive weapons and weapons trade; strengthen the United Nations and international efforts for cooperation and human rights; foster just and sustainable economic development.

Even more radically, Stassen suggests the possibility of taking "transforming initiatives" that can break one out of the vicious cycle of violence. As an example from bygone days, he suggests that Jesus' teaching in the Sermon on the Mount that "if anyone forces you to go one mile, go also the second mile" (Matthew 5:41) is such a transforming initiative. Noting that at that time "Roman soldiers could compel Jews to carry their packs a mile," Stassen quotes Pinchas Lapide, who has the following neglected take on this exhortation: by carrying the pack a second mile, a Jew was "transforming compulsory service into a voluntary escort after the prescribed mile so that the astounded Roman would be disarmed … by graciousness" (Stassen 1992, p. 66). Lapide goes on to say, "Here the initiative is taken away from the superior, evil is repaid with good, and, in all probability, in the course of the second mile a friendly conversation will begin to develop." *How is that for a creative transforming initiative? How would our world be different now if we had had sufficient moral imagination and courage to pursue transforming initiatives prior to September 11, and what might such transforming initiatives have looked like?*

Allow me to elaborate further by proposing some steps that could be taken now that could ameliorate the escalating threat of terrorism. It is my conviction that the U.S. Government has not adequately acknowledged or addressed all of the root causes of terrorism. The common view is that the Islamist terrorists hate us because of our western lifestyles, our democratic freedoms, our intermingling of genders, our civil liberties, or our separation of church and state. There are elements of truth in this view. But, as has been provocatively elaborated in the book *Imperial Hubris* (written by Michael Scheuer, a former CIA agent who was anonymous at the time of publication), the primary reason they hate us may be because of our foreign policies that are destructive for many Muslims. But the U.S. government has chosen, for the most part, to ignore this line of reasoning. Examples of such destructive foreign policies include America's protection and support of corrupt and tyrannical Muslim governments and, in my estimation, an obvious imbalance in support of Israel in the Israeli/Palestinian conflict. I would also add the grievances of the poor, Muslim and otherwise, in underdeveloped countries concerning our efforts toward economic globalization that overemphasize free trade at the expense of fair trade, thereby inhibiting the economic development of poor nations. Our "war on terrorism" will be endless unless we adequately address these root causes. These are strong convictions on my part. I hope you will feel free to disagree as we continue our conversation.

May I respectfully suggest, Harold, that the fatal flaw in your proposal for peacemaking as an alternative to war is that it will not work in our real world of conflict, for two reasons. First, to suggest that one can pursue diplomacy and negotiation with terrorists is ludicrous. It is totally out of touch with present day realities. In the real world in which we live, you can only overcome strength that is evil with greater strength. Second, while there might be a slight glimmer of hope for your strategies for peacemaking if you could mobilize the majority of Americans around your cause, that mobilization will never happen. You are essentially suggesting that your Christian understanding on this matter, which is very much a minority view among Christians, should be embraced by all Americans, whatever their worldview commitments, religious or secular. If you will pardon me for being so blunt, it amounts to you and I and all of us around this table having the freedom to debate this issue, in the abstract, in the safety of this location, because young Americans are willing to fight our wars for us, dying far away from home and loved ones.

Your critique is cogent and compelling. I am not convinced that I have an equally compelling response. But let me share a few reflections.

First, possibly the most outrageous assertion in all of the Bible, in light of present day realities in our world, is its teaching that the only ultimate way to overcome evil is with good (Romans 12:21). I can't think of any biblical teaching that is more naive and impractical. What am I, a professing Christian, to make of this teaching? I can only believe that it is true, despite my inability to understand how it can possibly be true. I live with the hope that one day its truth will be fully manifest. In the meantime, I am compelled to live *as if* it were true, living faithful to my understanding of the implications of that truth.

I point to the life and death of Jesus as my prime example of seeking to overcome evil with good. Jesus rejected the use of violence as a means for accomplishing good. In stark contrast, he gave powerful expression to the efficacy of a nonviolent response to violence as a force for restoration in our broken world. As a Christian who desires to be a "follower of Jesus," I can aspire to nothing less, recognizing that I will fall far short of this ideal.

Secondly, I understand and appreciate your observation, shared by a majority of humans, that my position is totally impractical in our conflict-ridden world. It just won't work. I have suggested that I must be faithful to my commitment to be a peacemaker even if I don't have clarity as to how well that will work, in the light of unforeseen and unintended consequences. But I live in the hope that in the long run, nonviolence will work. Amazingly, there is a growing body of empirical evidence that pursuing nonviolent alternatives to war can also work in the short run. Consider first the largely nonviolent overthrow of apartheid in South Africa, due primarily to the suffering love exemplified by Nelson Mandela and others. Other examples include the nonviolent people's movements that brought down the communist governments in Poland, East Germany, and Central Europe; the nonviolent role of church leaders in ousting dictator Ferdinand Marcos in the Philippines; and the nonviolent overthrow of various military regimes in Latin America. Consider also the abolition of slavery in the British Empire without a catastrophic civil war, brought about by persistent and patient debate, moral persuasion, and political pressure in Parliament over many decades, led by William Wilberforce. Of course, such examples are not necessarily transferable to regions of conflict and injustice in other concrete places and times. But it is my hope that if we exercise sufficient moral imagination, we can devise workable nonviolent means to address gross forms of evil and injustice in other parts of the world that are currently ridden by conflict, if we are committed to trying to do so.

American citizens would know more about nonviolent alternatives to war, on our own soil, that were proposed and rejected if American history books did not ignore them. As noted by James Juhnke: "Decisions for war in the American past were not inevitable, even though the master narrative of our textbooks makes it appear that way." Juhnke cites two examples. Whereas we all know about the Boston Tea Party that set the stage for the War for Independence, *how many of us know about the Philadelphia Tea Party, where a tea crisis was resolved nonviolently under the leadership of Quaker merchants? Also, how many of us know that at a meet-*

ing of colonial leaders in the First Continental Congress in Philadelphia, Joseph Galloway, leader of the Quaker party of Pennsylvania, "proposed a bold plan to change the Constitution of the British Empire" that could conceivably have prevented the War for Independence? As Juhnke notes, "Galloway has been all but expunged from our national memory" (Juhnke 2003, pp. 110–111).

To bring such examples up to date, there is a poignant recent example of the U.S. government's lack of willingness to entertain an alternative to war in Iraq, as reported by Jim Wallis in his book *God's Politics*. Wallis and four other U.S. church leaders formulated a six-point plan for a nonviolent alternative to war in Iraq. They had the opportunity to discuss this plan in person with Tony Blair. Since this plan was published in the *Washington Post* on March 14, 2003, it was reported by a White House contact that "everyone over there had seen it." Yet the U.S. government chose not to give this plan serious consideration. (Pages 43–55 of Wallis' book can provide you with more details.) In summary, nonviolent alternatives to war are indeed feasible if we have the moral imagination to devise them and the moral commitment to implement them.

You are correct, however, in observing that my understandings about war and violence in general are clearly minority points of view, even among Christians. I am not intent on imposing my point of view on others. But I do believe it is important for me to share my point of view and my rationale for holding it in the public realm, including the political process. It is my hope that through such open, honest, and respectful conversations in the political process, we may be able to collectively discern a response to war and violence that best reflects our common humanity in the midst of the brokenness and evil in our real world.

Finally, let me address your suggestion, at least implicitly, that those who aspire to be peacemakers, like me, are fortunate that there are others who are willing to fight our wars for us. My only response is that I must be open to the possibility that my vocation should be to pursue the scariest of all peacemaking options—putting myself in harm's way, vigorously opposing injustice, albeit with nonviolent means. For a moving story of one Christian peacemaker who put herself in harm's way in Iraq, I refer you to the book *Iraq: A Journey of Hope and Peace* by Peggy Faw Gish. To be sure, vigorously opposing injustice perpetrated by violent people using nonviolent means could also get one killed, far away from home and loved ones. I honestly think that more people who aspire to be peacemakers, like me, need to choose this option. I am currently struggling with the question of whether I have the courage to do so, willing to take as great a risk as that currently taken by U.S. soldiers.

◆ ◆ ◆

Well, there is a second example, concocted in my own imagination, of what a portion of a respectful conversation about an important contemporary issue could look like.

I now invite you, the reader, to take proactive steps in your own spheres of influence to orchestrate actual respectful conversations about the two issues I have addressed and the many other important contemporary issues that press upon us as human beings. My purpose in telling you my story will be fully realized only if many of you accept my invitation. It is my hope and prayer that you will do so.

PART IV

Improving Christian Higher Education

As my friend said many years ago, no matter how good things are, I can always envision them being better. Although there are institutions of Christian higher education that struggle, often due to financial challenges, the general state of Christian higher education is good. Enrollments are generally growing and the quality of faculty is impressive. But, things could be better.

Part I of this volume contained many hints as to ways to strengthen Christian higher education. These can be viewed as implicit recommendations. In this concluding section, I present some focused explicit recommendations, all of which emerge from the story of my pilgrimage.

In particular, I call for institutions of Christian higher education to be more diligent about creating structures that will enable faculty to flourish as scholars as well as teachers. An increased emphasis on faculty being scholars necessitates clarity as to the nature of scholarship. Chapter 22 is a progress report on the results of my lifelong attempt to attain a more nuanced understanding of knowledge from my perspective as a Christian. In it, I address the meaning I now ascribe to the hotly contested phrase "Christian scholarship."

My recommendations for making Christian higher education better also call for more in-depth study of what it could possibly mean to administer higher education from a Christian perspective, and concrete strategies for improving the actual practice of the *integration of faith, learning, and living*, and *holistic education* that are highlighted in most of our rhetoric.

I conclude my recommendations, and this volume, with a call for institutions of Christian higher education to make a vigorous commitment to becoming "welcoming places for respectful conversation."

22

Christian Scholarship

o o o o o o o o o o o o o o o o o o o o o o o o o o o o o o o o o o

Christian scholars may significantly improve the chances of the results of their faith-informed research gaining a respectful hearing in the larger academy if they will take the time and effort needed to engage their colleagues face-to-face, building relationships of mutual trust.

If institutions of Christian higher education are to be more hospitable to faculty being scholars as well as teachers (a recommendation I present in the next chapter), then they need to engage in more in-depth conversation about the possible meaning of "Christian scholarship." My ongoing struggle with what this could possibly mean came to a head when I helped to formulate a mission statement for the Center for Christian Studies at Gordon College that called for facilitating Christian scholarship.

What is it, if anything, that makes scholarship Christian? Does Christian scholarship just refer to any kind of research that happens to be done by professing Christians? Or, does the research itself have to be influenced by a Christian faith commitment for the results to qualify as Christian scholarship? During my years as CCS director, I gradually forged a position on these questions, primarily influenced by the work of three prominent Christian scholars: Nick Wolterstorff, George Marsden, and Stephen Evans.

In brief, I now embrace a definition of Christian scholarship that is a variation on a proposal by Stephen Evans (Evans 2003, p. 34): Christian scholarship is any creative work (breaking new ground) that fosters God's restorative purposes for Creation. This definition encompasses a wide variety of research projects. I can best illustrate this variety by introducing the idea of scholarship being "perspectival" (see Wolterstorff 2004, pp. 172–198, and Marsden 1998, for elaboration).

Scholarly work is perspectival when the research is influenced by the particular worldview beliefs of the scholar, be they Christian or otherwise, as well as other elements of the scholar's social location.

George Marsden has proposed that there are three ways in which the particular perspective of the scholar can influence her research. For the time being, I will limit myself to the first two influences. First, the perspective of the scholar can influence the choice of a topic to be researched. Second, the scholar's particular perspective can influence the questions she decides to ask about the chosen topic. Allow me to illustrate with a few examples, which will also help me to illuminate the variety of research projects that qualify as Christian scholarship under my definition.

Consider the case of a Christian chemist who chooses to do experimentation on the results of combining certain chemical compounds, an example of what may loosely be called technical scholarship. In light of Marsden's proposed first influence of perspective, it is important to explore the reasons that my hypothetical Christian chemist might give for doing such experimentation. Two possibilities come to mind. She may choose to do such experimentation because of a desire to understand better one aspect of God's Creation. If so, this experimentation qualifies as Christian scholarship, since one of God's restorative purposes is to gain greater understanding of Creation.

On the other hand, our Christian chemist may choose to do such research as one element of a research program that is seeking a cure for some form of cancer. If that is the ultimate motivation of the Christian chemist, then that surely qualifies as Christian scholarship under my definition, since such research fosters the physical well-being of humans, a crucial element of the restorative value of the healthy growth of persons.

Consider now a hypothetical Christian historian. Suppose that her Christian commitment motivates her to do research on a particular historical period in a particular geographical location when the cultural influence of Christianity seemed to be increasing (or decreasing). Suppose further, that the questions she then asks focus on how the ascendancy (or descendancy) of Christian influence was related to the particular expressions of the Christian faith that were prevalent in the time and place being studied. Here, both of Marsden's first two perspectival influences are operative. This project qualifies as Christian scholarship since it fosters greater understanding of the role that Christianity has played, and can play, as a restorative influence (or not) in culture.

Note carefully that in these various examples of Christian scholarship that illustrate Marsden's first two perspectival influences, the actual results of the research (after the topic and questions have been chosen) will not, as far as I can tell, be influenced by the worldview perspective of the scholar. In other words, a hypothetical non-Christian chemist or historian, using the research methods appropriate to her academic discipline, should obtain the same research results as a Christian chemist or historian. From now on, I will refer to Christian scholarship that is "only" influenced by a Christian perspective in Marsden's first two ways (the choice of research topic and the research questions asked about the topic) as "weakly perspectival." The use of this awkward phrase is not meant to denigrate this important form of perspectival Christian scholarship. Rather, it is meant to indicate that while these two perspectival influences are operative, their influence does not extend to the actual results of the research. A non-Christian scholar choosing to explore the same topic and questions should arrive at the same answers as a Christian scholar.

In contrast, I believe there is a category of Christian scholarship that can be called "strongly perspectival," meaning that not only is the choice of topic and questions influenced by the Christian commitment of the scholar, but so are the actual results of the research. One subcategory of such strongly perspectival scholarship is captured by Marsden's third proposal for perspectival influence: Christian perspective makes a difference when Christian scholars do the theoretical work of proposing or evaluating theories to explain observed phenomena. I will illustrate this form of strongly perspectival theoretical Christian scholarship by noting the scholarly work of Jim Waller, professor of Psychology at Whitworth College (WA) in Holocaust and Genocide Studies. Waller focuses on the timely question of why ordinary people sometimes do extraordinary evil.

Waller notes that in the contemporary scholarly debate in Holocaust and Genocide studies, alternative theories as to why ordinary people come to commit extraordinary evil typically propose what is called an "alteration process," which can take one of two forms.

One view of the alteration process includes "divided-self theories," which hypothesize that an ordinary person can only commit extraordinary evil by creating some other self to do that evil. An alternative theory about an alteration process rejects the idea that a person can create a second self. Rather, an alteration process that takes place is that the primary (and only) self is fundamentally altered as a result of the power of potent social forces, like those unleashed by Hitler in Nazi Germany.

Note that different theories can be proposed to explain the same observed data. Waller has proposed an alternative theory on evildoing that is deeply informed by an orthodox Christian belief that our present human nature is flawed or fallen. Put simply, this theory implies that any one of us is capable of committing extraordinary evil under certain conditions (Waller 2002). But it is not only Waller's theory that is informed by a particular worldview commitment. I believe that if one digs beneath the surface of the alternative alteration theories, one will also uncover assumptions as to the nature of human nature.

Of course, the realm of scholarship is not limited to evaluating the merits or demerits of theories. There are other forms of strongly perspectival Christian scholarship beyond the "theorizing" category exemplified by Waller's research. Whereas Waller's work is an example of "descriptive" research, theorizing about the way things are or have been, other Christian scholars have pursued strongly perspectival scholarship having a "normative" focus, daring to venture into hotly contested issues related to "how things ought to be" (see for example, the work of John Hare, cited by Evans 2003, p. 35).

The reason I have dwelt in some depth here as to the nature of strongly perspectival scholarship is that fostering such scholarship emerged as my passion in my nine years as CCS Director. While wishing to facilitate all forms of Christian scholarship, on a continuum between highly technical and strongly perspectival scholarship, it was the latter category to which I was most deeply committed. The category of strongly perspectival Christian scholarship, where the actual results of the research are influenced by a Christian faith commitment, is too often neglected at Christian colleges (and elsewhere in the larger community of Christian scholars). This neglect is more than a bit ironic since Christian colleges say that one of their primary distinctives is to draw out relationships between biblical and academic insights, and such relationships are especially pertinent to Christian scholarship that is strongly perspectival.

My experience seeking funding for CCS projects from foundations that are sympathetic to the work of Christian scholars suggests that some of these foundations are a bit wary of supporting scholarship by Christians that is strongly perspectival. This reluctance may reflect a fear that the dissemination of the results of such work will prove to be divisive. I can understand that concern. Over recent years, a number of outstanding Christian scholars have gained respectability, even preeminence, in their disciplinary guilds. In a number of cases, but not all, this respect has been accomplished through focusing on research that is not strongly perspectival (and I applaud such accomplishments). Won't such respectability be endangered if these accomplished scholars are encouraged to pursue research that is strongly perspectival, since the dissemination of such research can lay bare deep worldview differences among scholars about religious commitment? I have two responses to this legitimate question.

First, it appears to me that it is precisely those Christian scholars who have gained respectability in the larger academy through high quality research that is not strongly perspectival who have the greatest potential to gain a fair hearing from non-Christian scholars as they seek to disseminate the results of strongly perspectival scholarship.

Second, whether the attempt of Christian scholars to disseminate the results of strongly perspectival scholarship is divisive or not depends on how Christian scholars go about disseminating the results of their work. To be sure, some attempts at dissemination can prove to be divisive, or even obnoxious. But, as I have proposed, there may be forms of dissemination that exemplify the noblest of Christian virtues and, thereby, can prove to be restorative.

It may be helpful for me to situate my views on Christian scholarship within a debate on the nature of such scholarship precipitated by the book *Scholarship & Christian Faith: Enlarging the Conversation* (Jacobsen & Jacobsen 2004). In this provocative book, the authors discuss what they perceive to be the strengths and limitations of what they call the "integration model" for Christian scholarship, the essence of which they describe as "the philosophical task of comparatively analyzing the ideas and theories (i.e., doctrines and theological systems) of Christian faith in relation to the ideas and theories of the various academic disciplines" (Jacobsen & Jacobsen 2004, p. 27). They associate this integration model with a Reformed, or Calvinistic, vision of Christian scholarship. While appreciating the many contributions of this integration model, the Jacobsens propose that this Reformed emphasis needs to be complemented by approaches that reflect the emphases of other Christian traditions, such as the Catholic, Anabaptist, and Wesleyan Holiness traditions. In brief, they wish to "enlarge the conversation" by recognizing "three styles of scholarship" that divide scholarship "along the lines of ideas, actions, and feelings:" "Analytic styles of scholarship are idea-oriented … strategic styles of scholarship are action-oriented … empathetic styles of scholarship are feeling-oriented, focusing on the need to connect with others and the world that are more subjective and aesthetic"—citing the work of the Harvard psychologist Robert Coles on the moral development of children as an example of the latter category (Jacobsen & Jacobsen 2004, pp. 124–129).

Where do I stand relative to this debate? First, since I have stood on the shoulders of Arthur Holmes, Nick Wolterstorff, and George Marsden, Christian scholars cited by the Jacobsens as exemplars of the integration model, I applaud their efforts to understand relationships between biblical insights and academic insights at the level of ideas and theories. For the Jacobsens to describe the integration model solely in cognitive terms does not do justice to these Reformed luminaries. For neither they nor I would take the position that the research of a Christian scholar should be viewed as the work of a disembodied intellect, divorced from actions and feelings (as a case in point, consider Wolterstorff's *Until Justice and Peace Embrace*, a work brimming with deep feelings and a call to action—Wolterstorff 1983).

In terms of the integration of faith and learning theme that I began unpacking in Chapter 4, such integration does indeed include a cognitive dimension, the drawing out of relationships between biblical and academic insights that I label the integration of knowledge. But such integration should also include affective and volitional dimensions, with all three dimensions related in what I have called personal integration.

My own view is that a significant way in which such personal integration manifests itself for a Christian scholar is in her choice of a topic for research. Analogous to the way in which I encouraged students to pursue "integrative questions" that were existentially important to them, so I would now encourage faculty to pursue research topics that flow from their whole beings. For example, a Christian scholar working in political science in South Africa in the aftermath of apartheid may feel deeply about the integrative question "What is the role of forgiveness in national or international settings?," not as an intellectual exercise, but as a prelude to becoming actively involved as an "agent for forgiveness" in her country. An Anabaptist Christian scholar working in Criminal Justice may invest her whole being in the integrative question, "In what ways can the present penal system in our country be more restorative, not just retributive?" (For a listing of some other integrative questions that may be found compelling by Christian scholars in a few other academic disciplines, see Heie 2002, p. 102).

I do concur with the Jacobsens' conclusion that members of the Christian academy need to embrace an expansive view of Christian scholarship that accommodates analytic, strategic, and empathetic approaches. I would add that the particular approach to be taken by a Christian scholar in a given time and place will emerge from her social location, which includes, but is not exclusively defined by, her particular Christian tradition. May I even be so bold as to suggest that the scholarship that is reported on in this book, which is primarily synthetic in nature (connecting related ideas into a complex whole), is an example of the expansive view of Christian scholarship that the Jacobsens call for, reflecting my attempt to integrate the intellectual, affective, and volitional aspects of who I am as a person.

Can Knowledge Claims Informed by Religious Beliefs Gain a Fair Hearing in the Academy?

Our world has a growing population of "religious dogmatists," those who will abort any possibility of conversation by saying, "Here is what my Holy Book says and that settles it." What their Holy Book says may indeed provide the most adequate perspective on the issue at hand, but they are not willing to let that possibility emerge as a result of conversation, along with the possibility of their learning something new. Christian scholars who are dogmatists will not likely be welcomed to the table for conversation within the larger academy, nor should they be.

But my concern here is with a second set of dogmatists, those "secular dogmatists" who are not willing to discuss any claim to knowledge that is informed in any way by religious beliefs (see Litfin 2004, pp. 254–273 for an analysis of such dogmatists that bears similarities to what follows).

The extent to which secular dogmatism pervades the larger academy is argued by Christian scholars working at major research universities. Having never served as a faculty member in such a setting, I am not qualified to address that disagreement. It is probably safe to say that there are at least strong pockets of secular dogmatism in the larger academy.

One form of secular dogmatism is commitment to philosophical naturalism, the view that all that exists is nature, a closed system that cannot be influenced by anything outside the system, like a God of religion. Another dogma held by some in the academy is an extreme form of rationalism that will not allow for any claim to knowledge that does not emerge from human cognitive faculties, thereby precluding any claim informed by "Christian revelation." A third possible dogma is a radical form of empiricism that rejects any claim to knowledge that cannot be directly supported by evidence from the senses (see Smith 2003, pp. 108, 109, 114–116 for other secular dogmas, referred to as "theoretical traditions," that are prevalent in the social sciences).

One effect of most of these secular dogmas in the academy is that they lead to rules of the academic game that impose on scholars a truncated view of possible sources of claims to knowledge. For example, these dogmas preclude the possibility of a Christian scholar appealing to any of her Christian beliefs as at least one possible source of her claims to knowledge. You can hold to your Christian beliefs in private, or in the company of other Christians, but there is no place for them in public discourse in the academy. This position essentially precludes the possibility of a Christian scholar presenting to non-Christian scholars the results of "strongly perspectival scholarship" in which the actual results of the scholarship are informed by a Christian faith perspective.

Another way to look at this obstacle is that it points to an apparently irreconcilable conflict relative to standards for evaluating claims to knowledge within the academy. The unyielding initial evaluative test for the secular dogmatist is whether the claim to knowledge is influenced in any way by a religious influence. If it is, the test is flunked, and any further discussion is ruled inappropriate. In contrast, as I have already argued, I think the issue of the sources of a claim to knowledge ought to be bracketed, and the claim ought to be evaluated based on its merits, or demerits, using other appropriate publicly accessible standards for evaluation within the disciplinary guild, independent of the source of the claim.

How can I get beyond this apparent impasse? I will respond by imagining myself seated around a table with other scholars, a number of whom are secular dogmatists, to discuss alternative views on a given topic of research.

As I have already suggested, when there is disagreement around the table as to the appropriate standards for evaluating competing claims to knowledge, as there obviously is in this imaginary conversation, those disagreements regarding evaluation must first be sorted out before there is much hope for fruitful further conversation. In such an initial discussion, I would say something like the following, as an attempt to relax the overly narrow rules of the academic game embraced by the secular dogmatists who have joined me around the table.

◆ ◆ ◆

Philosophical naturalism and extreme forms of rationalism and empiricism also represent worldview commitments, as do religious beliefs. All of us around the table have fundamental beliefs, albeit differing ones, about the nature of reality, our place within that reality, and how one can know any of these things. Therefore, no particular worldview should be privileged, a priori, in a way that discounts, without discussion, a proposal influenced by a differing worldview.

It is likely that despite our differing worldview commitments, we share a number of beliefs that are not empirically verifiable directly, such as that "humans should have equal rights regardless of race or gender, that it is wrong to murder infants, or that one should be especially concerned for the poor" (Marsden 1997, p. 12). Surely, we would not preclude discussion of such beliefs and their implications just because one can point to a worldview, religious or secular, as the "source" of such beliefs. Therefore, as George Marsden has asserted, any of these beliefs ought to be able to be introduced into the academy, provided they are "defended with arguments and evidence that are publicly accessible" (Marsden 1997, pp. 10, 11).

We are not disembodied intellects. Human experience is too rich to be reduced to the cognitive. We need to be open to insights from a variety of sources, like our feelings, life experiences, and worldview commitments (religious or secular). Of course, claims to knowledge and proposals for action based on such sources are not self-authenticating. They need to be assessed based on publicly accessible standards for evaluation. We diminish our humanity if we categorically rule out such claims without further conversation.

◆ ◆ ◆

I would like to think that arguments such as these could persuade the scholars around the table that it is acceptable to discuss the merits, or demerits, of a proposal that has a "religious source." But, to the extent that secular dogmas are pervasive within the academy, this persuasion may well not happen. If so, this particular conversation may end prematurely. Hopefully, there will be further opportunities for similar conversations in the future that will move the academy further toward refining its prevailing academic rules of the game in ways that will make it generally permissible to discuss the results of scholarly work that are substantially informed by religious faith perspectives. In the meantime, many secular scholars may have little interest in allowing Christian scholars to give voice to knowledge claims that are informed by their faith perspective. There is at least one marvelous exception to which I can point, which exemplifies an interpersonal strategy that may open up the possibility for more Christian scholars to be invited to high-level conversations in the larger academy.

An Interpersonal Model for Disseminating the Results of Christian Scholarship

The third case study for the *Christians Engaging Culture* project reported on in chapter 16 dealt with the work of Jim Waller in engaging scholars in Holocaust and Genocide Studies, the substance of which I summarized above. My concern now is with the interpersonal strategy Waller chose to disseminate the results of his faith-informed scholarship.

Recall that Waller's research focused on the question "Why is it that ordinary people sometimes do extraordinary evil?" about which he has developed a theory that was informed by his Christian faith perspective. His theory gained a respectful hearing within an elite group of scholars specializing in Holocaust and Genocide Studies. His report on how this openness occurred reflects the efficacy of an interpersonal approach at two levels.

The first level was his way of engaging secular scholars relative to their differing worldviews. Professor Waller sought to exemplify three forms of humility. "Worldview humility" involved his willingness to be self-critical—ready to state his beliefs, but not with an absolute certainty that precludes conversation; open to listening to the differing worldviews of others. "Intellectual humility" involved his willingness to admit to his own "limited cognitive access" that reflects his particular social location. "Relational humility" included his refusal to accept the common stereotypes that Christians have of those who do not share their faith commitments and working to dispel the common stereotypes of Christians that others may have.

The second level of Professor Waller's interpersonal mode of engaging others, related to "relational humility," focused on developing friendships with his secular colleagues. For example, he decided early on that he would not go to a professional conference just to present a paper and then retreat to his room. Rather, he would take the time to get to know his fellow scholars as persons, not just scholars. At times that meant a quiet dinner with a co-presenter, or better yet, someone who was a vocal critic of his presentation. This approach even involved his being a designated driver for a group that wanted a night out on the town at the end of a long conference day. He began building friendships that went beyond the formality of conference attendees, including seeing pictures of children and grandchildren, hearing stories of campus politics, and sharing soccer coaching tips for six-year-old daughters.

So what? Professor Waller found that when he befriended those who disagreed with him, they were more open to listening respectfully to his point of view. That correlation should surprise no one, for we all know that we can best say what is on our minds with friends we trust (see Ellis 2000). Unfortunately, that has not been a dominant approach to discourse in the academy.

Of course, neither of these two levels of interpersonal engagement is a substitute for doing good scholarly work. Schmoozing is not a good substitute for a bad scientific theory. With his newfound friends, Professor Waller still had to present a compelling public rationale for his theory in light of the prevailing standards for evaluation within his disciplinary guild. But, rationale-giving and relationship-building provide a cogent combination in any conversation. The lesson to be learned is that Christian scholars may significantly improve the chances of the results of their research gaining a respectful hearing in the larger academy if they will take the time and effort needed to engage their colleagues face-to-face. This investment will ameliorate the very human tendency to ignore or even demonize persons you don't know who disagree with you, a particularly strong temptation when such persons have deeply held religious beliefs that you do not share.

I would even press my proposal so far as to suggest the need for a refinement of the prevailing paradigm for disseminating the results of Christian scholarship. The time-honored way for disseminating scholarship of any kind is for scholars to write essays and books we hope other scholars will read. Such written dissemination is often complemented by scholars making oral presentations at meetings of scholarly societies, which generally includes some modest engagement between scholars through a question-and-answer session following the presentation. So far, so good! I do not question the continuing importance of these traditional modes of dissemination. In addition to these typical modes, Christian scholars would do well to create more interpersonal forums for respectful conversation in which Christian scholars can befriend and engage, face-to-face, other members of the academy who do not share their Christian faith commitment.

Dialogic Pluralism

It may be helpful to some readers if I situate my proposal for respectful conversation in the academy within three alternatives for ways in which Christian scholars can engage, or choose not to engage, other scholars in the larger academy. David Claerbaut has classified these three strategies as assimilation, seccessionalism, and pluralism (Claerbaut 2004, pp. 77–89). In my own words, the assimilationist Christian scholars accommodate themselves to the prevailing secular dogmas of the academy. The seccessionalist Christian scholars view the academy as bankrupt due to the prevalence of secular dogmas and withdraw to the more hospitable spaces occupied only by other Christian scholars. The Christian scholars committed to pluralism want all perspectives, religious or secular, to be allowable in academic conversations, provided they can be discussed on the basis of publicly accessible standards for evaluation. I obviously embrace the pluralist position.

The most complete discussion of and argument for this pluralist strategy is presented in George Marsden's book *The Outrageous Idea of Christian Scholarship* (Marsden 1997B). Nick Wolterstorff also argues for this position, which he calls "dialogic pluralism," "a plurality of entitled positions engaged in dialogue which is aimed at arriving at truth" (Wolterstorff 2002, p. 14). An eminent scholar who is not committed to the Christian faith, Richard Bernstein, describes a similar pluralist strategy as "engaged fallibilistic pluralism," which represents his "vision of a democratic society." His proposed pluralism is "fallibilistic" because of "its rejection of all forms of fundamentalism that appeal to absolute certainty, whether they be religious or secular." And it is "engaged" because it requires "real encounter, a serious effort to understand what is other and different" (Bernstein 2002, pp. 150, 151).

In a recent reflection on his past (and present) advocacy of the legitimacy of Christian scholarship in a pluralist academy, George Marsden makes two observations that are relevant to my emphasis on the importance of establishing personal relationships of mutual trust with those within the academy, and elsewhere, with whom you disagree (Marsden 2005). First, he now sees how his using the term "Christian scholarship" was "problematic in the academic world," partly because "[w]hen we say 'Christian' a lot of other people hear 'Fundamentalist.'" He now favors the phrase "intentionally faith-related scholarship." Secondly, he states that "[a]nother thing [he] has learned over the years is the importance of the personal dimension if we [Christian scholars] are to have a positive influence within university culture." Marsden now endorses the idea "that for Christians to successfully engage culture, they must do so by personally getting to know and take seriously people of other outlooks," further suggesting that "the personal dynamics of acting as a loving Christian are as important as what one says" (Marsden 2005, pp. 6–7).

23

Recommendations for Christian Higher Education

o o o o o o o o o o o o o o o o o o o o o o o o o o o o o o o o o o

To integrate means that you have uncovered integral connections ... Coexistence is not integration

Integration of Faith, Learning and Living

Over the past twenty or so years, I have had the privilege of speaking or consulting at over forty Christian colleges and universities, mostly member institutions of the CCCU. A favorite strategy of mine has been to ascertain before my visit what it is that an institution says is important, by reading their catalog and other promotional materials, and then encouraging the faculty and administration at the institution to seek ways to be better at doing what they already say is important.

Invariably, CCCU institutions claim that one of the goals they consider to be most important is the integration of faith, learning, and living, or words to that effect. There is a significant body of literature on what this phrase may mean and how to foster such integration for students, as well as for faculty (see the "Christian Higher Education" segment of my Further Recommended Reading), to which I have made a modest contribution (see, for example, Wolfe and Heie 1993). It is my hope that the discerning reader will conclude that this present book is an extended example of what I take that phrase to mean, without my having yet offered an explicit definition. In this concluding chapter, let me simply state that for you to integrate two or more things means that you have uncovered integral connections between those things. Unfortunately, much of what is passed off as "integration" in Christian higher education is no better than coexistence. *Coexistence is not integration.* Putting two good things side-by-side is not integration. A student or faculty member is making progress toward the noble and daunting goal of integrating faith, learning, and living only to the extent that she has uncovered integral connections between her understanding of her Christian faith, her understanding of knowledge claims in the various academic disciplines, and the manner in which she lives her daily life.

In that light, I present two recommendations for consideration by those who say that the integration of faith, learning, and living is important, making explicit that which is already implicit in the story of my pilgrimage relative to the integration of knowledge.

Provide students with more opportunity to deal with questions that arise in their experience of trying to live well. Start by helping students to elaborate on their questions in ways that will require them to draw significantly from their Christian faith beliefs (or the beliefs they hold based on other religious or secular worldviews) and their understanding of knowledge claims in relevant academic disciplines.

The ways in which these opportunities to grapple with what I have called integrative questions can be provided for students may be as varied as the imaginations of faculty and administrators. My experience suggests that students can best deal with such integrative questions in their upperclass years, when they have attained some intellectual maturity and have studied sufficiently to have accumulated an adequate storehouse of knowledge related to their faith commitment and the various academic disciplines. The possible vehicles for such attempts at "integration of knowledge" can include a senior seminar course or a senior thesis project.

Provide opportunities for students to deal with "integrative questions" pertinent to their academic disciplinary specialization, starting in their first year and proceeding though their senior year in more sophisticated and nuanced ways.

Once again, faculty and administrators can find innovative ways to implement this recommendation, if so desired. I have proposed a rather radical method for implementation at a number of institutions of Christian higher education. To the best of my knowledge, no institution has adopted this radical methodology. But I am persistent. Have the faculty in any given department decide on a handful of integrative questions, perennial or contemporary, that they believe their students should have grappled with in a significant way before they graduate. For example, in my former teaching field of mathematics, these questions could include the following: Can the deductive nature of mathematics be used to do Christian apologetics? Is mathematical knowledge created or discovered? Why should a Christian do mathematics? What is the status of the classical laws of two-valued logic? What is the meaning of "infinity" in mathematics, and is there any relationship between the mathematician's use of "infinity" and the meaning of the theologian who refers to God as "infinite"?

The departmental faculty can then decide where in the departmental curriculum it is most appropriate to first introduce these questions, and then reintroduce them in other courses (what has been called a "spiral approach") as the sophistication of the student increases in the particular academic discipline. These questions could be first introduced in a seminar for first-year majors, and then be re-introduced in appropriate courses throughout the four-year curriculum. (e.g., the question as to whether mathematical knowledge is created or discovered would be very pertinent to courses in Abstract Algebra and non-Euclidean Geometry). The spiral could then be completed by requiring majors in a senior seminar to write a term paper that responds to these questions with significant sophistication.

To be sure, this proposed methodology swims upstream against two strong tendencies at institutions of higher education: The tendency for students to want immediate answers to any questions posed in a given class, and the tendency of faculty to not seek for coordination between the isolated courses that they teach. But, I would be delighted if some institution(s) of Christian higher education would give it a try.

Holistic Education

The buzz words holistic education have been so abused as to be almost useless. So I need to make clear how I am using these words. What I mean is the personal integration that combines with the integration of knowledge to constitute my understanding of the phrase integration of faith, learning, and living. By personal integration I mean the integration of a student's cognitive, affective, and volitional capacities. The best means to help students grow toward such personal integration is through coherent connections between curricular and co-curricular programming.

Unfortunately, the current situation at many Christian institutions of higher education is that there is very little in the way of partnership between those educators responsible for the curriculum (the teaching faculty) and those educators responsible for the co-curriculum (student development staff, spiritual formation/campus ministries staff, and athletic staff). As a result, settling for coexistence of good things, rather than true integration, is the rule and not the exception. Consider the following telling examples of coexistence. Christian colleges typically have chapel programs, the content of which is seldom coordinated with the college curriculum. Service-Learning programs are also gaining in popularity at Christian colleges—a good thing. One approach to such programming is truly integrative, where active service activities are built into a course syllabus, and the course includes a dialectic between theory and practice. It is very rare to find intentional connections being sought between the volunteer service activities of students and courses in the college curriculum that are related to the type of service being rendered (sometimes causing students to roll up their sleeves working in a soup kitchen who have never been asked to examine the societal structures that lead to soup kitchens). My recommendation for overcoming the tendency to settle for coexistence between curricular and co-curricular programming is simple to state, albeit difficult to put into practice.

Provide forums for teaching faculty and staff responsible for co-curricular programming to talk to each other, with the goal of refining curricular and co-curricular programming to make each complement and enrich the other in helping students to attain agreed-upon educational goals.

I am appalled at the extent to which teaching faculty and co-curricular staff are typically compartmentalized. The tendency is for each group to go its own way, to do its own thing. Sometimes there isn't even harmonious coexistence, but instead competition for limited institutional funds and for the time and energy of students. Even when the two groups are committed to cooperation, they quickly run into the limitations of the coexistence ideal. For example, at one college I am familiar with an attempt was made to define two sets of educational goals for the student, one for the curriculum and one for the co-curriculum. I disagree.

The starting point for the type of partnership I envision is for the college to decide on one set of educational goals for the student. For each such goal, the teaching faculty and co-curricular staff should sit down together to explore ways in which each group can help students to attain that goal, one group working inside the classroom, and one group working outside the classroom. To take this strategy beyond the level of abstraction, allow me to give one concrete example.

Northwestern College in Iowa has agreed upon the following goal: the student "should value the diversity of the human family and seek opportunities for learning, growth, and transformation through intercultural relationships." This goal obviously has cognitive, affective, and volitional components. It requires that students learn a great deal about other cultures and the intercultural competencies needed to effectively engage persons from other cultures. It requires that students develop a deeply felt sense of empathy for those who differ from them, enabling them to see things from the perspective of the other. In addition, it requires actual engagement with those steeped in other cultures. I believe that the importance of a diversity goal of this type cannot be overstated since there is compelling empirical evidence attesting to the significant educative influence of "exposure to otherness."

For this goal, and for all other agreed upon learning goals, the teaching faculty should ask how these multiple, interrelated outcomes can best be fostered by means of curricular classroom instruction, and the co-curricular staff should ask how these very same outcomes can best be fostered by co-curricular activities outside the classroom. For each particular goal, how can you connect each group's respective initiatives in such a way that each set of initiatives complements and enriches the other set of initiatives relative to the kind of persons you want your students to become? Only then will the college have effected an integration of curricular and co-curricular programming. Only if a college effects such an integration can it be said with a straight face that out-of-class activities are co-curricular rather than merely extra-curricular.

Northwestern College, and other Christian colleges who do likewise, are to be commended for basing their programming decisions on a careful articulation of agreed-upon educational goals for the student. When deliberations about curricular and co-curricular programming are not based on such first principles, they often deteriorate into turf battles (especially when the deliberations are about revising General Education requirements for all students—I have some battle scars that can attest to that struggle).

More conversations between teaching faculty and co-curricular staff could also help a Christian college get beyond truncated definitions of spirituality and liberal arts that come with the faulty coexistence model. The meaning of spirituality is not exhausted by what takes place in chapel or residence hall Bible studies and prayer meetings, as good as these things are. To be spiritual also includes intellectual pursuits informed by one's Christian faith perspective and working tirelessly to address the needs of the poor and marginalized in society and other social problems. The liberal arts are not just those studies that liberate the mind. A comprehensive liberal arts education must also liberate the student who doesn't feel deeply and who doesn't act on her beliefs. Such broad views could emerge if teaching faculty and co-curricular staff would talk more to each other.

Faculty as Teachers and Scholars

You may feel that I have already harped enough on the need for Christian institutions of higher education to enable faculty to be both effective teachers and productive scholars (as in chapter 13). But my consideration of Christian scholarship (in chapter 22) adds new urgency to my plea. In addition to helping students become agents for God's restorative purposes, a faculty member at a Christian college should be an agent for redemption by doing Christian scholarship and disseminating the results of that scholarship to the larger academy and, upon suitable translation, to the Christian Church and to the broader culture. Hence my next recommendation:

Create institutional structures that will enable faculty to flourish as both effective teachers and productive scholars.

Of course, to create new institutional structures is much easier said than done, especially given the limited resources of most Christian institutions of higher education. Administrators and faculty will have to be extremely creative. For beginners, Christian colleges have to avoid the easy path of simply adding new expectations for faculty scholarship on top of already stringent expectations relative to teaching, such as large teaching loads. I recall consulting at one Christian university that had recently revised its expectations for the granting of tenure to include enormous expectations for both teaching and scholarship. My immediate gut level reaction was to say that "only God need apply." Something in our current institutional structures "has to give" to enable faculty to be both teachers and scholars.

What I personally think has to be relaxed are the inordinately heavy teaching loads at most Christian institutions of higher education. If I could design a Christian college from scratch, my "ideal" for faculty workload would be as follows: I would expect each faculty member to teach five courses during the academic year; give each faculty member a twelve-month contract (which doesn't mean pay for nine months of work spread out over twelve months), expect faculty to devote their summer months (except for a one-month vacation) to scholarly work; and develop criteria for faculty advancement (promotion and tenure) that hold faculty accountable to demonstrate that they are both effective teachers and productive scholars. Lest you think that scenario is an impossible wish, there is at least one institution of Christian higher education, the King's University College in Edmonton, Alberta, Canada, that instituted such a set of faculty expectations a number of years ago. The interested reader may want to ask them how that plan is currently working.

Of course, one does not have to be a rocket scientist to figure out that such a plan for faculty assignments and expectations for performance comes with a considerable price tag. If it is judged that the "ideal" faculty workload I propose is too expensive, more Christian colleges could implement some modest initiatives that already exist at a number of Christian colleges, such as faculty summer research grants, awarded on a competitive basis, and selected release time from teaching during the academic year to pursue approved scholarly projects.

The bottom line question is whether a given Christian college judges that the goal of faculty being both effective teachers and productive scholars is of sufficient value to warrant the cost, even if it means that costs have to be cut in other areas of the college operation. Furthermore, significant steps have to be taken to convince the college's supporting constituency that faculty scholarship is important in light of God's restorative purposes. As I have provocatively claimed, colleges do seem to find the money for that which they consider to be important. To date, not many Christian colleges have accepted this considerable challenge. I hope more will.

Leadership in Christian Higher Education

I am perplexed that for all the talk and writing about the meaning of the integration of faith, learning, and living for faculty and students at Christian colleges, there is almost a deafening silence about what it may mean to administer from a Christian perspective. Although the CCCU offers leadership institutes for administrators at their member institutions, I am not aware of any major literature that has emerged from these seminars. Hence, the following recommendation.

The CCCU should commission the preparation of a book (or two) that deals with selected aspects of what it means to administer from a Christian perspective at institutions of Christian higher education.

I cannot resist sharing some of what I would say if asked to write such an essay, reflecting some of my good and bad experiences as an academic administrator. In broad terms, I would propose two theses, both of which would require considerable elaboration.

- *A leader in Christian higher education should start with a vision as to how she and her institution can best contribute to the realization of God's restorative purposes.*

The pages of my narrative lay bare my vision as to how I and the enterprise of Christian higher education can most effectively contribute to God's restorative purposes. Current leaders in Christian higher education do not have to embrace my vision. They need to shape and articulate their own vision for themselves and Christian higher education. That vision has to be the starting point for all that they attempt to do as leaders. There are few things as sad as an administrator in Christian higher education who does not have a vision. He is simply tossed to and fro by external influences and forces, barely able to keep up with the myriad managerial details of college administration.

After a leader has forged a vision for herself and for Christian higher education, the huge question is how to implement that vision. Hence, my second thesis.

- *A leader in Christian higher education should enable her "followers" to refine her vision, then empower them to work together with her toward the implementation of that vision, with each person provided a welcoming space to exercise her particular gifts.*

This thesis is contrary to the command and control model that characterizes too much of the current leadership in both religious and secular contexts, despite the fact that much of the current literature on leadership calls that model into question. In that old model, the leader is the primary, or only, decision-maker, who then passes his decisions down to "followers" for implementation. To be sure, certain decisions need to be made by the "boss," where the buck stops. However, that reality does not preclude the primary focus of leadership being the empowerment of followers to do the best work of which they are capable.

The above reflects my understanding of the primary overarching characteristics of a Christian perspective on leadership in Christian higher education in two ways. Christian leaders, along with all Christians, are called to be agents for God's restorative purposes in their particular social locations. And, the focus on empowering other people comports with my understanding of what it means to love another person.

The above is not meant to present too simple a take on the complex issue of governance at a Christian institution of higher education. As I found out the hard way, there needs to be clarity as to who at the institution is responsible for which decisions. Implementing such an agreed-upon governance structure does not, however, preclude broad conversations before decisions are reached. My own experience as both a faculty member and an administrator suggests that the role that faculty would like to play relative to decisions that ultimately lie with the administration is that of discussing issues that affect them and the institution, thereby giving them the opportunity to provide some input before an administrative decision is made (if not via face-to-face conversation, at least electronically).

As you may well expect by now, I believe that a major dimension of the task of empowering others is for a leader to provide welcoming spaces for "followers" to have a voice in matters important to them and the institution by orchestrating forums for respectful conversation.

Christian Colleges as Welcoming Places for Respectful Conversation

There are many important topics that should be talked about at Christian colleges. A partial list emerges from my narrative in this book:

- the meaning of peace and how to be a peacemaker in a world torn by conflict.
- the meaning of justice and how Christians can play a meaningful role in the political process toward fostering justice, especially for the poor and marginalized of the world.
- means for being agents for the realization of all God's restorative purposes.
- means for avoiding the rampant stark relativism of our age by seeking for appropriate standards for evaluating competing claims to knowledge.
- the meaning of spirituality in light of God's restorative purposes.
- the meaning of liberal arts education from a Christian perspective.
- means for creating genuine collaborative partnership between teaching faculty and co-curricular staff.
- means for constructively addressing the thorny issue of homosexuality that is tearing the Christian church apart.
- means for getting beyond "integration of faith, learning, and living" and "holistic education" being only slogans.
- means for faculty and students steeped in a given Christian tradition to learn from the best insights of other Christian traditions while being true to their own tradition.

The list could go on. In that light my next-to-last recommendation to those involved in Christian higher education is the following.

Provide welcoming places where students, faculty and administrators can have respectful conversations about important contemporary issues, starting with the strategy of building interpersonal relationships of mutual trust.

As John Tagg reminds us, "[t]he word 'college' comes from the word 'collegium': 'a group, the members of which pursue shared goals while working in a framework of mutual trust and respect' (*American Heritage College Dictionary*, 3rd ed.)" (Tagg 2003, p. 324).

This collegium ideal is difficult to attain at Christian institutions of higher education (not to mention everywhere else) since equally committed Christians can, and do, disagree strongly about most contemporary issues, including all those noted above. One's position on any of these issues should not be taken as a litmus test of whether one is a Christian or how good a Christian one is. We need to get to know each other well enough to see that those who disagree with us have not jettisoned their Christian faith. Rather, they have a different understanding of the implications of their Christian faith relative to the issue at hand. We need to learn to listen to them, trying to see things from their perspective, in preparation for talking to them about our differences.

Of course, it is easier to encourage Christian colleges to create welcoming spaces for respectful conversation about important issues than it is to make it happen. Some of these issues, like homosexuality, are extremely controversial, and even allowing for conversation about them is sometimes taken as a slide into apostasy. It will take both personal courage and institutional courage to welcome such conversations. At the institutional level, Christian colleges need to resist the temptation to take an official "institutional" stance on controversial issues about which equally committed Christians disagree, even in the face of growing external constituency pressures to do so.

To provide welcoming places for such respectful conversations on Christian college campuses will require that everyone on campus be given a voice—be given permission to speak, however controversial their views may be. This invitation raises the thorny "academic freedom" question of whether there should be limits on the views that can be expressed by someone affiliated with a Christian college. Space does not permit me to say much about that here, possibly just enough to be misunderstood and create some controversy. My brief reflections draw on a four-fold taxonomy that Robert Benne has proposed relative to church-related institutions of higher education (Benne 2001). Church-related colleges can be "orthodox" (requiring shared beliefs on matters viewed as fundamental to their faith tradition among all faculty and staff, and sometimes among students); or "critical-mass" institutions (Christianity or a specific Christian tradition is given a privileged voice at the institution, embodied in a majority, or a sizable minority, of their faculty and students). Church-related institutions can also be "intentionally pluralist" (likely to describe themselves as having a Christian heritage rather than emphasizing Christianity or a particular faith tradition as part of their present identity). Or they can be "accidentally pluralistic" (there being virtually no public acknowledgment of the institution's religious heritage).

I claim that my recommendation to create welcoming spaces for respectful conversations is appropriate, in some form, for church-related institutions that fall in any one of Benne's four categories. However, since the four colleges at which I served fall into Benne's orthodox category (as do all member institutions of the CCCU, by virtue of the CCCU criteria for membership), I will limit my brief remarks on academic freedom to such institutions. As private institutions, such orthodox colleges have the right to expect all faculty and administrators (and even students, if so desired) to share certain beliefs judged to be essential to the Christian faith (e.g., a belief that "Jesus Christ is pivotal to the accomplishment of God's redemptive purposes"). My own opinion is that such a set of expected shared beliefs should be minimalist in nature, allowing community members to disagree about matters not deemed essential to the Christian faith (in which category I would place beliefs on all the issues I identified above). Of course, the fact that what is non-essential to one Christian may be considered essential by another Christian makes the implementation of this distinction complicated (possibly another topic for respectful conversation at the college). For those who judge that my take on academic freedom at orthodox colleges is no freedom at all, compared, let's say, to secular institutions of higher education, I can only assert that there is no institution of higher education where community members are free to say whatever they want. Every institution places some kind of limits on what can be said; they just define their limits differently. For example, it can be argued that in certain academic departments at some secular universities, you are not free to make knowledge claims rooted in your particular religious beliefs.

To summarize this line of thought, for respectful conversations at Christian colleges to give a fair hearing to alternative viewpoints, members of the college community must be given a welcoming space to say whatever is on their minds, however controversial, within the context of whatever they have agreed to by voluntarily choosing to join that community.

You will note that the issues I raise as examples of topics that need to be discussed at Christian colleges are interdisciplinary in nature; they do not fit neatly into the domain of exploration defined by any one academic discipline. Extremes of academic specialization work against interdisciplinary conversations. Thankfully, the days are long gone when a Christian college hires an engineer to teach mathematics full time, with a few physics courses thrown in for good measure. In the forty plus years since my first opportunity to become involved in Christian higher education, monumental strides have been made in the credentials expected of those who teach at Christian colleges. Christian college faculty now typically have degrees from outstanding research universities in specialized fields, and they are hired to teach primarily in their fields of specialization. That expertise is a good thing. But it comes with a price. It generally makes it harder to generate interdisciplinary conversations on our Christian college campuses. If the kind of interdisciplinary conversation I call for on the topics noted above is to become a reality, faculty need to be willing to move out of their disciplinary comfort zone, and even be willing to do some personal study in areas outside of their areas of expertise.

"Time out," you say. How can I be expected to do any personal study outside my area of expertise and devote significant quantities of time to respectful conversations about interdisciplinary issues, in light of the numerous responsibilities for teaching in my discipline, scholarly work, and institutional service that I already have? An excellent and fair question. To be blunt: If the faculty are too busy to be reading anything outside of their area of specialization and are too busy to participate in the forums for respectful conversation that I call for, then the faculty are too busy. The institution needs to make some creative workload adjustments to make such activities possible. As in my call for finding more time for faculty to do scholarly work, providing faculty with time for preparing for and engaging in institutional forums for respectful conversation will require that an institution examine its value priorities and, hopefully, make creative adjustments in its assignments for faculty. As an example, I will present a brief description of one model that has been successful at Gordon College, a model that takes us back to the need for greater partnership between teaching faculty and co-curricular staff.

This model is based on the work of Gerald Graff (1992). He argues that rather than camouflaging disagreements between members of a college community, which can easily happen when isolated courses in the formal curriculum are taught as "ships passing in the night," colleges need to "teach the disagreements," both in the curriculum (e.g., periodic joint meetings of two different classes) and in the co-curriculum.

One of the co-curricular strategies Graff proposed was to create out-of-class conferences focusing on student participation, similar to the professional conferences attended by faculty off campus. This idea became the seed for the annual Gordon College Symposium coordinated by the Center for Christian Studies. In the spring semester each year at Gordon (since 1998), a week is devoted to this symposium, including evening programming all week and one full day (for which all classes are cancelled). An interdisciplinary symposium theme is announced each fall. (Some of the past chosen themes have been Who is my Neighbor?; Money and Possessions; Embodiment as Blessing, Offense and Constraint; Peace, Justice and Reconciliation; The Coming of Global Christianity; Art at the Millenium.) Students are then turned loose to design symposium sessions that they judge to be pertinent to the given theme. The designs have included lecture-type presentations (with students at the podium and some faculty sitting in the student chairs), poetry readings, a panel of students from a given class dealing with an interdisciplinary issue related to the course material, musical compositions, art exhibits, and other venues as varied as the imaginations of students (including a pig roast on the quad one year).

This annual event has featured as many as 70 student-initiated projects over the one-week period, with conversations about the materials presented expected as part of each design. Student attendance for the week's events has exceeded 3000, for a student body of about 1500 (mostly on a voluntary basis, although some required chapel credits could be obtained for a limited number of events). The total cost for this week of events is minimal because it typically involves no outside speakers. It is a co-curricular vehicle for students to take more responsibility for their own learning (their projects typically emerge from their own deeply felt "need to know") and for making students and faculty equal co-participants in the educational process. I am convinced that with a bit of imagination, the faculty, administration, and students at many Christian colleges can develop similar low-cost initiatives that enable these colleges to be welcoming places for respectful conversation.

My last recommendation for Christian higher education is the climax to this volume.

Provide welcoming places where Christians can have respectful conversations about important contemporary issues with those having different religious commitments or no religious commitment.

I have a dream (a 10) that many readers of this book will accept my invitation to respectful conversation and will embark on numerous initiatives to orchestrate such conversations in the arenas of politics and public policy practice, religious communities, and the academy. The more focused dimension of my dream is that a good number of Christian colleges will embrace my vision and will invite those who do not share their Christian faith commitment to join the conversations on their campuses.

Christian colleges could exert a more significant redemptive influence in our world if they would create such welcoming places for respectful conversation within the larger human community, especially if such conversations model the combination of commitment and openness that is so rare in our times. It is the lack of this rare combination that is devastating our world. Commitment without openness leads to fanaticism, even terrorism. Openness without commitment leads to stark relativism. Christian colleges should have as a high priority the creation of forums for respectful conversation that consistently model both commitment and openness.

Postscript

This book surprised me. Ever since my unpublished *My Star* manuscript in the 70s, I had it in the back of my mind that someday I would again tackle the daunting task of writing a manuscript that seeks to create a synergy between the personal and the scholarly. But, since then I have been so busy with other tasks that I have had scarce opportunity to do extensive writing of any kind.

Around the time of my retirement as Director of the Center for Christian Studies at Gordon College in the early summer of 2003, a few trusted colleagues at Gordon encouraged me to write about my forty years of experience in Christian higher education. I was flattered, and the dormant urge resurfaced.

But it was my circumstances later that summer that made concentrated writing a possibility. Pat and I were in the midst of all the choices we needed to make for a home we were having built in Orange City, Iowa. We were moving our stuff, one pickup truck load at a time, from temporary storage. Doing such things more than a few hours at a time was more than my mind or back could bear. So I just started writing. Each morning for two months I put blue felt-tip pen to legal pad paper of various colors. Although my son Jonathan and others are slowly dragging me into the twenty-first century, kicking and screaming, by making me more computer literate, I preferred writing the old-fashioned way (now, many drafts later, I am reasonably proficient at word processing).

What surprised me was how the words just poured out, nonstop. When I wasn't writing, I was thinking about what I would write next. Contrary to my usual way of writing, I didn't start with notes or any outline beyond a tentative list of chapter titles for what proved to be about one-third of the book. I just wrote what came to mind in a stream of consciousness, one chapter at a time. Sometimes, I would wake up in the middle of the night, and I couldn't get back to sleep because my mind was racing. On occasion, I would get up and write notes on my "Palm Pilot," a blue felt tip Pilot pen applied to my left hand. It was as if the words had been inside me for a long time, screaming to get out. Like most of what I have done in life, my writing came from deep within me, without much initial concern for who my audiences might be.

The resulting first draft was rich with autobiography. But the point of my telling my story was far from clear. A good friend who read my first draft helped me to clarify my main purpose in writing by asking, in effect, what I hoped might result if this book was eventually published and read. The answer was so obvious to me because it has become such an integral aspect of who I am. But, I had failed to articulate it well to others. Since I learned to love the cause of Christian higher education, I want to be an agent for improving that noble enterprise. But more specifically, my career in Christian higher education has converged on a passion to orchestrate respectful conversations among those who disagree about important issues. My primary goal is to invite readers to also embrace that project. I restructured all subsequent drafts around this main point. It is my fondest hope that your reading of this book will encourage and empower you to accept this invitation, whatever your sphere of influence.

In addition to potential readers I do not know personally, I also write this book for my family and circle of friends, some of whom may have been trying for years to figure out what makes Harold tick. Although this latter audience will not create a marketing bonanza, my story would be incomplete if I didn't tell you why this audience is very important to me.

Unless you ask me to talk about the distinctives of Christian higher education (when my eyes light up and you can't shut me up), I tend to be quiet. I have even been known to just say "yup" a few times. Like Pop I don't go around saying much about my framework of beliefs, unless solicited to do so. If solicited, I have difficulty talking about my beliefs as if they were abstract entities to be trotted out upon request, because my beliefs and my life are all of one piece. It is not clear why I believe as I do outside the context of my Christian pilgrimage. So, when I am asked questions about my beliefs on particular issues and my reasons for holding them, I am inclined to give long answers that frame my response within the story of my life. Having enough social sense to know that my inquisitors are not usually looking for long answers, I tend to say less than I would like to. Sometimes I say just enough to make the listener wonder where those strange ideas came from. In these pages, I have let it all hang out. I hope that my family and friends now have a better understanding of what makes me tick.

I enjoyed immensely writing this book. I hope you have found enjoyment and even some illumination in its pages.

Harold Heie
Orange City, Iowa
July 2007

Annotated Works Cited

In the annotations presented below, I have not attempted to give a complete summary of each work cited in the body of this book. Rather, I have generally highlighted those aspects that are most pertinent to my own narrative.

Appiah, Kwame Anthony. *Cosmopolitanism: Ethics in a World of Strangers.* New York: W.W. Norton & Company, 2006.

Inspired by the ancient Greek ideal of cosmopolitanism, Appiah offers an ethics for a global era in an engaging manner that reflects his experience of life on three continents.

Audi, Robert and Nicholas Wolterstorff. *Religion in the Public Square: The Place of Religious Convictions in Political Debate.* Lanham, MD: Rowman & Littlefield, 1997.

Audi and Wolterstorff present views on the role that religious convictions should have in public debate that reveal some common ground, but significant disagreements. As one reviewer said, "Their debate is itself a model of the richer political discourse our society needs" (Charles Larmore, Columbia University).

Balmer, Randall. *Thy Kingdom Come: How the Religious Right Distorts the Faith and Threatens America—An Evangelical's Lament.* New York: Basic Books, 2006.

Combining ethnographic research, theological reflections, and historical context, Balmer argues that the progressive political causes promoted by nineteenth-century evangelicals have been abandoned by contemporary evangelicals who have embraced an agenda virtually indistinguishable from the Republican Party platform. Balmer offers an alternative contemporary evangelical voice, calling all Christians to reclaim the noblest traditions of their faith.

Barbour, Ian G. *Myths, Models, and Paradigms: A Comparative Study in Science & Religion*. New York: Harper & Row, 1974.

A comparative study of the use of language in science and religion, focusing on the role of models and paradigms in both scientific and religious language.

Barker, Stephen F. *Philosophy of Mathematics*. Englewood Cliffs, NJ: Prentice-Hall, 1964.

A brief introduction to Philosophy of Mathematics that deals with the nature of Euclidean and non-Euclidean geometries, and literalistic and non-literalistic views of numbers.

Belmonte, Kevin. *Hero for Humanity: A Biography of William Wilberforce*. Colorado Springs, CO: NavPress, 2002.

A biography of William Wilberforce emphasizing Wilberforce's character as a Christian political leader dedicated to the moral and social improvement of England, culminating in his success in the abolition of Britain's slave trade.

Benhabib, Seyla. Ed. *Democracy and Difference: Contesting the Boundaries of the Political.* Princeton, NJ: Princeton University Press, 1996.

This volume brings together a group of distinguished thinkers who rearticulate and reconsider the foundations of democratic theory in light of the debates about identity and difference that challenge democracies everywhere.

Benne, Robert. *Quality With Soul: How Six Premier Colleges and Universities Keep Faith with Their Religious Traditions*. Grand Rapids, MI: Eerdmans, 2001.

Based on a typology of four different categories of church-related institutions of higher education, Benne provides a multi-dimensional assessment of Christian colleges in six different Christian traditions, concluding with proposed "Strategies for Maintenance and Renewal." For a fascinating case study of one college (Hope College in Michigan) against the backdrop of Benne's typology, see *Can Hope Endure? A Historical Case Study in Christian Higher Education.* James C. Kennedy and Caroline J. Simon. Grand Rapids, MI: Eerdmans, 2005.

Bernstein, Richard J. "Religious Concerns In Scholarship: Engaged Fallibilism In Practice." In *Religion, Scholarship and Higher Education: Perspectives, Models, and*

Future Prospects. Ed. Andrea Sterk. Notre Dame, IN: University of Notre Dame Press, 2002, pp. 150–158.

Featuring the work of eighteen scholars from diverse institutional, disciplinary, and religious backgrounds, this book presents a wide diversity of viewpoints on the role of religion in higher education and different approaches to religiously informed scholarship and teaching. In his essay, Bernstein argues that since "we are always already shaped by the multiple traditions to which we belong," the challenge is to "distinguish productive and enabling prejudgments and traditions from those that are distorted and unwarranted." He suggests that such discernment is a "fragile and temporary achievement ... that emerges in and through our critical encounters with different and opposing perspectives."

Booth, Wayne. "The Rhetoric of War and Reconciliation." In *Roads to Reconciliation: Conflict and Dialogue in the Twenty-First Century*. Eds. Amy Benson Brown and Karen M. Porenski. Armonk, NY: M. E. Sharpe.

In this collection of essays, the authors attempt to understand the process of reconciliation in many different contexts, from international political conflicts to racial and religious struggles within one culture to the internal conflicts of individuals dealing with powerful, unresolved feelings in the wake of traumatic events. In his introductory essay, Booth maps various aspects of the concept of reconciliation and proposes a "rhetoric of reconciliation" that, contrary to "war language," "pursues understanding of the kind that results only when there is genuine *listening* to the opponent's position" (p. 9).

Boyd, Gregory A. and Paul R. Eddy. *Across the Spectrum: Understanding Issues in Evangelical Theology*. Grand Rapids, MI: Baker, 2002.

This book brings together in one volume a very useful summary of the main theological debates within evangelical Christianity, demonstrating that there is no single evangelical viewpoint on a wide range of controversial issues. For each issue, divergent views are summarized in a succinct, fair, and compelling manner.

Buechner, Frederick. *Wishful Thinking: A Theological ABC*. New York: Harper & Row, 1973.

Buechner provides a provocative "dictionary for the restless believer, for the doubter, for anyone who wants to redefine or define more concretely those words that have become an integral part of our daily language—words that we use about God, the universe, and last, but never least, man." Words addressed include agnostic, charity, Christian, Devil, grace, guilt, joy, omniscience, Trinity, and virgin birth.

Cahoy, William J. "A Sense of Place and the Place of Sense." In *Professing in the Postmodern Academy: Faculty and the Future of Church-Related Colleges.* Ed. Stephen R. Haynes. Waco, TX: Baylor University Press, 2002, pp. 73–111.

This edited volume examines the landscape of religiously affiliated higher education from the perspective of fourteen faculty members willing to imagine a creative and vibrant future for the American church-related college. Particularly helpful is its fair and balanced view of "postmodernism," noting both its weaknesses and strengths, including consideration of the present "postmodern opportunity" for Christian scholars. In his essay, Cahoy embraces the postmodern insight on "the importance of location in our knowing" ("where one stands affects what one sees"), which "opens up the possibility of rethinking the idea and rationale of the church-related college" (pp. 74–75). For a companion volume that presents contrasting views of six Christian scholars on "postmodernism," see *Christianity and the Postmodern Turn.* Ed. Myron B. Penner. Grand Rapids, MI: Brazos Press, 2005.

Claerbaut, David. *Faith and Learning on the Edge: A Bold New Look at Religion in Higher Education.* Grand Rapids, MI: Zondervan, 2004.

Claerbaut argues against worldviews governing contemporary research and academe that insist that faith has no place in the quest for knowledge. He then proposes ways to apply a faith-and-learning approach across a broad spectrum of disciplines in the physical sciences, the arts and humanities, and the behavioral sciences.

Cunningham, David S. *Faithful Persuasion: In Aid of a Rhetoric of Christian Theology.* Notre Dame, IN: University of Notre Dame Press, 1990.

Cunningham explores the relationship between Christian theology and rhetoric—the study of persuasive argument. Drawing chiefly on the rhetorical insights of Aristotle, Cunningham argues that "Christian theology can best be understood as a form of persuasive argument." He then explores the implications of a rhetorical method for doctrinal formulations, biblical exegesis, and church history.

Ellis, Joseph J. *Founding Brothers: The Revolutionary Generation.* New York: Vintage Books, 2000.

Through an analysis of six fascinating episodes in the early history of the United States, Ellis brings to life the personalities of the statesmen who shaped our country. Of particular interest is his account of post-presidential correspondence (a fourteen-year exchange of 158 letters) between John Adams and Thomas Jefferson ("The Friendship," pp. 206–248). Ellis notes that "[i]n the summer of 1813 the dialogue ceased being a still-life picture of posed patriarchs and became an argument between competing versions of the revolutionary legacy. All the unmentionable subjects were now on the table because *a measure of mutual trust had been recovered"* (p. 230, italics mine).

Evans, Stephen C. "The Calling of the Christian Scholar-Teacher." In *Faithful Learning and the Christian Scholarly Vocation.* Eds. Douglas V. Henry and Bob R. Agee. Grand Rapids, MI: Eerdmans, 2003, pp. 26–49.

In this essay, Evans presents a compelling argument for Christian faculty members to be productive scholars as well as effective teachers, and identifies the various dimensions of Christian scholarship. Especially helpful is his description of a "relevance continuum" in which the influence of a Christian scholar's faith commitment on her scholarship increases as one proceeds from the academic discipline of mathematics; to the natural and human sciences; to history, literature and the arts; and then to philosophy and theology.

Fee, Gordon D. and Douglas Stuart. *How To Read The Bible For All Its Worth: A Guide to Understanding the Bible.* 2nd ed. Grand Rapids, MI: Zondervan, 1983.

This very readable book will help the Christian lay person understand the different types of literature (genres) that are found in the Bible. Especially helpful is the attempt to bridge the "hermeneutical gap … moving from the 'then and there' of the original text to the 'here and now' of our own life settings."

Fish, Stanley. *The Trouble with Principle.* Cambridge, MA: Harvard University Press, 1999.

Fish has a quarrel with "neutral principles." He argues that there is no realm of higher order impartiality—no neutral or fair territory on which to stake a claim. It is history and context that determines a principle's content and power. In this light, Fish addresses issues such as academic freedom, hate speech, affirmative action, multiculturalism, and the boundaries between church and state.

Fretheim, Terence E. *God and World in the Old Testament: A Relational Theology of Creation.* Nashville: Abingdon Press, 2005.

Fretheim argues that the Old Testament portrays God as a "Relational Being" (p. 16) and creation as having a fundamental "relational character" (p. 13). This portrayal precludes thinking of humans as either "passive overseers" or "dominating subjects in control of the created order" (p. 14). Rather, the relationship of God to humans is one of "mutuality" in which humans play a significant role as co-agents with God toward the realization of God's purposes for Creation.

Gaede, Beth Ann. Ed. *Congregations Talking about Homosexuality: Dialogue on a Difficult Issue.* Bethesda, MD: Alban Institute, 1998.

This book identifies the difficulties in discussing controversial issues and deals with the preparations and procedures necessary for discussing contentious issues in a church congregation. It relates the experiences of seven mainline Christian congregations that have dealt with the issue of homosexuality, leading in each case to a decision to be "open and affirming" to gays and lesbians.

Gaede, S. D. *When Tolerance Is No Virtue: Political Correctness, Multiculturalism & the Future of Truth & Justice.* Downers Grove, IL: InterVarsity Press, 1993.

Gaede affirms the commitment of Christians to truth and justice. In that context, he considers the issues of multiculturalism and PC (political correctness), helping Christians to understand the current emphasis on diversity and to sort out what they should laud and what they should be wary of in the rush toward tolerance.

Gish, Peggy Faw. *Iraq: A Journey of Hope and Peace.* Scottsdale, PA: Herald Press, 2004.

In this compelling book, Gish recounts the moving experiences of those working with the Christian Peacemaker Teams in Iraq before, during, and after the 2003 war and occupation. Told as her personal account, Gish makes real the story of prisoner abuse, the character of the Iraq people she got to know personally, and a passionate vision for peace.

Graff, Gerald. *Beyond the Culture Wars: How Teaching the Conflicts Can Revitalize American Education.* New York: W.W. Norton & Company, 1992.

Graff responds to the torrent of criticism in recent years of American higher education. He argues that we should stop lamenting current conflicts about multiculturalism, political correctness, and which books belong to the canon. Rather, we should "teach the conflicts," drawing students into both curricular and co-curricular conversations about disagreements.

Gutman, Amy and Dennis Thompson. *Democracy and Disagreement.* Cambridge, MA: Harvard University Press, 1996.

In response to the deep disagreements that pervade American society, the authors propose a form of "deliberative democracy." They explore principles for "reasonable argument" with application to actual cases that they believe will help us to resolve some of our present moral controversies and live with those that will inevitably persist. Their procedural principles are *reciprocity, publicity,* and *accountability.* Their substantive principles are *basic liberty, opportunity,* and *fairness.*

Habermas, Jürgen. *Moral Consciousness and Communicative Action.* Cambridge, MA: The MIT Press, 1990.

Habermas "aims to show that our basic moral intuitions spring from something deeper and more universal than contingent features of our tradition, namely from normative presuppositions of social interaction that belong to the repertoire of competent agents in any society." For a helpful collection of essays that reflect on the work of Habermas, see *Habermas and the Public Square.* Ed. Craig Calhoun. Cambridge, MA: The MIT Press, 1992.

Hasker, William. *Metaphysics: Constructing a World View.* Downers Grove, IL: InterVarsity Press, 1983.

Hasker introduces readers to the nature of metaphysical questions as to the ultimate nature of the universe and the people in it. He then explores how one answers such questions and proposes standards for evaluating the adequacy of competing responses. In that light, he then examines various metaphysical theories, including naturalistic, pantheistic, and theistic views of the relationship between God and the world.

Hauerwas, Stanley. *Performing the Faith: Bonhoeffer and the Practice of Nonviolence.* Grand Rapids, MI: Brazos Press, 2004.

Hauerwas offers a provocative reading of Dietrich Bonhoeffer's political theology and the relationship between "Truth and Politics." In the words of one reviewer: "Contending that truth depends on performance far more than on theory, Hauerwas steps forward as a pacifist gadfly for a more truly faithful and a more recognizably democratic society" (George Hunsinger, Princeton Theological Seminary).

Heie, Harold. "Mathematics: Freedom Within Bounds." In *The Reality of Christian Learning: Strategies for Faith-Discipline Integration.* Eds. Harold Heie and David L. Wolfe. Grand Rapids, MI: Eerdmans, 1987, pp. 206–230.

This book first presents a typology of various strategies for faith-discipline integration, which are then exemplified by two essays in each of seven academic disciplines. A principal essayist addresses a significant issue in the discipline from a Christian perspective. A respondent then analyzes that essay, suggesting at least one alternative approach to integration. In the principal essay in mathematics, it is argued that the doing of mathematics is an exemplification of "freedom within bounds," and that the exercise of such freedom fits well within a broader perspective on the nature of Christian living.

Heie, Harold. "Values in Public Education: Dialogue Within Diversity." *Christian Scholar's Review* XXII:2 (December 1992): 131–143.

In the context of current debates relative to public vs. private education and the values, if any, that publicly supported education should exemplify and inculcate, this essay proposes a model in which a diversity of publicly supported schools, each proclaiming and promoting its own value and worldview commitments, will engage in a continuous "public dialogue on alternative viewpoints on issues affecting the public good."

Heie, Harold. "The Postmodern Opportunity: Christians in the Academy." *Christian Scholar's Review* XXVI: 2 (Winter 1996): 138–157.

This essay argues that the postmodern epistemological turn toward perspectivalism, the view that our claims to knowledge unavoidably reflect our particularities and social location, provides a window of opportunity for Christian voices to gain a hearing in the academy. Concrete suggestions are then made for how Christian colleges can model communities of conversation and then invite non-Christian scholars to join the conversation.

Heie, Harold. "What Can the Evangelical/Interdenominational Tradition Contribute to Christian Higher Education?" In *Models for Christian Higher Education: Strategies for Survival and Success in the Twenty-First Century*. Eds. Richard T. Hughes and William B. Adrian. Grand Rapids, MI: Eerdmans, 1997, pp. 245–260.

This book of essays provides historical narratives of how fourteen Christian colleges representing seven major faith traditions are "integrating faith and learning" on their campuses. These narratives are preceded by introductory essays that define the worldview and theological heritage of each faith tradition. In this introductory essay on the Evangelical/Interdenominational tradition, it is argued that since colleges in this tradition attract faculty and students representing a wide diversity of Christian faith traditions, these colleges are in an ideal position to create vibrant "communities of conversation" where similarities and differences in various Christian perspectives can be discussed.

Heie, Harold. "Developing A Christian Perspective on the Nature of Mathematics." In *Teaching As an Act of Faith: Theory and Practice in Church-Related Higher Education*. Ed. Arlin C. Migliazzo. New York: Fordham University Press, 2002.

This book contains essays that consider the relationship between the Christian faith and higher learning from the vantage point of fourteen different academic disciplines. The essay in Mathematics proposes a teaching strategy (pedagogy) for initiating students into exploring questions that relate faith and learning, whatever their disciplines (with in-depth examples taken from mathematics). It concludes with a suggestion that good teaching must go beyond good pedagogy by modeling that learning, teaching, and living are all of one piece.

Heskins, Jeffrey. *Face to Face: Gay and Lesbian Clergy on Holiness and Life Together*. Grand Rapids, MI: Eerdmans, 2005.

In this provocative book, Heskins takes a step back from the heated rhetoric within the Anglican Church regarding homosexuality by providing a safe space for persons committed to both ordained ministry in the Anglican

Church and same-sex partners to tell their stories and reflect on their experiences.

Holmes, Arthur F. *The Idea of a Christian College.* Grand Rapids, MI: Eerdmans, 1975.

Holmes presents a concise case for the Christian college, defining its distinctive mission and contribution, with an emphasis on the importance of liberal arts education. Written in language accessible to all readers, it has been widely discussed by students, faculty, education administrators, and Christian laity.

Holmes, Arthur F. "The Just War." In *War: Four Christian Views*, Ed. Robert G. Clouse. Downers Grove, IL: InterVarsity Press, 1981, pp. 117–135.

In this edited volume, four Christian scholars address the question "Should Christians ever go to war?," presenting and discussing the alternative views of Biblical Nonresistance, Christian Pacifism, Just War, and Preventive War. Professor Holmes argues for a Just War position.

Holmes, Arthur F. "The Closing of the American Mind and the Opening of the Christian Mind: Liberal Learning, Great Texts, and the Christian College." *In Faithful Learning and the Christian Scholarly Vocation.* Eds. Douglas V. Henry and Bob R. Agee. Grand Rapids, MI: Eerdmans, 2003, pp. 101–122.

In this edited volume, eleven prominent Christian teacher/scholars provide a theological foundation for understanding faith-and-learning integration, and discuss major challenges and opportunities facing Christian higher education in the twenty first century. In his essay, Holmes proposes various dimensions of "the opening of the Christian mind" against the backdrop of Allan Bloom's influential book *The Closing of the American Mind.*

Huebner, Chris K. "Patience, Witness, and the Scattered Body of Christ: Yoder and Virilio on Knowledge, Politics, and Speed." In *A Mind Patient and Untamed: Assessing John Howard Yoder's Contribution to Theology, Ethics, and Peacemaking.* Eds. Ben C. Ollenberger and Gayle Gerber Koontz. Telford, PA: Cascadia Publishing House, 2004, pp. 56–74.

This book is a collection of essays that analyze the far-reaching ethical and theological writings of the late eminent Mennonite scholar John Howard Yoder. In his essay, Chris Huebner examines "Yoder's appeal to the practice of patience as a way of resisting the violent logic of speed" that is not willing to risk the possibility that truthfulness can emerge gradually from "ongoing, timeful 'open conversation.'" Yoder thereby rejects "the essentially violent temptations toward closure, finality and purity that haunt so much contemporary theology."

Hulse, Carl and Robert Pear. "3 Months of Tense Talks Led to Immigration Bill." *The New York Times.* May 19, 2007, p. A11.

Hulse and Pear report on the dynamics of the engagement between Democrat and Republican senators on the ad hoc committee that formulated the May 2007 proposal for immigration reform for Senate consideration.

Jacobsen, Douglas and Rhonda Hustedt Jacobsen, Eds. *Scholarship and Christian Faith: Enlarging the Conversation.* New York: Oxford University Press, 2004.

This book argues that most of the recent literature on the nature of Christian scholarship has focused on a "Reformed and evangelical" orientation. While recognizing the strengths and significant contributions of this orientation, the editors and essayists argue that a broader view of Christian scholarship is needed, one that respects the insights of a variety of different Christian faith traditions, such as the Catholic, Lutheran, Anabaptist, Wesleyan, and Pentecostal traditions.

Jacobsen, Douglas and Rodney J. Sawatsky. *Gracious Christianity: Living the Love We Profess.* Grand Rapids, MI: BakerAcademic, 2006.

This book presents an intelligent, readable, and winsome introduction to the Christian faith as a grace-filled and peaceable way of life, and not as an argumentative and tensely held dogma. The authors intend to engage readers in conversation by posing probing questions throughout their narrative.

Juhnke, James C. "How Should We Then Teach American History? A Perspective of Constructive Nonviolence." In *Must Christianity Be Violent? Reflections on History, Practice, and Theology.* Eds. Kenneth R. Chase and Alan Jacobs. Grand Rapids, MI: Brazos Press, 2003, pp. 107–118.

In this book, thirteen Christian scholars respond to those who argue that the Christian faith is inherently violent, or that Christian doctrines inevitably lead to sacrifice, conquest, and war. The contributors explore the history of Christian violence and advocate the need for an uncompromised biblical theology in the search for peace. In his essay, Juhnke "rejects the myth of redemptive violence as a metanarrative for teaching U.S. History ... [and] suggests multiple strategies ... for Christians to promote constructive nonviolence in the study of history ..." (Introduction, p.15).

Kauffman, Richard A. "Foreword." In *To Continue the Dialogue: Biblical Interpretation and Homosexuality*. Ed. C. Norman Kraus. Telford, PA: Pandora Press U.S., 2001, pp. 7–11.

In the forward to this edited volume (cited under Kraus in this bibliography), Kauffman encourages Mennonites (and other Christians) to find a "third way between Fight and Flight," proposing that seeking a third way will require confession, empathy, humility, patience, and prayer.

Keim, Paul A. "The Ethos of Anabaptist-Mennonite Colleges." In *The Future of Religious Colleges*. Ed. Paul J. Dovre. Grand Rapids, MI: Eerdmans, 2002, pp. 264–280.

In this essay, Keim identifies some characteristics that are shared by the variety of institutions of higher education working out of the Anabaptist-Mennonite theological tradition.

Kierkegaard, Søren. *Fear And Trembling* and *The Sickness Unto Death*. Princeton, NJ: Princeton University Press, 1954.

This book contains two of Kierkegaard's works. In *Fear and Trembling,* Kierkegaard deals with that difficult biblical passage in Genesis 22 that recounts the story of Abraham's willingness to sacrifice his son Isaac in response to a command from God. The thorny issue is whether Abraham was "suspending the ethical" for the sake of a higher "religious calling."

King, Michael A. *Fractured Dance: Gadamer and a Mennonite Conflict over Homosexuality.* Telford, PA: Pandora Press U.S., 2001.

This book "is not about homosexuality per se. Rather, it is about talking about homosexuality." King reports on a difficult series of conversations on homosexuality within the Mennonite Franconia Conference. While reporting that these conversations did not resolve strong differences in beliefs about homosexuality, King "holds out hope that traditional Mennonite commitments to community, humility, and ... yieldedness" will eventually yield redemptive results. King appeals to the principles for dialogue embraced by the eminent philosopher Hans-Georg Gadamer, including the view that "[g]enuine conversation ... seeks to find that commonality within differences when each participant is open to question his or her own truth and to consider the truth of the other."

King, Michael A., Ed. "Special Issue: Toward a Genuine Conversation on Homosexuality." In *DreamSeeker Magazine: Voices from the Soul.* Telford, PA: Cascadia Publishing House. 6.1 (Winter 2006).

This special issue presents eleven essays by Mennonite Church leaders and scholars that take contrasting positions relative to the ongoing discussion of homosexuality within that Christian tradition. As noted by the editor, his hope for this issue "was to catalyze a genuine conversation, from multiple points of view, within which authors modeled ability to respect and learn from each other even in disagreement" (p. 2).

Koop, C. Everett and Timothy Johnson. *Let's Talk: An Honest Conversation on Critical Issues.* Grand Rapids, MI: Zondervan, 1992.

A lively conversation between two highly respected Christian doctors, in which agreements and differences are laid bare relative to the controversial issues of abortion, euthanasia, AIDS, and Health Care. In contrast to the typical strident public debate about these difficult issues, Koop and Johnson model the ancient adage that "one must not see eye to eye to walk arm in arm."

Kraus, C. Norman. Ed. *To Continue the Dialogue: Biblical Interpretation and Homosexuality.* Telford, PA: Pandora Press U.S., 2001.

This volume presents fifteen essays, with eight responses, in which Mennonite Christians present contrasting views on homosexuality. The book is organized into the two categories of "The Need for Continuing Dialogue," and "Framing the Theological Questions." It is a splendid example of allowing a multiplicity of diverse voices to be heard, in preparation, hopefully, for loving dialogue.

Kuyper, Abraham. "Souvereiniteit in Eigen Kring." Amsterdam: Kruyt, 1880.

This quote from Kuyper is cited in James D. Bratt and Ronald A. Wells, "Piety and Progress: A History of Calvin College" in *Models For Christian Higher Education: Strategies for Survival and Success In the Twenty-First Cen-*

tury. Eds. Richard T. Hughes and William B. Adrian. Grand Rapids, MI: Eerdmans, p. 143.

Lakoff, George and Mark Johnson. *Metaphors We Live By*. Chicago: The University of Chicago Press, 1980.

A study of the way in which various metaphors structure our most basic understandings of our experience, often shaping our perceptions and actions without our noticing them. Numerous examples are given of various types of metaphors that "we live by."

Levang, Joseph H. *The Church of the Lutheran Brethren 1900–1975: A Believers' Fellowship—A Lutheran Alternative*. Fergus Falls, MN: Lutheran Brethren Publishing Company, 1980.

A historical account of the formation of the Church of the Lutheran Brethren in America in 1900 and the development of this "Lutheran alternative" through 1975. The roots of this movement are traced to the revival in Norway in the late nineteenth century led by Hans Nielsen Hauge.

Litfin, Duane. *Conceiving the Christian College*. Grand Rapids, MI: Eerdmans, 2004.

In this book, the current president of Wheaton College (IL) presents his vision for Christian Higher Education. Litfin distinguishes between an "umbrella model" and "systemic model." While recognizing the important contribution of both models, Litfin elaborates on the meaning of integration of faith and learning within the systemic model.

MacIntyre, Alasdair. *Whose Justice? Which Rationality*? Notre Dame, IN: University of Notre Dame Press, 1988.

MacIntyre argues persuasively that there is no such thing as a rationality that is not the rationality of some tradition. He examines the problems presented by the existence of rival traditions of inquiry in the cases of four major thinkers: Aristotle, Augustine, Aquinas, and Hume. Particularly helpful is his consideration of how those working out of rival traditions can engage one another despite their differing rationalities (pp. 349–403).

Macmurray, John. *The Self as Agent.* London: Faber and Faber Limited, 1957.

This is Volume One of Professor Macmurray's 1953–54 Gifford Lectures on *The Form of the Personal.* In this volume, Macmurray seeks to establish the primacy of "action," arguing that different forms of reflective activity are derived from and related to action, thereby emphasizing the "importance of the practical in human experience."

Macmurray, John. *Persons in Relation.* London: Faber and Faber Limited, 1961.

In this second volume of his Gifford Lectures, Macmurray starts from the practical standpoint elaborated in *The Self as Agent* to "show that the form of personal life is determined by the mutuality of personal relationship, so that the unit of human life is not the 'I' alone, but the 'you and I.'"

Marsden, George M. "Christian Advocacy and the Rules of the Academic Game." In *Religious Advocacy and American History.* Eds. Bruce Kuklick and D.G. Hart. Grand Rapids, MI: Eerdmans, 1997A, pp. 3–27.

In this book, some leading historians of American religion and culture address two related questions: How do personal religious convictions influence one's own research, writing, and teaching? What place, if any, should personal beliefs have within American higher education? In his essay, Marsden proposes that "various Christian and other religious outlooks be evaluated on the same grounds as other academic outlooks" using "some widely accepted rules for judgments of academic merit" that need not marginalize explicit reference to religious viewpoints.

Marsden, George M. *The Outrageous Idea of Christian Scholarship.* New York: Oxford University Press, 1997B.

In this groundbreaking and controversial book, Marsden rebuts various arguments given for excluding religious viewpoints from the scholarly enterprise. He argues that scholars with a religious commitment have both a religious and intellectual obligation not to leave their deeply held religious beliefs at the gate of the academy, and such beliefs can make a significant difference in scholarship.

Marsden, George M. "What Difference Might Christian Perspective Make?" In *History and the Christian Historian.* Ed. Ronald A. Wells. Grand Rapids, MI: Eerdmans, 1998, pp. 11–22.

In this essay, Marsden carefully distinguishes between scholarship where the faith perspective of the scholar makes no difference and scholarship where the scholar's faith perspective can have a "pervasive influence." Helpful examples of each type of scholarship are provided.

Marsden, George M. "Being an Intentional Christian Scholar Today." Unpublished manuscript, presented as a paper at a Whitworth College (WA) conference on *Christians Engaging Culture: Models for Public Policy Practitioners, Politicians and Scholars.* 25 October 2005.

Marsden reflects back on his earlier books, *The Soul of the American University* (New York: Oxford University Press, 1994) and its sequel *The Outrageous Idea Of Christian Scholarship* (New York: Oxford University Press, 1997). He reiterates his earlier position that "having a religious source for one's views" should "not automatically exclude one's views from acceptance in the academy so long as one argues for them on other, more widely accessible grounds."

Marshall, Christopher D. *Beyond Retribution: A New Testament Vision for Justice, Crime, and Punishment.* Grand Rapids, MI: Eerdmans, 2001.

Based on a careful examination of New Testament teachings on justice and punishment, Marshall encourages a fundamental rethinking of many common assumptions about the place of punishment in the Bible and in society. The author makes a case for a Restorative Justice approach to dealing with criminal offenders.

Monsma, Stephen V. *Pursuing Justice in a Sinful World.* Grand Rapids, MI: Eerdmans, 1984.

Drawing on his eight years of service in the Michigan legislature, Monsma examines ways to reconcile political ideals with the gritty world of political action. He argues that Christians need to address structural evils by becoming politically involved, working to create a just society.

Monsma, Stephen V. *Positive Neutrality: Letting Religious Freedom Ring.* Grand Rapids, MI: Baker, 1993.

After summarizing current case law and the historical development of church-state theory and practice in the U.S., Monsma proposes "positive neutrality" as a paradigm for church-state relations, in which government policy is neutral toward all persons, irrespective of faith.

Monsma, Stephen V. and Christopher J. Soper, Eds. *Equal Treatment of Religion in a Pluralistic Society.* Grand Rapids, MI: Eerdmans, 1998.

In this edited volume, eight leading scholars of constitutional law provide an analysis of a new paradigm for discussing church-state relations—equal treatment, also sometimes referred to as neutrality—that has recently been used in several Supreme Court decisions. This paradigm allows governmental accommodation and assistance to religiously based groups and activities, as long as such accommodation and assistance are offered equally to all religious and nonreligious groups.

Monsma, Stephen and Mark Rodgers. "In the Arena: Practical Issues in Concrete Political Engagement." In *Toward an Evangelical Public Policy.* Eds. Ronald J. Sider and Diane Knippers. Grand Rapids, MI: Baker, 2005, pp. 325–341.

In this essay, two Christians who have had extensive legislative experience at the state or national levels address practical issues related to political engagement, including the roles of compromise and coalition building in the real world of politics.

Moran, Tom. "The Kean Legacy: Clarity, Compassion, Class." *The Star-Ledger,* New Jersey Section. June 10, 2005, pp. 21, 27.

Moran reflects on the political legacy of Thomas Kean, former Governor of New Jersey and member of the 9/11 Commission.

Mouw, Richard J. *Uncommon Decency: Christian Civility in an Uncivil World.* Downers Grove, IL: InterVarsity Press, 1992.

Mouw acknowledges that it is not easy to hold to Christian convictions and treat sometimes vindictive opponents with civility and decency. He presents very helpful insights about what Christians can appreciate about pluralism, the theological basis for civility, and how Christians can communicate with people who disagree with them on critical issues.

Nation, Mark Thiessen. "Fruit of the Spirit or Works of the Flesh? Come Let Us Reason Together." In *To Continue the Dialogue: Biblical Interpretation and Homosexuality*. Ed. C. Norman Kraus. Telford, PA: Pandora Press U.S., 2001.

In this essay intended to facilitate ongoing conversations about homosexuality within the Mennonite and other Christian communities, Thiessen Nation argues that we must first seek to discern what we agree on, and he suggests eight points that he believes most Christians would agree upon. He then proposes that by starting with such common ground, we will be better able to identify our "differences within the agreement," thereby facilitating ongoing conversation.

Nation, Mark Thiessen. "Discipleship In a World Full of Nazis: Dietrich Bonhoeffer's Polyphonic Pacifism As Social Ethics." In *The Wisdom of the Cross: Essays in Honor of John Howard Yoder*. Eds. Stanley Hauerwas, Chris K. Huebner, Harry J. Huebner, and Mark Thiessen Nation. Grand Rapids, MI: Eerdmans, 1999, pp. 249–277.

In this essay, Thiessen Nation rejects the common view that Bonhoeffer rejected his lifelong pacifism when he involved himself in the plot to assassinate Hitler. He argues that Bonhoeffer was a consistent pacifist throughout his life, even unto his being executed by the Nazis.

O'Donovan, Oliver and Joan Lockwood O'Donovan, Eds. *From Irenaeus to Grotius: A Sourcebook in Christian Political Thought*. Grand Rapids, MI: Eerdmans, 1999.

In this edited volume, the tradition of Christian thought about the political order, in all its extraordinary richness and diversity, is made available in primary sources to nonspecialist readers. That portion of Martin Luther's *The Sermon On the Mount* quoted in my narrative is translated from sermons delivered by Luther in Wittenberg between November 1530 and April 1532 (pp. 595–602). In it, Luther seeks to reconcile the tension between living out Christ's commands in the Sermon On the Mount and his understanding of a Christian's social obligations.

Palmer, Parker J. *The Active Life: A Spirituality of Work, Creativity, and Caring*. San Francisco: Harper & Row, 1990.

Palmer critiques the view that Christian spirituality must involve a withdrawal from the world. In contrast, Palmer "articulates a bracingly vital, down-to-earth spirituality for persons who live busy, active lives—at home or work, in the arts or politics, serving others or working for social change."

Pearcey, Nancy. *Total Truth: Liberating Christianity from Its Cultural Captivity.* Wheaton, IL: Crossway Books, 2004.

Pearcey critiques the common cultural assumption that religion is strictly a private matter that should not impinge on public life. She argues that attempts at personal and cultural renewal are thwarted by this untenable private/public bifurcation. Pearcey proposes that Christianity is not just religious truth, but truth about total reality.

Pirsig, Robert M. *Zen and the Art of Motorcycle Maintenance.* New York: Bantam Books, 1974.

A moving story of the journey of a father and son as they seek to understand themselves and the nature of "truth."

Placher, William C. *Unapologetic Theology: A Christian Voice in a Pluralistic Conversation.* Louisville, KY: Westminster/John Knox Press, 1989.

Placher examines religion and the search for truth in a pluralistic society. Among the issues he considers are science and its relation to belief, dialogue among various religions, and theological method. This book presents a cogent philosophical/theological foundation for my invitation to respectful conversation.

Popper, Karl R. *Conjectures and Refutations: The Growth of Scientific Knowledge.* New York: Harper & Row, 1963.

Popper argues that the way in which knowledge progresses, especially scientific knowledge, is by our making conjectures that "are controlled by criticism; that is by attempted refutations, which include severely critical tests." Therefore, "as we learn from our mistakes our knowledge grows," and "those among our theories which turn out to be highly resistant to criticism, and which appear to us at a certain moment in time to be better approximations to truth than other known theories, may be described … as the 'science' of that time," despite the fact that "none of them can be positively justified."

Potok, Chaim. *The Chosen.* New York: Ballantine Books, 1967.

A marvelous story of the pilgrimage from boyhood to manhood of an emerging Jewish intellectual seeking to forge an expression of his Jewish faith that he can live by. It provides sympathetic insights into Jewish family life, and Jewish tradition and heritage. Particularly poignant is a portrayal of the tragedy of a person being "a mind without a soul."

Potok, Chaim. *My Name Is Asher Lev.* New York: Ballantine Books, 1972.

A deeply moving story of the need for a religious Jewish boy to draw, to paint, to render the world he knows and the pain he feels on canvas for everyone to see. It chronicles Asher Lev's struggles to be an artist without shaming his people or relinquishing any part of his deeply felt Judaism.

Potok, Chaim. *The Gift of Asher Lev.* New York: Alfred A. Knopf, 1990.

A sequel to *My Name is Asher Lev*, this story portrays how Asher Lev, having become a painter of international renown, continues to struggle with negotiating a demanding and ultimately exalting balance between both his religious and artistic impulses.

Ramsey, Paul. *The Just War: Force and Political Responsibility.* New York: University Press of America, 1983.

A collection of works by the late eminent ethicist Paul Ramsey on the subject of Just War doctrine and the responsible use of force, intended as a complement to his 1961 book *War and the Christian Conscience: How Shall Modern War Be Conducted Justly?* (Duke University Press, Durham, NC).

Rodin, Judith and Stephen P. Steinberg, Eds. *Public Discourse in America: Conversation and Community in the Twentieth-First Century.* Philadelphia: University of Pennsylvania Press, 2003.

A collection of essays that evaluates the current condition of public discourse in America and identifies the features and principles that could characterize more productive discourse in the twenty-first century. Essays outline how public conversations can be used to reintegrate fragmented communities and bridge barriers of difference and hostility among communities and individuals.

Rogers, Carl R. *Freedom to Learn.* Columbus, OH: Charles E. Merrill Publishing Company, 1969.

Rogers encourages teachers to create a learning environment that gives students "freedom to learn within limits." Teachers are encouraged to "risk themselves in experimentation with their classes." The book concludes with a proposal "for bringing about self-directed change in an educational system."

Roth, John D. *Beliefs: Mennonite Faith and Practice.* Scottdale, PA: Herald Press, 2005.

A succinct and engaging introduction to the core elements of Anabaptist/ Mennonite perspectives on theology, ecclesiology, and Christian discipleship.

Sacks, Jonathan. *The Dignity of Difference: How to Avoid the Clash of Civilizations.* New York: Continuum, 2002.

Going back to the roots of biblical monotheism, Sacks presents a theological basis for a "respect for difference, based not on relativism but on the concept of covenant" (p. VIII). He argues that this respect for difference is necessary to check the potential abuses of globalization and to help realize the possibilities of globalization for fostering human well-being. Particularly pertinent to my narrative is his proposal that *conversation* is the key to living with moral difference while sustaining an overarching community (p. 83).

Scheuer, Michael. *Imperial Hubris: Why the West is Losing the War on Terror.* Washington, D.C.: Brassey's Inc., 2004.

According to Scheuer, the greatest danger for Americans confronting the radical Islamist threat is to believe that Muslims attack us for what we are and what we think rather than for what we do. He then elaborates on some specific U. S. policies, and their military, political, and economic implications, about which a growing segment of the Islamic world strenuously disapprove.

Schroch-Shenk, Carolyn. "Commanded to Keep Wrestling and Wrestling and Wrestling." In *To Continue the Dialogue: Biblical Interpretation and Homosexuality.* Ed. C. Norman Kraus. Telford, PA: Pandora Press U.S., 2001, pp. 245–255.

Schrock-Shenk proposes that to rebuild the "necessary relationships" needed for future discussion on homosexuality within the Mennonite Church to be fruitful, fellow believers need to "Understand Each Other's Fears, Reluctance, Suspicions," "Recognize Our Finiteness," and "Commit to Staying Connected … for the Long Haul."

Schroeder, David. "Homosexuality: Biblical, Theological and Polity Issues." In *To Continue the Dialogue: Biblical Interpretation and Homosexuality.* Ed. C. Norman Kraus. Telford, PA: Pandora Press U.S., 2001, pp. 62–75.

Schroeder first presents brief "Exegetical Notes" on biblical passages taken to pertain to homosexuality and extends his reflections to Biblical and Systematic Theology. He concludes by considering implications and challenges for church polity in our time.

Sider, Ronald J. "Justice, Human Rights, and Government: Toward an Evangelical Perspective." In *Toward an Evangelical Public Policy.* Eds. Ronald J. Sider and Diane Knippers. Grand Rapids, MI: Baker, 2005, pp. 163–193.

Edited by the co-chairs of the "Toward an Evangelical Framework for Public Engagement" initiative of the National Association of Evangelicals (NAE), this book of essays written by 21 Christian scholars challenges Christians to pursue political strategies that will foster the health of America. The essay by Sider deals with the nature of justice and human rights, and the relationship between society and government.

Skillen, James W. *The Scattered Voice: Christians at Odds in the Public Square.* Grand Rapids, MI: Zondervan, 1990.

Skillen explores the question, "Who speaks for Christians in politics?" by examining seven political perspectives held by Christians ranging from "pro-American conservatives" to "theonomic reconstructionists." He then concludes by urging Christians to move from contention to communication in the development of a more coherent and consistent approach to politics.

Skillen, James W. *Recharging the American Experiment: Principled Pluralism for Genuine Civic Community.* Grand Rapids, MI: Baker, 1994.

Starting with a vision for "principled pluralism," Skillen argues that the "American experiment" can be "recharged" through three reforms: restoring full religious freedom to public life, establishing educational pluralism that allows coexisting public and private education to flourish, and refining the electoral system to be more truly representative.

Skillen, James W. *In Pursuit of Justice: Christian-Democratic Explorations.* Lanham, MD: Rowman & Littlefield, 2004.

Working within an American context, Skillen explores the implications of a Christian-democratic approach to the meaning of civil society. Considering issues such as racial justice, environmental responsibility, welfare, education, and political participation, Skillen argues that the roots of a Christian-democratic approach are neither liberal nor conservative but pluralistic, opening the way to a healthy regard for both social complexity and government's responsibility to uphold political community.

Smith, Christian. *Moral, Believing Animals: Human Personhood and Culture.* New York: Oxford University Press, 2003.

Smith argues that humans are animals with an inescapable moral and spiritual dimension. He presents a critique of rational choice theory, sociobiology, and other accounts of human social life drawn from naturalistic and noncultural traditions of Western social theory. In contrast, Smith argues that all people are believers whose lives, actions, and institutions are constituted, motivated, and governed by narrative traditions and moral orders on which they inevitably depend. Of particular interest is Smith's summary of how seven eminent scholars, in a variety of academic fields, have proposed engaging and judging "rival presuppositions and narratives" (pp. 90, 91).

Smucker, Marcus G. "Psychological Dynamics." In *To Continue the Dialogue: Biblical Interpretation and Homosexuality.* Ed. C. Norman Kraus. Telford, PA: Pandora Press U.S., 2001, pp. 45–61.

Based on conversations with gays and lesbians, including his daughter, Smucker describes five "psychological dynamics" experienced by persons who are homosexual, as well as by their families, and suggests four "Implications for the Church."

Stassen, Glen H. *Just Peacemaking: Transforming Initiatives for Justice and Peace.* Louisville, KY: Westminster/John Knox Press, 1992.

Stassen proposes an agenda for "just peacemaking" to prevent war, with emphasis on "transforming initiatives," drawing on Jesus' Sermon on the Mount and other New Testament passages. He concludes by considering the relationships between just peacemaking, just war, and pacifism. The quotation from Pinchas Lapide is taken from *The Sermon On the Mount: Utopia or Program for Action.* Maryknoll, NY: Orbis Books, 1986, pp. 112–113.

Stassen, Glen H. *Just Peacemaking: Ten Practices For Abolishing War.* Cleveland, OH: The Pilgrim Press, 1998.

Stassen proposes ten practices for abolishing war, directed to individuals, grassroots groups, voluntary associations, and religious organizations. He challenges pacifists to be peacemakers and just war theorists to spell out the resorts that should be tried before the last resort of war.

Stassen, Glen H. "The Ethics of War and Peacemaking," In *Toward an Evangelical Public Policy.* Eds. Ronald J. Sider and Diane Knippers. Grand Rapids, MI: Baker, 2005, pp. 284–306.

Stassen seeks to supplement the views of those holding to pacifism or just war theory by noting their implicit commitment to peacemaking. He concludes with a summary of "ten effective practices of peacemaking."

Swartley, Willard M. *Covenant of Peace: The Missing Peace in New Testament Theology and Ethics.* Grand Rapids, MI: Eerdmans, 2006.

In this comprehensive book, Swartley explicates virtually all of the New Testament, relating peace and the associated emphases of love of enemies and reconciliation to core theological themes such as salvation, christology, and the reign of God.

Tagg, John. *The Learning Paradigm College.* Boston: Anker Publishing, 2003.

Tagg argues that a paradigm shift is taking place in American higher education, away from simply providing instruction to the focused mission of producing learning in students. Descriptions of the features of the Learning Paradigm are paired with concrete examples of how selected institutions of higher education are transforming themselves into Learning Paradigm colleges. A number of these examples can be viewed as possible ways to implement some of the "Recommendations for Christian Higher Education" that I present in chapter 23.

Volf, Miroslav. *Exclusion and Embrace: A Theological Exploration of Identity, Otherness,* and *Reconciliation.* Nashville: Abingdon Press, 1996.

Volf proposes "the idea of embrace as a theological response to the problem of exclusion" that distorts "our perceptions of reality ... causing us to react out of fear and anger to all those who are not within our (ever-narrowing) circle." In light of this problem, he proposes that Christians must "take the dangerous and costly step of opening ourselves to the other, of enfolding him or her in the same embrace with which we have been enfolded by God."

Waller, James. *Becoming Evil: How Ordinary People Commit Genocide and Mass Killing.* New York: Oxford University Press, 2002.

After calling into question many of the standard explanations for antisocial behavior, Waller proposes a theory to explain why ordinary people sometimes commit extraordinary evil. The ingredients of this theory include an "ancestral shadow," the "cultural belief systems" and "social context" of would-be perpetrators, and the "social death" of intended victims, "characterized by 'us/them' thinking, blaming, and dehumanization."

Wallis, Jim. *God's Politics: Why the Right Gets It Wrong and the Left Doesn't Get It.* San Francisco: Harper San Francisco, 2005.

Drawing on his analysis of the 2004 presidential election, Wallis argues that the "Right gets it wrong" by almost exclusively focusing on moral issues related to abortion and same-sex marriage, and the "Left doesn't get it" because of its unwillingness to express its broader social concerns in terms of morality and values. He then issues a strong call for religious communities and the government to be accountable to key values in the prophetic religious tradition, such as those embracing justice, peace, environmental flourishing, equality, and broad, consistent views of being pro-life and pro-family.

Walzer, Michael. *Just and Unjust Wars.* New York: Basic Books, 1977.

In what is arguably the most widely respected book on just war theory, Walzer "bases just war theory on justice as the right to life, liberty, and community, and opposition to dominion," as cited in Glen H. Stassen, "The Ethics of War and Peacemaking," in *Toward an Evangelical Public Policy.*

Eds. Ronald J. Sider and Diane Knippers. Grand Rapids, MI: Baker 2005, p. 292.

Webb, William J. *Slaves, Women & Homosexuals: Exploring the Hermeneutics of Cultural Analysis.* Downers Grove, IL: InterVarsity Press, 2001.

Webb addresses some of the most difficult issues that have faced the Christian church by proposing a "Redemptive-Movement Hermeneutic" that seeks to distinguish that which is cultural in Scripture from that which is timeless.

Wilson, Marvin R. *Our Father Abraham: Jewish Roots of the Christian Faith.* Grand Rapids, MI: Eerdmans, 1989.

Wilson is a biblical scholar who has for many years been at the forefront of facilitating conversation between Jews and Christians. In this book he "delineates the link between Judaism and Christianity, between the Old and the New Testament, and calls Christians to reexamine their Hebrew roots so as to effect a more authentically biblical life-style."

Wolfe, David L. *Epistemology: The Justification of Belief.* Downers Grove, IL: InterVarsity Press, 1982.

Wolfe first examines traditional and current approaches to justifying one's beliefs. He then proposes standards for evaluating competing systems of beliefs, and applies his method to systems of religious beliefs.

Wolfe, David L. and Harold Heie. *Slogans or Distinctives: Reforming Christian Higher Education.* Lanham, MD: University Press of America, 1993.

Wolfe and Heie examine five phrases that have been slogans in Christian Higher education, including "All Truth Is God's Truth," "Integration of Faith and Learning," and "Holistic Education." They challenge Christian educators to make these slogans true distinctives by adopting far-reaching proposals for faculty development, faculty-student relations, and curricular change, including an "Ambrose House" model for outstanding students who are the Christian scholars and faculty of the future.

Wolterstorff, Nicholas. *Until Justice and Peace Embrace.* Grand Rapids, MI: Eerdmans, 1983.

Wolterstorff uses the biblical concept of shalom to address the question of how a Christian can set goals and determine courses of action that are conducive to the establishment of a just and peaceful social order. He argues for the vital relationship that must exist between liturgy and social action in the life of a Christian, concluding with reflections on the relationship between theory and practice.

Wolterstorff, Nicholas. "Scholarship Grounded In Religion." In *Religion, Scholarship and Higher Education: Perspectives, Models, and Future Prospects.* Ed. Andrea Sterk. Notre Dame, IN: University of Notre Dame Press, 2002, pp. 3–15.

In Wolterstorff's essay in this book (See the Bernstein citation), he argues against the "self-understanding of the modern Western academy" that "learning is a *generically human* enterprise." In contrast, Wolterstorff argues that learning unavoidably reflects the particularities of scholars in the academy. That being so, "particularist learning of many forms should be allowed to flourish in the academy," leading to his proposal for a "dialogic pluralism."

Wolterstorff, Nicholas. *Educating For Shalom: Essays on Christian Higher Education.* Eds. Clarence W. Joldersma and Gloria Goris Stronks. Grand Rapids, MI: Eerdmans, 2004.

The editors present a comprehensive collection of essays on the nature of Christian higher education written by Nicholas Wolterstorff over the course of many years. These essays converge toward a focus on "educating for Shalom." His essay titled "The Mission of the Christian College At the End of the Twentieth Century" (pp. 27–35) traces three stages in the evolution of the mission of Christian higher education, from an emphasis on personal piety through a focus on developing Christian perspectives on all aspects of culture, to a focus on reforming society, with each later stage building on the previous stage.

Wood, Jay W. *Epistemology: Becoming Intellectually Virtuous.* Downers Grove, IL: InterVarsity Press, 1998.

In the context of examining current views on epistemology, Wood argues that "knowing" is closely related to living out various "intellectual virtues." He concludes with examining the relationship of epistemology to religious belief, and the role of emotions and virtues in proper cognitive functioning.

Woodiwiss, Ashley. "Deliberation or Agony? Toward a Postliberal Christian Democratic Theory." In *The Re-Enchancement of Political Science: Christian Scholars Engage Their Discipline.* Eds. Thomas W. Heilke and Ashley Woodiwiss. Lanham, MD: Lexington Books, 2002, pp. 149–166.

In this collection of essays, Christian scholars in political science consider whether and to what extent the community of Christian scholars can add a distinctive and significant dimension to the academic discipline of political science. In his essay cited above, Woodiwiss points to the limitations of a "deliberative model" in politics, arguing that "deliberative democracy … [is] inextricably involved in an exclusionary project similar to the liberalism it claims to have overcome" (p. 150). Woodiwiss proposes consideration of an alternative "agonistic model," proposed by Chantel Mouffe, which recognizes that "[p]luralism implies the permanence of conflict and antagonism" (p. 254 in Chantel Mouffe, "Democracy, Power, and the 'Political,'" In *Democracy and Difference: Contesting the Boundaries of the Political.* Ed. Seyla Benhabib. Princeton, NJ: Princeton University Press, 1996, pp. 245–256).

Yoder, John Howard. "The Hermeneutics of Peoplehood: A Protestant Perspective." In *The Priestly Kingdom: Social Ethics as Gospel.* Notre Dame, IN: University of Notre Dame Press, 1984, pp.15–45.

In this collection of his essays, Yoder presents a powerful and provocative case for the "radical reformation" as the demonstratively classical form of Christian faith. In the essay cited, he argues for the centrality of the "voluntary Christian community," "which has … neither the coercive givenness of establishment nor the atomistic isolation of individualism." Such communities seek "communal moral discernment" through patient, ongoing conversation, the "shape" of which Yoder helpfully delineates in terms of the various gifts of those in conversation (pp. 28–34). For an extremely helpful companion volume that will introduce the reader to the voluminous writings of this late Mennonite scholar, see *John Howard Yoder: Mennonite Patience,*

Evangelical Witness, Catholic Convictions. Mark Thiessen Nation. Grand Rapids, MI: Eerdmans, 2006.

Young, Iris Marion. "Communication and the Other: Beyond Deliberative Democracy." In *Democracy and Difference: Contesting the Boundaries of the Political.* Ed. Seyla Benhabib. Princeton, NJ: Princeton University Press, 1996, pp. 120–133.

In her essay in this volume, Young proposes "an expanded conception of democratic communication," recognizing that "[g]reeting, rhetoric, and storytelling are forms of communication that in addition to argument contribute to political discussion" (p. 120).

Zehr, Howard. *Changing Lenses: A New Focus for Crime and Punishment.* Scottdale, PA: Herald Press, 1990.

Zehr examines the prevailing assumptions about crime and justice that are primarily informed by a "retributive lens." He then proposes a "restorative justice lens" based on biblical principles and consideration of the needs of victims and offenders and their respective communities.

Zeleny, Jeff. "Testing the Water, Obama Tests His Own Limits." *The New York Times.* December 22, 2006, p. 1.

Zeleny reflects on the possibilities and challenges that Barack Obama will face as a presidential candidate in 2008.

Further Recommended Reading

It has been my experience that the footnotes, end notes, or bibliographies in a good book suggest multiple additions to my never-ending list of more good books to read. I liken it to a snowball growing as it rolls down a hill. In case your experience is similar, I offer the following bibliography of books that may be of interest to you. The books recommended represent only a small fraction of possible entries. They are chosen based on my judgment that they complement well the books already cited. This second bibliography is organized according to various categories that are prominent in my narrative.

It is my hope that what I have said in this book will be a catalyst for extensive ongoing study and many respectful conversations about the ideas presented. The references in my two bibliographies provide some places to start such further study. Hopefully you will not view them as places to finish your own pilgrimage of faithful learning.

Christian Higher Education

Anderson, Chris. *Teaching as Believing: Faith in the University.* Waco, TX: Baylor University Press, 2004.

Burtchaell, James Tunstead. *The Dying of the Light: The Disengagement of Colleges and Universities from Their Christian Churches.* Grand Rapids, MI: Eerdmans, 1998.

Carpenter, Joel A. and Kenneth W. Shipps, Eds. *Making Higher Education Christian: The History and Mission of Evangelical Colleges in America.* Grand Rapids, MI: Eerdmans, 1987.

Dockery, David S. and David P. Gushee, Eds. *The Future of Christian Higher Education.* Nashville: Broadman & Holman, 1999.

Garber, Steven. *The Fabric of Faithfulness.* Downers Grove, IL: InterVarsity Press, 1996.

Harris, Robert A. *The Integration Of Faith and Learning: A Worldview Approach.* Eugene, OR: Cascade Books, 2004.

Heie, Harold. "Wanted: Christian Colleges For a Dynamic Evangelicalism." *Christian Scholars Review* XXI: 3 (March 1992): 254–274.

Holmes, Arthur F. *Shaping Character: Moral Education in the Christian College.* Grand Rapids, MI: Eerdmans, 1991.

Hughes, Richard T. *How Christian Faith Can Sustain the Life of the Mind.* Grand Rapids, MI: Eerdmans, 2001.

Klassen, Norman and Jens Zimmerman. *The Passionate Intellect: Incarnational Humanism and the Future of University Education.* Grand Rapids, MI: BakerAcademic, 2006.

Mannoia, V. James Jr. *Christian Liberal Arts: An Education That Goes Beyond.* New York: Rowman & Littlefield, 2000.

Marsden, George. *The Soul of the American University: From Protestant Establishment to Established Nonbelief.* New York: Oxford University Press, 1994.

Moore, Steve. Ed. *The University Through the Eyes of Faith.* Indianapolis, IN: Light and Life Communications, 1998.

Palmer, Parker J. *The Courage to Teach: Exploring the Inner Landscapes of a Teacher's Life.* San Francisco: Jossey-Bass, 1998.

Peterson, Michael L. *With All Your Mind: A Christian Philosophy of Education.* Notre Dame, IN: University of Notre Dame Press, 2001.

Plantinga, Cornelius Jr. *Engaging God's World: A Christian Vision of Faith, Learning, and Living.* Grand Rapids, MI: Eerdmans, 2002.

Poe, Harry Lee. *Christianity in the Academy: Teaching at the Intersection of Faith and Learning.* Grand Rapids, MI: Baker, 2004.

Schaefer Riley, Naomi. *God on the Quad: How Religious Colleges and the Missionary Generation Are Changing America.* New York: St. Martin's Press, 2005.

Schwehn, Mark R. *Exiles from Eden: Religion and the Academic Vocation in America.* New York: Oxford University Press, 1993.

Williams, Clifford. *The Life of the Mind: A Christian Perspective.* Grand Rapids, MI: Baker, 2002.

Perspectives on Reformed Theology

Hesselink, I. John. *On Being Reformed: Distinctive Characteristics and Common Misunderstandings.* Ann Arbor, MI: Servant Books, 1983.

Osterhaven, M. Eugene. *The Faith of the Church: A Reformed Perspective on Its Historical Development.* Grand Rapids, MI: Eerdmans, 1982.

Worldviews

Fackre, Gabriel. *The Christian Story: A Narrative Interpretation of Basic Christian Doctrine.* Grand Rapids, MI: Eerdmans, 1978.

Holmes, Arthur F. *Contours of a World View.* Grand Rapids, MI: Eerdmans, 1983.

Naugle, David K. *Worldview: The History of a Concept.* Grand Rapids, MI: Eerdmans, 2002.

Pepper, Stephen C. *World Hypotheses: A Study in Evidence.* Berkeley: University of California Press, 1942.

Sire, James W. *The Universe Next Door: A Basic Worldview Catalog.* 3rd ed. Downers Grove, IL: InterVarsity Press, 1997.

Smart, Ninian. *Worldviews: Crosscultural Explorations of Human Beliefs.* New York: Charles Scribner's Sons, 1983.

Walsh, Brian J. and Richard J. Middleton. *The Transforming Vision: Shaping a Christian Worldview.* Downers Grove, IL: InterVarsity Press, 1984.

Wolters, Albert M. *Creation Regained: Biblical Basics for a Reformational Worldview.* Grand Rapids, MI: Eerdmans, 1985.

Evangelical Christianity

Carpenter, Joel A. *Revive Us Again: The Reawakening of American Fundamentalism*. New York: Oxford University Press, 1997.

Hunter, James Davison. *American Evangelicalism: Conservative Religion and the Quandry of Modernity*. New Brunswick, NJ: Rutgers University Press, 1983.

Hunter, James Davison. *Evangelicalism: The Coming Generation*. Chicago, University of Chicago Press, 1987.

Marsden, George M. *Understanding Fundamentalism and Evangelicalism*. Grand Rapids, MI: Eerdmans, 1991.

McGrath, Alister. *Evangelicalism & the Future of Christianity*. Downers Grove, IL: InterVarsity Press, 1995.

Noll, Mark A. *The Scandal of the Evangelical Mind*. Grand Rapids, MI: Eerdmans, 1994.

Noll, Mark A. *American Evangelical Christianity: An Introduction*. Oxford, UK: Blackwell Publishers, 2001.

Smith, Christian. *American Evangelicalism: Embattled and Thriving*. Chicago: University of Chicago Press, 1998.

Stackhouse, John G. Ed. *Evangelical Futures: A Conversation on Theological Method*. Grand Rapids, MI: Baker, 2000.

Faculty Scholarship

Boyer, Ernest L. *Scholarship Reconsidered: Priorities of the Professoriate*. Princeton, NJ: The Carnegie Foundation for the Advancement of Teaching, 1990.

Perspectives on or Related to Epistemology

Belenky, Mary Field; Blythe McVicker Clinchy; Nancy Rule Goldberger; Jill Mattuck Tarule. *Women's Ways of Knowing: The Development of Self, Voice, and Mind*. New York: Basic Books, 1986.

Clouser, Roy A. *The Myth of Religious Neutrality: An Essay on the Hidden Role of Religious Belief in Theories.* Notre Dame, IN: University of Notre Dame Press, 1991.

Haskell, Thomas L. *Objectivity Is Not Neutrality: Explanatory Schemes in History.* Baltimore: The John Hopkins University Press, 1998.

Kuhn, Thomas S. *The Structure of Scientific Revolutions.* 2nd ed., Enlarged. Chicago: University of Chicago Press, 1970.

Palmer, Parker J. *To Know As We Are Known: A Spirituality of Education.* San Francisco: Harper & Row, 1993.

Plantinga, Alvin and Nicholas Wolterstorff, Eds. *Faith and Rationality: Reason and Belief in God.* Notre Dame, IN: University of Notre Dame Press, 1983.

Plantinga, Alvin. *Warranted Christian Belief.* New York: Oxford University Press, 2000.

Polanyi, Michael. *Personal Knowledge: Towards a Post-Critical Philosophy.* New York: Harper & Row, 1958.

Wolterstorff, Nicholas. *Reason Within the Bounds of Religion.* Grand Rapids, MI: Eerdmans, 1976.

Christian Perspectives on Homosexuality

There are strong disagreements among Christians relative to issues related to homosexuality. The following is a small sampling of books that reflect some of these disagreements.

Balch, David L. Ed. *Homosexuality, Science, and the "Plain Sense" of Scripture.* Grand Rapids, MI: Eerdmans, 2000.

Bradshaw, Timothy. Ed. *The Way Forward? Christian Voices on Homosexuality and the Church.* 2nd ed. Grand Rapids, MI: Eerdmans, 2003.

Brawley, Robert L. Ed. *Biblical Ethics and Homosexuality: Listening to Scripture.* Louisville: Westminster/John Knox Press, 1996.

Grenz, Stanley J. *Welcoming But Not Affirming: An Evangelical Response to Homosexuality.* Louisville: Westminster/John Knox Press, 1998.

Hays, Richard B. "Homosexuality." In *The Moral Vision of the New Testament.* San Francisco, Harper Collins, 1996, pp. 379–406.

Helminiak, Daniel A. *What the Bible Really Says About Homosexuality.* San Francisco: Alamo Square Press, 1994.

Johnson, William Tracy. *A Time to Embrace: Same-Gender Relationships in Religion, Law, and Politics.* Grand Rapids, MI: Eerdmans, 2006.

Myers, David G. and Letha Dawson Scanzoni. *What God Has Joined Together? A Christian Case for Gay Marriage.* San Francisco: HarperSanFrancisco, 2005.

Nissenen, Martti. *Homoeroticism in the Biblical World.* Minneapolis: Fortress Press, 1998.

Rogers, Jack. *Jesus, the Bible and Homosexuality: Explode the Myths, Heal the Church.* Louisville, KY: Westminster/John Knox Press, 2006.

Scanzoni, Letha Dawson and Virginia Ramey Mollenkott. *Is the Homosexual My Neighbor? A Positive Christian Response.* San Francisco: Harper-Collins, 1994.

Schmidt, Thomas E. *Straight and Narrow? Compassion and Clarity in the Homosexuality Debate.* Downers Grove, IL: InterVarsity Press, 1995.

Smedes, Lewis B. *Sex for Christians: The Limits and Liberties of Sexual Living.* Rev. ed. Grand Rapids, MI: Eerdmans, 1994.

Swartley, Willard M. *Homosexuality: Biblical Interpretation and Moral Discernment.* Scottdale, PA: Herald Press, 2003.

Thompson, Chad W. *Loving Homosexuals As Jesus Would: A Fresh Christian Approach.* Grand Rapids, MI: Brazos Press, 2004.

Via, Dan O. and Robert A. J. Gagnon. *Homosexuality and the Bible: Two Views.* Minneapolis: Fortress Press, 2003.

Christians in Politics

There are enormous differences in beliefs among Christians as to the extent to which Christians should or should not become involved in politics, and the nature of such involvement. The following books reflect this broad spectrum of competing claims.

Bandow, Doug. *Beyond Good Intentions: A Biblical View of Politics.* Westchester, IL: Crossway Books, 1988.

Budziszewski, J. *Evangelicals in the Public Square: Four Formative Voices on Political Thought and Action.* Grand Rapids, MI: BakerAcademic, 2006.

Cromartie, Michael. Ed. *Caesar's Coin Revisited: Christians and the Limits of Government.* Grand Rapids, MI: Eerdmans, 1996.

Danforth, John. *Faith and Politics: How the "Moral Values" Debate Divides America and How to Move Forward Together.* New York: Viking Penguin, 2006.

Eidsmoe, John. *God and Caesar: Christian Faith and Political Action.* Westchester, IL: Crossway Books, 1984.

Fackre, Gabriel. *The Religious Right and Christian Faith.* Grand Rapids, MI: Eerdmans, 1982.

Gushee, David P. Ed. *Christians and Politics Beyond the Culture Wars: An Agenda for Engagement.* Grand Rapids, MI: Baker, 2000.

Heie, Harold, A. James Rudin and Marvin R. Wilson, Eds. *The Role of Religion in Politics and Society.* Wenham, MA: Center For Christian Studies of Gordon College and the Interreligious Affairs Department of the American Jewish Committee, 1998.

Koyzis, David T. *Political Visions & Illusions: A Survey and Christian Critique of Contemporary Ideologies.* Downers Grove, IL: InterVarsity Press, 2003.

Lugo, Luis E. Ed. *Religion, Pluralism and Public Life: Abraham Kuyper's Legacy for the Twenty-First Century.* Grand Rapids, MI: Eerdmans, 2000.

Macedo Stephen. Ed. *Deliberative Politics: Essays on Democracy and Disagreement.* New York: Oxford University Press, 1999.

Marshall, Paul. *God and the Constitution: Christianity and American Politics.* New York: Rowman & Littlefield, 2002.

Mouw, Richard J. *Politics and the Biblical Drama.* Grand Rapids, MI: Eerdmans, 1976.

Neuhaus, Richard John. *The Naked Public Square: Religion and Democracy in America.* Grand Rapids, MI: Eerdmans, 1984.

Reed, Ralph. *Politically Incorrect: The Emerging Faith Factor in American Politics.* Dallas: Word Publishing, 1994.

Schansberg, D. Eric. *Turn Neither to the Right nor to the Left: A Thinking Christian's Guide to Politics and Public Policy.* Greenville, SC: Alertness Books, 2003.

Sherratt, Timothy R. and Ronald P Mahurin. *Saints as Citizens: A Guide to Public Responsibilities for Christians.* Grand Rapids, MI: Baker, 1995.

Sider, Ronald J. *Genuine Christianity.* Grand Rapids, MI: Zondervan, 1996.

Skillen, James W. and Rockne M. McCarthy. *Political Order and the Plural Structure of Society.* Atlanta: Scholars Press, 1991.

Stassen, Glen H. and David P. Gushee. *Kingdom Ethics: Following Jesus in Contemporary Context.* Downers Grove, IL: InterVarsity Press, 2003.

Thomas, Cal and Ed Dobson. *Blinded By Might: Can the Religious Right Save America?* Grand Rapids, MI: Zondervan, 1999.

Wallis, Jim. *The Soul of Politics: A Practical and Prophetic Vision for Change.* New York: The New Press and Orbis Books, 1994.

Wogaman, J. Phillip. *Christian Perspectives on Politics.* Philadelphia: Fortress Press, 1988.

Yoder, John Howard. *The Politics of Jesus.* Grand Rapids, MI: Eerdmans, 1972.

Zwier, Robert. *Born-Again Politics: The New Christian Right in America.* Downers Grove, IL: InterVarsity Press, 1982.

Peacemaking and Restorative Justice

Friessen, Duane K. *Christian Peacemaking & International Conflict: A Realist Pacifist Perspective.* Scottdale, PA: Herald Press, 1986.

Jones L. Gregory. *Embodying Forgiveness: A Theological Analysis.* Grand Rapids, MI: Eerdmans, 1995.

Lederach, John Paul. *Building Peace: Sustainable Reconciliation in Divided Societies.* Washington, D.C.: United States Institute of Peace Press, 1997.

Lederach, John Paul. *The Little Book of Conflict Transformation.* Intercourse, PA: Good Books, 2003.

Mock, Ron. *Loving Without Giving In: Christian Responses to Terrorism & Tyranny.* Telford, PA: Cascadia Publishing House, 2004.

Yoder, John Howard. *Nevertheless: The Varieties and Shortcomings of Religious Pacifism.* Scottdale, PA: Herald Press, 1992.

Zehr, Howard. *The Little Book of Restorative Justice.* Intercourse, PA: Good Books, 2002.

About the Author

Nelly Olsen and Henning Heie emigrated separately from Norway to Brooklyn, New York in the 1920s. Mom came from the hamlet of Vik, near Grimstad, on the southern tip of Norway. Pop was born and raised on the island of Tysnes, near Bergen, on the southwest coast. They met, courted, and married in the Bay Ridge section of Brooklyn, not far from where the Verrazano Bridge to Staten Island now stands. I have a vague recollection of once being told that Mom, ten years older than Pop, proposed marriage, which Pop accepted. I never checked this story out, but it wouldn't surprise me. When Mom was 40, she gave birth to two boys, my brother John and I, born at approximately the same time (I am the younger son by 10 minutes). We had no other siblings. Mom said we were "quite enough" (claiming that during our infancy one of us cried most of the night, and the other cried most of the day). Mom was a homemaker her entire married life. Pop worked at the same factory for over 30 years. When Pop retired in the mid 1960s, they moved to Pasadena, California. Mom passed away in 1973, and Pop passed away in 1993.

My childhood, then, was set in the streets and schools of Brooklyn. My post-secondary schooling was in mechanical and aerospace engineering. I received a B.M.E. degree from the Polytechnic Institute of Brooklyn in 1957, an M.S.M.E. from the University of Southern California in 1959, and an M.A. and Ph.D. in mechanical and aerospace engineering from Princeton University in 1961 and 1965. I worked briefly in the aerospace industry, first for Hughes Aircraft in Culver City, CA and then at the General Electric Space Technology Center in King of Prussia, PA.

While at Princeton, I was inspired to pursue a career in teaching by the modeling of excellent teaching by Forman Acton, a professor of electrical engineering for whom I worked as a teaching assistant. This experience propelled me into a 40-year career serving at four Christian Colleges. I taught mathematics at The King's College in New York (1963–1975) and at Gordon College in Massachusetts (1975–1980). I then embarked on academic administration, serving two stints as a Vice President for Academic Affairs, first at Northwestern College in Iowa (1980–1988) and then at Messiah College in Pennsylvania (1988–1993). In the fall of 1994, I returned to Gordon College to serve as Founding Director of its Center for Christian Studies until my retirement from that position in the summer of 2003.

My wife Pat and I were married in the summer of 1962, and we nurtured three children. Our oldest, Jonathan, is married to Sheila and lives in Sioux Center, Iowa. Our second, Janice, lives in Aspen, Colorado, and our youngest, Jeff, is married to Tammy Krause and lives in Phoenix. We have five grandchildren: Stephanie and Lacey in Iowa, Noah and Samuel in Phoenix, and John Thomas in Aspen. Our great-grandaughter Averi lives in Sioux Center.

When I retired, sort of, in the summer of 2003, Pat and I moved back to Orange City, Iowa, where we had lived in the 1980s. Although I miss some splendid friends in New England and the Atlantic Ocean, we were lured back to Iowa by our love for small town living and our love and appreciation for the good people we knew in Iowa. The flat farmlands of Northwest Iowa around harvest time have their own kind of beauty. I didn't know what cold weather was until I moved to Iowa. So, as much as we have come to love Iowa, we have sense enough to travel to warmer places in January and February, thanks to the hospitality of relatives and friends. We are currently members of the American Reformed Church in Orange City, a congregation of the Reformed Church in America.

I still keep busy professionally, working as a Senior Fellow at both the Center for Christian Studies at Gordon College and the Council for Christian Colleges and Universities in Washington, D.C., typically designing and implementing selected projects on a contract basis. I also serve as a Trustee for the Center For Public Justice in Annapolis, MD.

In my spare time, I sometimes enjoy and sometimes endure exercising. Pat and I also like to travel, mostly by car, visiting family and friends from coast to coast. But the activity I still enjoy most is reading a good book.

I consider it a gift from God that during most of my professional career I have worked at tasks I believe God considers to be important. I love them so much that I would do them for nothing, but I have been fortunate enough to find people willing to pay me. I wish the same good fortune for you.

978-0-595-45546-1
0-595-45546-8

Printed in the United States
90004LV00004B/61-114/A

9 780595 455461